Chicken Soup for the Soul

On, Being a Parent

Our **101** BEST STORIES

Chicken Soup for the Soul® Our 101 Best Stories:
On Being a Parent; Inspirational, Humorous, and Heartwarming Stories about Parenthood
by Jack Canfield, Mark Victor Hansen & Amy Newmark

Published by Chicken Soup for the Soul Publishing, LLC www.chickensoup.com

The publisher gratefully acknowledges the many publishers and individuals who granted Chicken Soup for the Soul permission to reprint the cited material.

Front cover photo courtesy of Getty Images, ©Mike Kemp/Rubberball. Back cover photo courtesy of Jupiter Images/Photos.com. Interior illustration courtesy of iStockPhoto.com/Tomacco. Smiley-faces courtesty of Jedediah Owen Taylor.

Cover and Interior Design & Layout by Pneuma Books, LLC
For more info on Pneuma Books, visit www.pneumabooks.com

Distributed to the booktrade by Simon & Schuster. SAN: 200-2442

Publisher's Cataloging-in-Publication Data
(Prepared by The Donohue Group)

Chicken soup for the soul. Selections.
    Chicken soup for the soul : on being a parent : inspirational, humorous, and heartwarming stories about parenthood / [compiled by] Jack Canfield [and] Mark Victor Hansen ; [edited by] Amy Newmark.

    p. ; cm. -- (Our 101 best stories)

    ISBN-13: 978-1-935096-20-7
    ISBN-10: 1-935096-20-6

1. Parenthood--Literary collections. 2. Parenthood--Anecdotes. 3. Parents--Literary collections. 4. Parents--Anecdotes. I. Canfield, Jack, 1944- II. Hansen, Mark Victor. III. Newmark, Amy. IV. Title. V. Title: On being a parent

PN6071.P28 C48 2008
810.8/5/02/03525   2008934916

PRINTED IN THE UNITED STATES OF AMERICA
on acid∞free paper
16 15 14 13 12 10 09   02 03 04 05 06 07 08

Chicken Soup for the Soul®

On, Being A Parent

Our 101 BEST STORIES

Inspirational, Humorous, and
Heartwarming Stories about
Parenthood

Jack Canfield
Mark Victor Hansen
Amy Newmark

Chicken Soup for the Soul Publishing, LLC
Cos Cob, CT

Chicken Soup for the Soul

Contents

❶

~The Joys of Parenting~

❷

~Funny Times~

❸
~Moms Really Do Know Best~

❹
~Wise Dads~

❺
~They Grow Too Fast~

6

~Loss and Lessons~

7

~Parents by Choice~

8

~Parenting Wisdom~

❾

~Learning from the Kids~

❿

~Thank You~

⓫
~It Takes a Village to Raise a Child~

⓬
~No Place I'd Rather Be~

Chicken Soup for the Soul

A Special Foreword

by Jack and Mark

For us, 101 has always been a magical number. It was the number of stories in the first *Chicken Soup for the Soul* book, and it is the number of stories and poems we have always aimed for in our books. We love the number 101 because it signifies a beginning, not an end. After 100, we start anew with 101.

We hope that when you finish reading one of our books, it is only a beginning for you too—a new outlook on life, a renewed sense of purpose, a strengthened resolve to deal with an issue that has been bothering you. Perhaps you will pick up the phone and share one of the stories with a friend or a loved one. Perhaps you will turn to your keyboard and express yourself by writing a Chicken Soup story of your own, to share with other readers who are just like you.

This volume contains our 101 best stories and poems about parenting. We share this with you at a very special time for us, the fifteenth anniversary of our *Chicken Soup for the Soul* series. When we published our first book in 1993, we never dreamed that we had started what became a publishing phenomenon, one of the best-selling series of books in history.

We did not set out to sell more than one hundred million books, or to publish more than 150 titles. We set out to touch the heart of one person at a time, hoping that person would in turn touch another person, and so on down the line. Fifteen years later, we know that it has worked. Your letters and stories have poured in by the hundreds of thousands, affirming our life's work, and inspiring us to continue to make a difference in your lives.

On our fifteenth anniversary, we have new energy, new resolve, and new dreams. We have recommitted to our goal of 101 stories or poems per book, we have refreshed our cover designs and our interior layout, and we have grown the Chicken Soup for the Soul team, with new friends and partners across the country in New England.

In this new volume, we have selected our 101 best stories and poems about parenting from our rich fifteen year history. The stories that we have chosen were written by parents about their children and by children about their parents. There is a common thread of caring, humor, hard work, and joy of shaping young lives. New parents should enjoy these stories as they embark on their great adventure, and older parents will laugh, cry, and nod their heads as they recognize common experiences.

We hope that you will enjoy reading these stories as much as we enjoyed selecting them for you, and that you will share them with your families and friends. We have identified the 40 *Chicken Soup for the Soul* books in which the stories originally appeared, in case you would like to continue reading about parenting and families among our other titles. We hope you will also enjoy the additional books about families, children, pets, and life in "Our 101 Best Stories" series.

With our love, our thanks, and our respect,
~*Jack Canfield and Mark Victor Hansen*

Preface

The Smiley-Faces

We moved into our dream house, the one with the gigantic sycamore tree in the backyard and plenty of room for our three boys to run around. We had wanted an older home for a long time and ours came with classic doorknobs, big, heavy window frames, thick walls and thick paint.

We settled in and it became our home. Our home provided a studio office for my wife, Nina, and myself, a welcome change from commuting. I settled into my new studio and got down to work. We couldn't have been happier.

Jed is the youngest of my three boys and, at seven years old, moving into a new house was a grand adventure. I call him a hunter and gatherer. Hundred-year-old houses have many secrets to reveal.

He dug wherever he could. He had several shovels and a metal detector. The backyard of an old house reveals many small treasures for eager young men. "Bumstead's Worm Syrup: One Bottle has Killed One Hundred Worms. Children Cry for More. Try It." medicine bottles from the 1800s, matchbox cars from the 1960s, bones, army men, and much more began to fill Jed's many treasure chests.

Bold and active, Jed is a free spirit. "All boy" as they say. Always smiling and willing to take a dare. He'll tear anything apart to see how it is made. He tests everything to the limits and is not satisfied until he has carried out his plans. He's a skater kid. Unafraid. He likes to get dirty and tell naughty jokes. He's the first to jump off a roof and was recently busted for drawing his teacher as a Cyclops.

Since I am a creative director and my wife is a writer, there is plenty of freedom of expression around our home and we encourage lots of creative discovery. So we celebrate Jed in all his glory.

About nine months after we moved in, I made a creative discovery of my own. Indeed, hundred-year-old houses reveal many things. Each time I walk out of my office, I admire the bathroom door. They don't make doors like that anymore. "Solid wood, cast iron hinges, porcelain knobs... I love this house," I thought, as I usually do. And then I discovered it... two black dots and a curve in the middle of the right panel of my beautiful bathroom door.

"Is it a scratch in the paint? It looks like marker... Is that a smiley face? It's a smiley face on my beautiful bathroom door! Where the heck did that come from?"

My middle son, Silas, always has a marker in his hand for illustrating epic battle scenes between robots and aliens. He's not a smiley-face-drawing kind of artist. Jed. It had to be Jed because Noah is too old for that. Besides, Jed has been busted for drawing on the walls before!

I go out to the family room and as I am sitting in front of our new coffee table stewing over the smiley-face, I notice a smiley-face is staring back at me from the coffee table. No. It can't be... Yes. It is. Another smiley-face.

I skirt the room... oh man... one on the side-chest. And one on the entertainment cabinet. Wait... that's a sad smiley-face. And here's one that is sort of expressionless. Oh man.

I went to Nina. We looked at each other in astonishment with gaping mouths. Almost wordless. Our eyes locked and we both said, "Jed."

In the next second, we burst out laughing. We couldn't contain ourselves. Traveling from one smiley-face to the next, examining the intricacies and character of each, we were crying tears of laughter.

After Jed got home from school, we gathered in the family room. "Jed... I have a question for you... did you draw this on the new coffee table?"

"Yes," he said under his breath, bright red and rocking furiously in the rocking chair.

"When did you do this, Jed?" I asked.

"I dunno," his face filling up and the chair bucking faster.

"Why did you do it?"

"I dunno. I guess I just wanted to draw a smiley-face."

"Did you draw a lot of these?"

"Yes." Barely audible, the chair going into hyperspeed.

"How many?"

"I dunno. Ten or six, or more, maybe."

I couldn't help it. I burst into laughter. All of us were laughing. My heart became so full... Jed and his carefree spirit... I swooped him up in my arms and kissed him, almost crying. I put him to the ground and began to tickle him like I used to do when he was a baby. Squeals of delight filled the room. Images of him as a baby, always smiling, flooded my memory. We got up and went around the room together, laughing at all the smiley-faces.

I never did punish him. I couldn't. Those smiley-faces constantly remind me to appreciate the unique blessing each of my sons brings to our family. They were drawn with permanent marker, and what could be more fitting? Permanent marks on my life, expressions of who we are, making our marks along the way, on the world, and on each other's hearts. Besides, now when Jed does something reckless or foolish, I find it easier to bear in mind his silly and impulsive nature.

Now, when I walk out of my office and I admire that big, old, heavy bathroom door, I say something different... a smile crosses my face and I just say, "Jed."

~Brian Taylor,
Creative Director Chicken Soup for the Soul

Postscript: When I learned of this title within the Chicken Soup for the Soul line of books, I knew immediately what I wanted to do... As I designed and produced this book, I placed Jed's actual smiley-faces on random pages, giggling as I did it, so you can also appreciate the silly and impulsive nature of kids everywhere, and celebrate the blessings of parenthood.

Chapter 1

On, Being a Parent

The Joys of Parenting

You don't really understand human nature unless you know why a child on a merry-go-round will wave at his parents every time around— and why his parents will always wave back.

~William D. Tammeus

The Day It All Came Together

Life is tough enough without having someone kick you from the inside.
~Rita Rudner

arch can be cold in Texas. I hadn't expected that. A transplanted Yankee, by way of a slight if forgivable detour through Virginia, I viewed Texas with the same avidity I did a pit viper. In my imagination, Texas was a land of endless deserts. Rattlesnakes curled up on the porch, and armadillos wandered the streets. My move to San Antonio, courtesy of the Air Force, to which I owed my time if not my soul, might as well have been a one-way shot to the moon.

It was in that alien landscape of cacti, fire ants, scorpions, armadillos, rattlesnakes, and a purposeful, somewhat lunatic roadrunner that traversed our cul-de-sac every afternoon at three without fail, that I became pregnant with our first child. We hadn't exactly been trying, but we hadn't exactly been careful either. We had sidled up to parenthood gradually, practicing first on three cats and a golden retriever. The baby was conceived during a playoff game between the Washington Redskins and the Chicago Bears, somewhere in the third quarter, around the twentieth yard line of the Bears. The Redskins went on to win the Super Bowl that year, a prelude of things to come, and after our initial astonished exchange ("Are you sure?" "Of course,

I'm sure. Look, the stick is blue!"), we accepted that the pregnancy just was, like morning coffee or taxes.

But I was not excited. I was a professional. I had a career. Ergo, pregnancy was a temporary way station on the road to something called motherhood, a hazy concept blurred at the margins by images of June and Ward, and Archie and Edith. After a wretched first trimester, when one sympathetic obstetrician observed that if men had to endure the raging hormonal imbalances pregnant women did, they would end up gasping on the floor like beached fish, I had adopted a somewhat detached attitude. There was nothing I could do about the alien invader whose presence reshaped my body before my eyes. She—for I knew "it" was a "she" by the sixteenth week—was a nameless entity that squiggled and kicked and rolled and had a knack for getting up when I most wanted to sleep.

Predictably, my parents were thrilled. My in-laws gushed. I received countless, indulgent smiles as I waddled back and forth, though men stopped whistling. (That was discouraging. Of course, wandering around in an Air Force maternity uniform wasn't helpful. The uniform was like a light blue parachute: a pull of the ripcord at the start of each month, and a new panel billowed out.) Total strangers approached me in the supermarket and patted my belly, as if I were their private Buddha. Yet despite my pediatrician-husband's assurances that I would soon "glow," I wasn't in the least bit incandescent. I didn't place my hands protectively across my abdomen the way women did in the movies. I didn't coo, and I didn't knit booties. There was one bad moment, in my fourth month, when I had an almost irresistible urge to buy a sewing machine. I paced the floor in front of a row of Singers and gnawed my nails. I think I finally wandered over to the living room section of the store, found a sleeper sofa on sale, and lay down, waiting for that feeling to go away. It did.

I remember, too, that my mother assured me that the anonymous lump in my stomach would develop her own little personality. I was not convinced, and to prove who was in charge here, I resisted picking a name.

One thing I did religiously was exercise. No puffy ankles for me, no hundred-pound weight gain. I swam incessantly. The one thing I did enjoy about Texas, besides breakfast fajitas, was the fact that I could swim outdoors year-round. There was a pool on the training side of the base, and I would swim a mile every day, without fail. As with naming the baby, I refused to buy a maternity suit and give in to what my aunt euphemistically called "my condition." My black Speedo stretched very nicely, thanks, and I think after his initial double take, the lifeguard got used to seeing the equivalent of a big, black water beetle.

Most of all, I wanted to prove that pregnancy was no obstacle. So one cold March afternoon—cold being a relative term in Texas—I pulled up to the pool, lugged my stuff into the locker room, and stuffed myself into my suit.

There was no one else insane enough to be at the pool except the lifeguard who had trudged out to his seat and huddled, miserable in a gray sweatshirt and beach towel. I wandered up to the edge of the pool and dipped my toe in. The water was like ice. I pulled my toe out. I caught the lifeguard looking hopeful.

Wrong-o, I thought. Just watch me.

I crossed to the steps, and gingerly let myself down into the water. The water wasn't just like ice; it was ice. Any sane person would have leapt from the water, called it a day and had a mug of hot chocolate.

Not me. Gritting my teeth, I persevered, and it was when the water hit the bottom of my belly that the baby reacted. Suddenly, my belly levitated. I was stunned. To be absolutely sure, I backed up the steps. The water receded, and my belly sagged. I counted to ten then got in again up to mid-abdomen. Now my belly didn't just rise; it lurched, and there was an odd, scrambling movement. It was as if the baby was trying to climb into my throat—anywhere it was warm. Then she kicked me, hard.

An image flashed in my mind: my baby yanking on her umbilical cord and yelping, "What the heck are you doing up there?"

I couldn't help it. I started to laugh. I'm sure the lifeguard thought I'd lost my mind. But in that instant, the baby went from being an anonymous alien fluttering around in my belly to assuming her own uniqueness, and she wanted to be very sure I understood that she was not amused.

So I didn't swim that day, or any other day in March of that year. And that night, my husband held me at arm's length and studied me with care.

"What?" I asked.

He folded me into his arms. "You glow."

We had chili that night, with lots of jalapeño peppers. Later, as my husband slept, my little daughter made very sure I understood she wasn't amused by jalapeño peppers, either.

No matter. As I drifted off to sleep, I thought of a name for her. And when she popped out four months later, she gave me a look that indicated that she wasn't amused by this little turn of events, either.

~Ilsa J. Bick
Chicken Soup for the Soul Celebrates Mothers

Change of Heart

All her friends were going to the baby shower, but my daughter, Kathy, wouldn't attend because she had a softball practice. Recently, there always seemed to be some reason why Kathy couldn't attend a baby shower. In my heart, I knew that something must be wrong.

Then I learned the sad truth. She and her husband, Kevin, desperately wanted to start a family and were having no luck. It was extremely difficult for them to talk about, and her father and I were sworn to secrecy. They had seen many doctors and undergone numerous tests, and still no reason for the problem had been found. With each new procedure, their hopes would build, only to end again in sad disappointment. They were on an emotional roller coaster ride.

Next, they traveled to a clinic in Vancouver, British Columbia, for in vitro fertilization—an expensive process in which a number of embryos from the couple are grown in a laboratory situation. The doctors then choose the healthiest embryos and implant several in the mother. The hope is that at least one will "take," and she will become pregnant. After three failed attempts, Kathy and Kevin became despondent and were ready to give up. And then, out of nowhere, a dim light of hope began to shine.

Carleen had been Kathy's closest friend from the time they entered high school. They had shared everything with each other ever since. She and her husband, Ward, had been there for Kathy and Kevin through all their hopes and disappointments. Carleen was the only friend Kathy confided in, so she experienced this roller coaster ride right at her side. When Kathy and Kevin returned from Vancouver, disappointed and heartbroken, she looked at her own good fortune and made a decision. She offered herself as a gestational surrogate mother. Kathy was overwhelmed at this unbelievable gesture made out of pure love from her best friend.

Could it be possible? After further medical, and some legal consultation, they realized this might be a real option. But when it came right down to it, would Carleen really be prepared to go through with it? She had a husband and two small daughters and knew she could not make this decision on her own. Her husband, Ward, began to struggle with what might happen. He felt for Kathy and Kevin, but he also cared very much for his wife. He had concerns about the drugs she would have to take, even though he was told they were safe. He feared for her health and emotional well-being after the birth. What if there were complications? Kathy made sure Carleen knew she had the option of changing her mind. There would be no questions asked and no hard feelings.

Still concerned, Ward finally decided to ask his wife to say no. He was on his way to phone her with his decision, when he suddenly stopped dead in his tracks. In that moment, he realized he might be preventing the only chance Kathy and Kevin would ever have of having a baby of their own. Ward then told Carleen, "Go ahead. I'll be with you all the way."

The planning began. By now, Carleen's parents knew, and Carleen's dad had many of the same concerns as Ward. I understood his concerns—as Kathy's mother, I had my own. I'd never heard of this kind of thing before; it was all new to me. I was worried about the relationships between the four people and how they might be affected in the future. Not wanting to make things any harder for them, I decided to remain silent, and instead, just sent all of them my prayers.

Leaving their two little girls with Carleen's parents, Ward and Carleen accompanied Kathy and Kevin to a fertility center in San Francisco. Those few of us who knew were sworn to secrecy. The two couples had just gone away for a two-week vacation. If this failed, Kathy was not prepared to handle all the talk and questions from well-meaning friends.

At the clinic, the doctors implanted four of Kathy and Kevin's embryos into Carleen, in the hopes that she would become pregnant. To increase their chances, Kathy underwent the same procedure.

The couples returned home hopeful and began the wait to see if either Carleen or Kathy was pregnant. The tension built as the days passed. And then the news finally came. Success! Carleen was carrying a single baby and Kathy was pregnant with twins. We were still sworn to silence, as something might yet go wrong. Seven weeks passed, and all was well. Twelve weeks passed — still all was well. Suddenly, the news was out, and in our small town this big news spread like wildfire. Fourteen weeks, and then crash — Kathy lost her twins. Again, Carleen was there for Kathy. But this time, Kathy knew that Carleen was carrying her baby, and that helped her make it through.

As the gossip made its rounds, I realized what a strong, special person Carleen was. People would ask her, "How can you give up this baby?" She would respond with no hesitation that it wasn't hers to keep. Because Carleen had two daughters, they would add, "What if this is a boy?" Carleen would answer simply, "It still isn't my baby." A local minister, who happened to meet Carleen, said, "This may work if you never see this baby again." Carleen laughed when she told Kathy, saying, "I think it's a pretty sure thing I'll see you and your baby after this!"

There was also enormous support from the community. One day, I heard Carleen's coworker say, "These girls will pull this off without a hitch. They are both so focused." It was true. Carleen paid no attention to the calendar and allowed Kathy to do all the work — just as she would have had to do had she been pregnant. Kathy accompanied Carleen on all her doctor's visits. As the months passed, the entire community began pulling for the two couples. One lady asked me when the baby was due, adding, "This may be Kathy and Kevin's baby, but it is also the whole community's baby!"

The baby was due January 10, 1998. By Christmas, Kevin was so excited, he was walking on clouds. January 10th came and went with no baby. On January 19th, the doctor decided to induce labor. Carleen entered the hospital, and Kathy stayed by her side the whole time. Four days later, Carleen gave birth by cesarean section to a healthy baby boy — 9 pounds, 15 ounces! Ten minutes later, Carleen leaned over to Kathy, gave her a big hug and kiss, and whispered, "Thank you for allowing me to do this for you." Kathy was so moved, she burst into tears of gratitude. Kathy and Kevin, along with the entire community, had a new son.

Carleen returned home to her family the following day to recuperate, and Kathy and Kevin took their little boy home a couple of days later. Tears of joy were shed everywhere as the news spread. A baby shower that was planned for a few close friends grew to a hundred! The whole community gave a special gift of appreciation to Carleen and Ward: a weekend at a resort.

What a story Kevin and Kathy have to tell their son when he is old enough to understand. They named him Matthew Edward, Edward after Ward whose change of heart made such a difference in the gift of life one friend gave another.

~Jane Milburn
Chicken Soup for the Girlfriend's Soul

Snow at Twilight

The sky had been gray all day, and now it was getting darker. Four feet of fresh snow lay over our town, a small city in a southern state that usually doesn't see a foot of snow all at one time, all winter long.

This was an unusual snow, a big snow, to which we had awakened that morning, and which had taken all day to accumulate. Anticipating it, the city had closed schools, and CJ and I had watched through the morning as showers of small grainy flakes were interrupted by windy swirls of large ones. By late afternoon, our mailbox was nearly drifted under and neither foot nor tire tracks disturbed the plane of snow we could see out the front window.

We decided to go sledding. Twilight was falling, but the snowfall had stopped, and the air was perfectly still. Bundled and booted, CJ and I skidded his new red plastic snow saucer behind us down the unplowed streets toward the sledding hill at the neighborhood park.

Slow work it was. Each boot fall cut a fresh break in the snow. We were the only ones out there.

But our snow hill was worth it. A nearly vertical drop that terminates in an open soccer field, it's about fifteen feet from the top of the hill to the wide flat below. The next day would surely see it crawling with kids, while moms in minivans drank coffee from carry-mugs and visited along the residential street at its crest.

"We're gonna have fun," I encouraged my six-year-old as he did his best to power himself through snow that reached, at times, to his thighs. We had to move with as much determination as the snow would allow, or dusk would overcome us before we got there.

But we never got to the snow hill. At least, not both of us.

Children's voices came to us as we approached a side street where a friend of CJ's lives. "Hey Mom, it's Kyle," CJ said. "I want to play with him."

Naturally, a friend one's own age is far more fun than the mom with whom you've been cooped up all day. And Kyle's driveway slopes; that was hill enough for a couple of little boys and Kyle's plastic toboggan. Kyle's mom said she was happy to have CJ come play for an hour before dinner.

So there I was, halfway to the sledding hill, but without my companion. I could have turned around and gone home to a house made quiet for the first time all day. But I didn't want to stop. And that's when I realized that taking CJ to the big hill was my excuse for going there myself.

So I continued.

Four teenage boys were the only ones at the park when I arrived. No other moms, no other kids. Mostly the boys were hanging around and jiving each other. But every so often, three boys watched as a fourth took a snowboard run down the side of the hill.

I might as well have been from another time zone, as little in common as I had with these boys in their neon fleece vests, tasseled knit caps and nylon ski suits. My old sweats and ancient peacoat were no match for fashion, and CJ's unadorned red saucer was a paltry counterpart to the logo-adorned snowboards they carried.

Together, the boys had dragged a tractor tire halfway up the hill, from the playground below where it usually functions as a climbing toy for children. Together, they had packed snow over and around it, to create a mogul for their snowboard runs. And individually, they tried to outdo each other as their snowboards hit the jump and went airborne.

Slyly, they eyed me. What could a mother possibly be doing at the snow hill without a child? I began to wonder about this myself as I folded my forty-one-year-old frame into a first-grader's snow saucer to push off. I hadn't bent my body into these angles in a dozen years or more.

If I end up spraining something, it serves me right, I thought.

But the saucer hadn't yet cut a gully into the snow, so my unhurried first run really required pushing my way down the hill. I hadn't injured any body parts when I reached bottom, but I hadn't really gone very fast. It was going to take another run or two before the saucer would gain any speed.

I picked up the saucer, trudged back to the top of the hill and learned afresh that no step routine at the gym matches the effect of taking oneself up a deeply snow-banked slope. But the second saucer run was more like it.

On the third run, my saucer sped down the hill and went a distance across the soccer field before stopping. Snow spray against my face refreshed it better than any fancy water spritzer at the cosmetics counter. My lungs filled with air that felt absolutely clean.

On the fourth run, the saucer's lip caught some snow on the way down and flipped me upside down into the soft powder. This is it, I thought, the moment I will have to explain to everyone from my neck brace. But instead, I found myself laughing out loud, sprawled on my back in the snow. My own victory whoops accompanied runs five and six.

The teenagers may have thought I had lost my mind. But no, instead I had found something else I had misplaced through my years of career advancement, motherhood and the advent of my forties: the freedom of going really fast through thin air.

It was nearly dark when I left the hill and made it back to Kyle's house for CJ. My son looked me over: my snow encrusted pants, wet gloves and flushed face. "What were you doing, Mom?" he asked.

"Me?" I answered. "I took myself sledding."

~Maggie Wolff Peterson
Chicken Soup for Every Mom's Soul

Pictures

A sister is a gift to the heart,
a friend to the spirit,
a golden thread to the meaning of life.
~Isadora James

I never had a sister, just two younger brothers. Now that we are adults, we get along well, even though it seems as though I spent much of my childhood trying to get rid of them. I wasn't exactly what you would call a benevolent older sister. But with a sister, I thought it would have been different. I envied the relationship that a few of my friends had with their sisters. When I had two daughters of my own, I hoped that they would have what I had only dreamed of.

It didn't start out that way at first. When the girls were young, although they got along most of the time, they weren't exactly soul mates. Maybe it was the difference in their ages—Shoshana was nearly five when Ilana was born—or maybe just a difference in personalities. As they got older, my dream of a special relationship between these two sisters seemed less important. After all, they were beautiful, bright children, and while they were not unusually close, they clearly loved each other.

But then, when I had almost forgotten the dream, things began to change.

It was June and Shoshana was fourteen, about to enter high school. Like many of the other teenagers in our small community, she had decided to attend a school in Chicago. The school had an excellent academic reputation, which helped offset our apprehension about sending our little girl nearly one hundred miles away from home, with her coming home only on the weekends.

It was hard at first to think of our child so far away, but my husband and I knew it would be good for her, and we gradually got used to the idea.

But Ilana didn't.

Actually, I didn't know that at the time. I was preoccupied with Shoshana's needs, and I didn't really stop to think about the effect this would have on Ilana. She was only nine, and it didn't occur to me that she would have such strong feelings on the subject. After all, in only four more years Shoshana would be going off to college anyway. It just didn't seem like such a big difference to me. But it was to Ilana.

I wish I could say that I knew this because I had many long, heartfelt discussions with Ilana on this subject or because Ilana confided in me, or because she told Shoshana how she felt. But that would be a lie. I only found this out by accident.

One morning, about a week before Shoshana was scheduled to leave for her new school, I went into Ilana's room to put away some clean laundry. I found Ilana sitting on the floor, surrounded by several piles of photographs. I looked more closely. I saw that they were the pictures from our family's summer camping trip. I hadn't even seen the pictures yet. They must have arrived in the mail just that morning. I was mildly annoyed that Ilana had taken them up to her room without telling me, but what I saw next made me really angry. Ilana had taken scissors and glue, and was carefully cutting out the figures on some of the pictures and pasting them onto a sheet of pink construction paper.

"What are you doing?" I yelled. "Stop that! Why are you cutting up those pictures?"

I didn't wait for an answer. I just grabbed the pictures and stormed out of the room. I was too angry to talk to Ilana at that moment. I just threw the pictures on the dresser in my room and stormed off.

Ilana stayed in her room the rest of the morning. When it got to be lunchtime, I decided that I should go up and talk with her. By now, I was more curious than angry.

I wanted to know why she had been cutting up the pictures.

When I opened the door to Ilana's room, I saw that she had fallen asleep on the bed. Lying beside her was the pink construction paper. I picked it up and turned it over. About half of the paper was covered with a collage of photographs that Ilana had cut out and assembled from the family vacation pictures, as well as a few older pictures from several years ago. Every picture was of her and Shoshana. Here they were, as infant and toddler, in the bathtub together. Here they were, in front of the mirror, with my lipstick and high heels. And in another, Shoshana was holding onto the back of Ilana's bike as she learned to ride without training wheels. I remembered that day. Ilana had come running into the house, beaming with pride. "I did it, Mommy!" she exclaimed. "Shoshana taught me!"

I sat down on the bed, and Ilana stirred and opened her eyes. "Hi, honey," I said gently.

Her lower lip quivered. "I'm sorry, Mommy," she said.

"I know, honey," I said. "It's okay. I'm sorry I got so angry. What were you making, anyway?" I asked her.

She took the pink paper from my hand and studied it. "It's for Shoshana," she said finally. "She can hang it up on the wall in her new room."

"That's a good idea," I agreed.

Then she looked up at me. "She's going to be really far away now. And she's going to be really busy; she'll have a lot of homework and a lot of new friends."

I reached out and hugged her. I knew what she was thinking, but it was too painful to say it out loud. How could I reassure her that things wouldn't change so much? How to tell her with confidence that her sister wouldn't forget about her? After all, I wondered those very same things myself. I didn't have the words to comfort her, but Ilana's next question provided the answer.

"Do you think she'll like it?" she asked. "I shouldn't have used pink. Shoshana hates pink. I like pink; that's why I picked it, but it's not for me."

"I think she'll love it," I answered gently. "She'll look at it every day and she'll think of you because you like pink." And I knew she would.

When Shoshana moved into her new room, it took her several weeks before she was settled in and found places for all of her things. But she hung up the pink paper the very first day.

And Ilana was right: Shoshana was very busy those first few months. We spoke on the phone every night, but we only saw her on weekends, and then she had homework and wanted to spend time with her friends. But she had that pink paper to remind her. And she remembered well. I found this out by accident, too. One evening, a few weeks after the start of the school year, I walked into the den. Ilana was sitting at the computer and she started giggling.

"What's so funny?" I asked. Ilana pointed to an e-mail from Shoshana.

"Remember the time I was teaching you to ride without training wheels?" the message began. "I let go of the bike, and you couldn't steer and you rode right through Mrs. Parker's flower bed. You squashed all of her tulips." By Thanksgiving, Ilana had a stack of e-mails an inch high from her sister. Each one started out with a reference to one of the pictures.

It took a physical distance between them to bring them closer emotionally. During the four years that Shoshana was away, Ilana became a teenager herself. The two girls found that they had more in common than just memories and a shared childhood. But it was precisely those memories and those shared experiences that formed the basis for their friendship, and that gave them something to build on. All of those years, when I had all but forgotten about the bond that I hoped they would develop, it was happening right under my nose and I didn't even recognize it.

When Shoshana went away to college, Ilana was just starting high school. She and Shoshana continued their frequent e-mail conversations. Ilana printed out and saved every one. And when Shoshana moved into her new dorm room, the first thing she hung up on the wall was the pink picture.

Last summer Shoshana got married. Ilana was her maid of honor. We have a whole album of beautiful pictures, including many of our two daughters together. But Ilana gave Shoshana and her new husband a picture of her own. It's a lovely picture of the two sisters, taken in front of our house on a soft spring morning. And on the frame, there is a lovely inscription: "A sister is a supportive companion, loyal and loving, protective and kind. A keeper of secrets, a one of a kind. A true friend in thought, and provider of memories."

When Shoshana and her husband moved into their new apartment I went over to help them unpack and settle in. The apartment was in chaos, filled with suitcases, partially opened gifts and half-eaten pizza. Shoshana had just started unpacking, and she had carefully laid out the important things the young couple would need as they started their new life together—toothbrushes, linens, a frying pan.

And of course, Ilana's pink picture.

We fill many roles throughout life, but just because we become something new—wives and mothers, for example, we never stop being what we were as children—daughters and sisters. Shoshana is a wife now. One day, God willing, she'll be a mother. But she is wise enough to know that the adult she is today owes much to the child she once was. She fills her home with the things of her own choosing that make her happiest, that bring her joy and remind her of those she loves and who love her. She and her sister still have time together, to giggle and share secrets and just be sisters with their own private language. There is enough love between them to share with others. Shoshana and her husband are in the process of writing their own history, of making memories together that they will share with their children and grandchildren in the years to come.

If she is very lucky, my daughter Shoshana will, one day, come across a child of hers cutting up pictures on the bedroom floor. And if I know Shoshana, she'll look at an old faded pink paper that will be framed and hung on the wall of some room in her house and she'll do what I should have done.

She'll smile to herself and softly close the door.

~Phyllis Nutkis
Chicken Soup for the Sister's Soul

Perfect Vision

My twin daughters have finally reached the age of two. And this means two things. First, they have control over language. Second, they have control over their bladders. In light of these latest acquisitions, one of their favorite pastimes recently has been to insult each other employing a combination of these newfound skills.

My darling girls now run around shouting, or just stating conversationally, "I pee on you!" followed by an illustrative, higher pitched, "PEE!" I honestly don't know where the seed that sprouted into this less-than-charming behavior came from. (Unless it was the isolated incident where an undiapered baby brother spritzed one of the girls in the head with, well, maybe you can guess. To say the least, it made quite an impression.)

Mostly, they say this to each other when they're bickering. Or sometimes when they're just plain bored. It is, happily, an idle threat unaccompanied by any action other than thrusting one's stomach out at the insulted party during the "PEE!" part.

In the privacy of our own home, and behind their backs, my husband and I are gently amused by our daughters' urinary shenanigans. However, this isn't exactly the type of conversation I'd say we encourage. Aside from the obvious objections, this one's got a high parental embarrassment factor. A public exhibition is bound to raise a few questioning eyebrows.

But it seems as if there are many things that two-year-olds do that don't need a lot of encouragement, and in my experience, they are frequently the very things that you would rather not have your offspring doing or saying in public. And with two two-year-old daughters, plus a one-year-old son, being the current equation of my life, I have ample opportunity to experience this particular phenomenon firsthand. Further, I'll have to admit that there are days when it feels as if the sum of this equation will be the loss of my desire to venture ever again into a public space.

Yes, with three kids under three years you greatly increase your odds that any given excursion into the public domain will involve loud conversations about bodily functions, declarations of nasal contents and the canvassing of total strangers to ascertain their anatomical correctness. This verbal barrage will likely serenade the complete devastation of at least one display or teaser table, and the attempted consumption of the (non-edible and expensive) merchandise displayed thereon.

It is also extremely likely there will be whining, followed by a smattering of biting and hair-pulling, and a diaper by-pass (or two or three), which will then be combined with excessive trips to the potty, leading to the need for new "big girl" pants anyway. These will have been accidentally left at home by yours truly. Hold the applause, please.

And that's all on a good day.

Believe me, I receive more than my fair share of stares, unhelpful comments and looks from passersby. So, my plate's full. And I try to limit the accretion of potentially embarrassing additions to it, such as shouts about voiding one's bladder on a sibling. But, of course, my kids have other ideas. And sometimes, it's these other ideas that teach me most about what being a parent is really all about.

Take, for example, last week at the drug store. Busily engaged seeking shampoo, it suddenly filters into to my brain that my twins are once again having their little "conversation." And have been for some time.

"I pee on you. Pee!" is countered by, "NO! I pee on you! Pee!"

They go back and forth and back and forth, as only two-year-olds can manage. It was actually a quiet discussion, and relatively civil, but I looked around furtively to see if anyone was eavesdropping.

It was then that I noticed two little old ladies staring at me. Lovely ladies, quintessential grandmotherly women, proper, upright pillars of the community they were. Ladies you'd like to drink tea and eat crumpets with, not offend by exposure to your overly bladder-minded toddlers.

They started slowly walking toward us purposefully and I could tell they meant to say something. Oh great, I thought, inwardly cringing, just what I need.

The oldest lady, a dear woman with a frail gray bun and a sturdy walker, reached me first. She bent over, peered at my daughters, and stuck a crooked finger out at them. My heart sank. Embarrassment aside, I rallied to defend my children from the onslaught of a stranger.

But she looked up, beaming. "I just wanted to tell you," she said "you have the two most precious little girls in this stroller! They are just beautiful, and so well-behaved!"

Her friend was nodding in agreement.

It was then that I noticed their hearing aids.

I was actually blushing, thinking, Ladies, if you only knew what these precious girls have been discussing for the past ten minutes. But then I smiled, and agreed, and thanked her because, of course, what she had said was true. I thought of the many times that my own "deaf ear" would serve my children and myself well.

"Oh, and look at the beautiful baby in the backpack!" They cooed over my son for a second.

Then one of them asked, "Are they all yours?"

I get this question a lot, but it is frequently worded more like "Are all these children yours?" and asked in a tone that implies that if the answer is "yes," then I should have my head examined. I nodded my head in the affirmative, or maybe my son nodded it for me, as he was, at that moment, ripping out handfuls of my hair.

Both their faces lit up at my answer, "Oh! What a blessing to have such a beautiful family!" one said.

"Yes, you're very lucky indeed," the other added.

They both smiled and sighed.

"Enjoy them. They grow up too fast."

Despite the day I'd been having, I knew I had just experienced great wisdom from women who knew a thing or two; women with impaired hearing but perfect vision. These women didn't need to see (or hear) the nitty-gritty sometimes-less-than-pretty details of life with toddlers. They had very likely been there themselves. And what they now saw was the forest, where I sometimes still only see the trees.

They saw the truth.

And that truth has become my four-sentence mantra, my reminder that the "I pee on you" days will not last forever. It's a bittersweet benediction.

"I am lucky."

"I am blessed."

"Enjoy them."

"They grow up too fast."

~Karen Driscoll
Chicken Soup for the Mother & Daughter Soul

A Mother's Mid-Summer Prayer

Labor Day is a glorious holiday because your child will be going back to school the next day. It would have been called Independence Day, but that name was already taken.

~Bill Dodds

Dear God,

Grant me the strength to last until Back to School Night.

Give me the energy to drive the swim team carpool, take knots out of wet shoelaces with my teeth and untangle the dog from the sprinkler hose.

Grant me the wisdom to remember the name of the redheaded kid from down the street who hasn't left our house since July.

Walk with me through the backyard over piles of wet bathing suits and empty ice cream cups, to rescue my good lipstick from the bottom of the wading pool.

Give me the courage to accept that everything in the refrigerator either has a bite out of it, had a finger stuck in it or is reproducing in the vegetable crisper underneath the expensive cheese.

Guide me down the hallway to the laundry room, where I can experience five minutes of peace and quiet by turning the lights out and climbing on the dryer so the kids can't see my feet underneath the door.

Help me accept that fact that even if I take the kids to the circus, install a pool in the backyard, go on a safari, and carve a redwood tree into a canoe and sail down the Congo, my children will end each day with "I'm bored."

Grant me the serenity to smile when my husband insists on tossing the Hamburger Helper on the gas grill because "everything tastes better barbecued."

In your infinite wisdom, show me how to disconnect the video game console that hasn't been turned off since June 22nd.

Comfort me when I realize the color of my earth-tone carpet has changed into a mixture of melted blue Popsicle and the remains of somebody's purple slushie.

And if I ask too much, God, just give me the foresight to know that one day — not too many years from now — the barbecue, television and sprinkler hose will be off; the refrigerator, front door and garage will be closed, and I will wonder where my children — and the little redheaded boy with the glasses — went.

~Debbie Farmer
Chicken Soup for the Mother's Soul 2

Just Another Day

God gave you a gift of 86,400 seconds today.
Have you used one to say "thank you?"
~William A. Ward

Is it morning already? I rub my eyes and get up to ready myself for just another day.

It's just another day. I look out my window to see the sun beaming down, caressing the Earth with its golden rays. Above, white clouds float in the brilliant blue sky. I hear a cardinal singing to his mate as he perches upon my back fence. And a bed of crocus open their purple heads to the heavens in joyful thankfulness.

It's just another day. My small daughter bursts into the room, her giggle ringing through the house as she hugs my neck tightly. Her small hand fits into mine as she pulls me to the kitchen to show me the card she has made. A stick figure with curly brown hair waves from the paper and beneath it; written in purple crayon are the words, "I love you, Mommy."

It's just another day as I stand quietly and watch a handicapped child. He struggles to get his special walker over the curb, but it won't budge. A well-meaning teacher offers assistance, but he brushes her away. With determination, he conquers the curb and is off to laugh and play with his friends. I weep inside for his handicap, but I am inspired by his courage. And I smile as I watch the children play, totally accepting their friend for who he is, not judging him for what he lacks.

It's just another day. My son proudly presents the report he did for school. He shares with me the hopes and dreams he holds for his future. His curiosity and excitement are contagious as we unfold the limitless possibilities that lay before him. I am encouraged that no dream is beyond our reach if we want it bad enough.

It's just another day. My beloved wraps his arms around me and surrounds me in love. I turn to look in the eyes that share my innermost feelings. What a special friend I have. Someone who loves me for who I am. Someone to lean on when I feel down. Someone to share my happiness. Someone to love.

Yes, it is just another day. A day to enjoy God's gracious beauty upon this Earth. A day to kiss the cherub cheeks of my children, and share in their hopes and dreams. A day to learn the value of determination and hard work. A day to learn the value of judging mankind for the quality he has, not what he has not. A day to learn the value of love.

Yes, it's just another day, I sigh. The stars dance in the velvet sky as a full yellow moon smiles cheerfully down. The house is quiet and still. The only sound is the soft even breathing of my spouse. I recall the scripture: "This is the day the Lord has made; let us rejoice and be glad in it." (Psalm 118:24) And as I lay at the side of my soul mate I pray that God will let me see "just another day"!

~Charlotte "Charlie" Volnek
Chicken Soup for the Christian Family Soul

On, Being a Parent

Funny Times

*Humor is the great thing,
the saving thing.
The minute it crops up, all our irritation and resentments slip away,
and a sunny spirit takes their place.
~Mark Twain*

Hamster on the Lam

He conquers who endures.
~Persius

F riday. The weekend beckoned. But when I walked through the door, I heard the sniffling of a traumatized child. Amy, our eight-year-old, was sobbing. And for good reason. Hammie the hamster was inside our bathroom wall.

One major complicating factor: Hammie was not ours. He was the class hamster. He had come to our house as part of the great second-grade pet cultural exchange, having survived more than a dozen home visits with the kids in Mrs. Blackwell's class. A hamster with peer pressure attached.

Now, though he had been in our house only a few hours, Hammie was performing his own version of the Hamster Olympics inside the walls of our home. He was where no paw should tread — on and under pipes, stirring up drywall dust, munching on whatever looked tasty.

As great tragedies often do, this one started with a small act of kindness. Amy had uncaged Hammie in the bathroom for an early-evening romp as she guarded the door. With only one exit, the bathroom had seemed the perfect place for a romp. Unfortunately there was the teeniest hole where the sink cabinet meets the wall. We'd never known it was there, but to Hammie, it must have looked like the Florida Turnpike.

A quick sprint and he was gone: down the linoleum, over the

baseboard and into the wall. And now the little squirt's telltale scratching seemed to move in rhythm to the sobs outside.

Midnight. The family was fast asleep while I maintained the hamster watch. Poking my finger into the hole, I felt a hamster paw. I bent over and, startled, gazed right into Hammie's eyes. He seemed to be smiling.

At first, I thought that by baiting Hammie with some hamster fast food — carrots, apple, a huge piece of lettuce — the little guy would pitter-patter back into the bathroom.

He went for the lettuce. Unfortunately, he took it right back into the hole.

After a restless night, we swore one another to a tell-and-you-die oath. We had forty-eight hours to capture Hammie. Monday would be bad enough without kick-starting the second-grade rumor mill.

Saturday afternoon brought a new plan of attack: Lure Hammie into the Mice Cube, a small plastic rectangle. Bait it. The hungry rodent goes in the trapdoor, but he doesn't come out. This night brought less sleep — more scratch, scratch, scratch — no Hammie. I guessed he still had plenty of lettuce.

Sunday morning. The pressure was on. We prayed for Hammie. Amy said that under no circumstances would she ever go to school again if we didn't catch him.

A visit to Dad's secret weapon, the Pet Store Guy, now seemed crucial. When I told him of our crisis, he barely batted an eye. Clearly he knew a lot about hamster psychology. In his opinion, Hammie was either (a) on the lam and loving it, (b) playing a game of catch-me-if-you-can or (c) lost in the wall. But he would come out. Hunger would win.

The Pet Store Guy told me to take a two-gallon bucket and place an apple inside. Douse a towel in apple juice. Put the bucket a few hamster steps from the hole and drape the towel over the side — a kind of hamster ramp, if you will. Just enough towel should stick into the bucket to allow the hamster to fall in but not crawl out.

Bedtime Sunday. The trap was in place, but the bathroom wall was eerily quiet. Was Hammie alive in there? I sat in a chair, feeling defeated. I had been beaten by a pint-size rodent. How would I break this news to sixteen second-graders?

Then, in what seemed like one of those slow-motion *Chariots of Fire* moments, my hamster-loving, sweet-hearted girl was motioning to us from the door. Amy had heard the hamster drop in the bucket.

She looked first. Her anxiety as she peered over the edge of the bucket, followed by the sheer euphoria of her realization that he was there, was indescribable.

Hugs and kisses. Hero Dad. Hero Mom. Hamster high-fives.

There are moments in your children's lives when your heart bounces through your throat—the first step, the first bicycle ride, the first sentence read, the first hamster drop.

I never did win a stuffed animal at the carnival for my sweetheart. But now I know how it feels.

~Amy and Jim Grove
Chicken Soup for the Cat and Dog Lover's Soul

Chickenpox Diary

Your day goes the way the corners of your mouth turn.
~Anonymous

Day 1: I'm starting a diary about the kids' upcoming experience with chickenpox. It all started this morning when Vicki called to tell me her kids have chickenpox. She knows I am undecided about whether to have my kids inoculated with the new vaccine, and she said if I wanted to just get it over with, we were welcome to come over and get exposed. She said the incubation period was a week or two, and when I looked at the calendar and counted the days, it turns out we'll have chickenpox right in the middle of our school's break.

Since the kids are going to be home anyway, I figured she was right—why not just get it over with? Plus, my husband is already planning to stay home that week to catch up on paperwork, so he'll be available to back me up when needed.

On the way to her house, I explained to the kids that we were having a playdate with sick friends because we want to get their germs. They asked if this meant there'd also been a policy change about chewing bubble gum that's been picked off the sidewalk.

Vicki made sure all the children shared juice cups, and we talked about how the timing of this was so perfect, it was almost like a miracle. Perhaps I will submit diary for publication in parenting magazine.

Day 2: Went to grocery store to stock up on calamine lotion and oatmeal bath called Aveeno. Told checker plan for having all four children get chickenpox during school break when husband is home to help. She said, "That's good planning."

Day 12: Keeping bottle of calamine in pocket since chickenpox expected to appear any minute.

Day 18: School break is over; daughters back in school. Husband back at work. Son home with chickenpox. New spots keep appearing; older ones shedding off. After dinner, I dashed to store for more calamine. Mentioned to checker that miracle plan is a bucket of hog slop. Then remembered Vicki's wise words: "It's a rite of passage" and vowed to remain positive.

Day 21: Daughter erupting with chickenpox, so she's staying home with brother. Children's only relief from boredom is connecting red dots on body with permanent marker and demanding exotic snacks.

Day 26: Husband left for out-of-town business trip. Son finished with chickenpox, now has flu. Daughter feeling fine but must remain in quarantine several more days. Second daughter also home with stomach ache. Am feeling kinship with pioneer women who gave birth in cornfield and shot rattlesnake off porch while husband away on cattle drive.

Day 30: All kids home from school—one with chickenpox, two with flu, one faking to get in on the snacks. Time together at home giving us a chance to get intimate understanding of each person's special idiosyncrasies, such as those observed by nurse on the job at lunatic asylum.

Day 32: Husband called early from nice hotel while waiting for morning room service. Very understanding when I was unable to remember his name. Described to him last night's dream about oatmeal in which pantry doors in kitchen swung open by themselves revealing huge container of Quaker Oats cereal. Portrait of friendly Quaker pictured on cereal box transformed into scary-looking image of Vicki, that contaminator of children.

Day... So tired... don't know what day it is and don't care anyway. Very concerned about last night's pizza order. Found pimply faced delivery boy's cap in bathtub and suspect he's the strong one I had trouble wrestling into Aveeno bath. Made note to give extra tip with next order.

~Janet Konttinen
Chicken Soup for the Mother's Soul 2

Sibling Rivalry

*A gorgeous example of denial is the story about the little girl who was
notified that a baby... sister was on the way.
She listened in thoughtful silence,
then raised her gaze from her mother's belly to her eyes and said,
"Yes, but who will be the new baby's mommy?"*
~Judith Viorst

When my wife, Deeptee, came home from the hospital
with our second baby, she hired Meena, a live-in nurse,
to come along and help out for the first few weeks.
Having read up on sibling rivalry, my wife watched our eighteen-
month-old daughter, Chinmya, for signs of jealousy or insecurity. But
Chinmya adored her little brother from the start. She loved to help
Meena feed and bathe the baby. She even offered to share her toys.

Several weeks passed and the mother of my two children, convinced that Chinmya was suffering no ill effects, decided she could
manage without a nurse. As she watched Meena walk out to her car
that last day, she heard an unmistakable cry of distress.

"Meena!" yelled Chinmya, running after her. "You forgot your
baby!"

~Deeptee and Vikrum Seth
Chicken Soup for Every Mom's Soul

A Forkful of Humor

If something has to go wrong, why does it have to happen while we're on vacation? It seems like every trip our family takes, we wind up making a visit to a hospital or clinic. It's one thing to visit these facilities while we're home and can utilize the comfort zone provided by our own family doctors, but while vacationing we are ultimately at the mercy of every student of the nearest medical school. It doesn't take a rocket scientist to diagnose an ear infection and prescribe some antibiotics. And it certainly was no rocket scientist who cared for my husband when our three-and-a-half-year-old daughter rammed the tines of her fork into his eye. For Dad and Elizabeth, it was no "tine-y" problem.

It was, of course, purely accidental. She's a sweet child who adores her daddy. However, she is animated, and she loves to talk. So while making conversation at dinner, her arms flailing to make a point, she pierced her father's eyeball with her salad fork.

"Owwww!" he screamed, pressing his hand to his instantly throbbing eye.

After persistent coaxing, I was finally allowed to look at the damage. There was obviously a serious problem at hand. My poor husband's eye was punctured and trickling blood. He needed immediate medical attention. Like rats in a maze, with our daughter in tow, we drove all over our tourist-infested region in search of a hospital or walk-in clinic. Soon we were seated in a nearby emergency room. The more seriously afflicted were seen first, and in comparison to heart attacks and severed limbs, a punctured eyeball was fairly low on the totem pole. Knowing we were in for a lengthy wait, we busied a guiltless Elizabeth with coloring books and crayons and waited. She immediately started drawing a stick figure of a man with a fork protruding from his eye. Her humor didn't go unnoticed.

"What seems to be the problem?" the male nurse asked when my hubby's name was finally called.

"My little girl stuck a fork in my eye," he explained.

"Any fever?"

"I don't think so."

"Any vomiting?"

"No, but I felt a little queasy when it happened."

"Any diarrhea?"

"From a fork in my eye?" my husband asked, partly amused, partly flabbergasted.

"Oh, that's right. Of course," the nurse jotted things on the chart and muttered constantly to himself.

Next he checked my husband's ears and throat, never looking at his eye, then turned and left the room. We assumed things would improve when the doctor got there.

"Looks like you've got a puncture wound here," the doctor said after a quick exam, indicating immediate pleasure in his quick diagnosis.

"Yes, I know," my husband said. "My daughter punctured my eyeball with a fork."

"Nope. It couldn't have been a fork," the doctor said, still peering from one eye to the next.

"I'm telling you, it was a fork," my husband said, by now becoming clearly disturbed.

"Looks more like a fishhook to me," the doctor said, ferociously scribbling his notes.

My husband shouted, "Look, I obviously was there when this accident happened. So was my wife. My daughter stuck a fork in my eye!"

"A fork!" Elizabeth chimed in.

The doctor didn't look up. He just kept writing.

"Does your husband have a drinking problem?" he asked me.

"What?" I asked. "No, he doesn't have a drinking problem. He hardly ever takes a drink."

By now Dad and daughter were headed for the door. I followed closely at their heels. We stopped by the desk and informed the secretary that since we'd received no service, we had no intention of paying the bill.

"Drinking problem," Elizabeth muttered, shaking her head like an adult rather than a child who had stabbed her daddy's eye.

As we headed out the door, the nurse stopped us once again.

"Here," he said, handing me a business card. "Please take this. And think about taking your little girl to Al-Anon."

On the card were the telephone numbers for the local human services office and the nearest chapter of AA. I couldn't believe what was going on! We were nearly at our car when we noticed a different nurse waving her arms frantically to get our attention.

"Excuse me, excuse me," she said.

"Yes?"

"I am so sorry. The receptionist mixed up your chart with someone else's. You were mistaken for a family where the father had repeatedly gotten drunk and drummed up a list of ailments a mile long," she explained. "Please, sir, accept our apologies and come back inside."

Everyone makes mistakes; we all have. We've always tried to practice the philosophy of forgiving and forgetting, so we went back into the hospital.

After waiting just a couple of minutes, the same male nurse came back out for my husband, greeting him with a smile and a profuse apology.

"It's okay," my husband said to him. "I just wish someone would do something for my incredible eye pain."

After we were made comfortable once again in a different examining room, we awaited the return of the doctor. When he arrived, he looked at my husband's chart and promptly asked how long his sinuses had been bothering him.

"They're never going to fix Daddy!" Elizabeth cried.

We quickly and quietly got up and walked out. There would be no looking back. There would be no going back. And there would obviously be no treatment for Dad's eye tonight.

A couple of days later when we were safely back at home, my husband, accompanied by Elizabeth, visited our family doctor.

"What seems to be the problem?" the doctor asked.

Elizabeth interjected quickly, "He has a drinking problem. What can we do to fix him?"

~Kimberly A. Ripley
Chicken Soup for the Father & Daughter Soul

The Family Ski Trip

Maybe I've been spending too much time watching television shows like *The X-Files* or something, but I'm trying to think how I would describe skiing to extraterrestrials.

Aliens: Take us to your leader.

Me: Can't right now, we're going skiing.

Aliens: What is skiing?

Me: Well, first you go to the top of this really, really high mountain that's covered with this cold, slippery stuff called snow. Then you strap these skinny little sticks on your feet, and try to go straight down the steep mountain in a standing position without killing yourself. And if you survive, you stand in a long line for the opportunity to do it again.

Aliens: Goodbye.

Me: Where are you going?

Aliens: In search of intelligent life.

It was crowded at the rental shop. Plus, with the temperature only twenty degrees outside, everyone was dressed like the Pillsbury Dough Boy—only in shades of mauve and lime green.

"Maybe we should have rented equipment back in town," my wife suggested.

"No way," I said. "Remember last time? They gave me two left skis and two right boots. All day long I kept running into myself. Besides, now that I'm more experienced, I need more sophisticated stuff."

"You and I never got off the bunny slope," she said. "The kids are the only ones who advanced."

"Well sure, but with better equipment I'll be skiing circles around everyone out there."

"That's what I'm afraid of," she said.

A young man approached us, wearing a ski hat pulled down to his eyebrows and a T-shirt that read "Ski Naked."

"Are you like into radical carving or do you get off by just dropping in and tucking?"

I hesitated.

"He kinda skis all over the place," my wife told him.

"Oh, right, vary the terrain, challenge the brain. Cool. Got just the set-up for you." He handed me a set of skis that looked like they might have been made by NASA. "Progressive force bindings with environmental friction control, and ultrafast racing skis with deep side cuts and a beta torsion core. You'll fly with these babies."

He turned to my wife. She glanced at me and my new racing outfit.

"I just want something for the other parent who can't afford to be out of work on crutches for six weeks," she told him.

To me, the worst part of skiing is getting from the ski lodge to the chairs. There's always a slope, and it's always slippery. Usually, after thirty minutes or so, I find I have actually lost ground and am now standing in the parking lot.

Apparently, the twelve-hundred-dollar skis helped, because in just minutes, we safely made it to the bunny slope and got into line with all the other five-year-olds.

That's when the rest of the family came barreling up, skidding to a stop right in front of us. I watched them for a second, smiled, then immediately fell down, taking the entire waiting line with me.

"Wow. Cool skis," Jon said. "But this is the wrong lift. You want that lift over there."

I followed the path of the chair lift up the mountain until it became a tiny speck that disappeared into the thick clouds.

"You're not... scared, are you?" asked Patrick.

"Of course not. It's just that these skis may not be fast enough to ski up there on...."

"Black Death Run...."

"Right. Black Death Run."

My wife opted for coffee instead of sheer terror, leaving me as parent-in-charge. Next thing I knew, we were standing somewhere that even mountain goats wouldn't go. I immediately issued a warning to the others.

"Don't get too close to the edge of that cliff," I shouted. "Follow me."

"This isn't a cliff," Christy said. "This is the trail. The cliff is over there somewhere... Dude?"

I've often wondered what my last words would be. I figured maybe something like "I did it for God and country," or "I'm sorry that I have but one life to give." As it turns out my last words contain only vowels, as in,

"Yiiiieeeeeooooooooo...."

I'm not exactly sure what happened over the next few minutes. I remember a lot of white, some muted voices, and being poked by a number of sharp objects all over my body. Fox Mulder of *The X-Files* would have called it an alien abduction. Maybe it was. Of course, why the aliens rolled me up like a giant snowball and dropped me off at the foot of the mountain I'll never know.

But everyone seemed glad to see me, including the rental-shop guy, who quickly removed my progressive force bindings and ultrafast racing skis, and returned to his shop muttering something about hotshot adults and why couldn't they be more sensible — like teenagers.

The rest of the family arrived just as my wife handed me a cup of something that looked like coffee, but tasted like brandy.

"Thanks, dear," I said. "And you'll be happy to know, I'm giving up skiing."

"We are, too," said Stacey.

"Really?" my wife asked.

"Yup," added Shane. "Tomorrow, we're all going snowboarding."

I sighed, pulled a pinecone out of my ear and then immediately downed the entire contents of the cup.

~Ernie Witham
Chicken Soup for the Father's Soul

Where Do Babies Come From?

Blessed are those who believe and see through the eyes of a child.
~Author Unknown

As Mercy Hospital's three-to-eleven nursing supervisor for forty years, I experienced just about every medical emergency. I donned my administrative hat when needed, but loved it most when I donned my nursing one.

Late one evening, I was paged by the understaffed emergency department saying a mom was threatening to deliver her fourth child while en route to the hospital. I hustled to the ER driveway just as a frantic husband sped their car into the ambulance driveway. He jumped out screaming, "The baby is coming! It's coming!"

I opened the door to the passenger's side to find the young mom leaning back in the seat, groaning and pushing—with three little boys gawking over her shoulder from the back seat. I raised her skirt. There was the baby's head. With one more groan and push, the infant was in my hands. People from the emergency-room staff raced to the car with medical supplies as I heard one little boy gasp, "Now I know where babies come from!"

His little brother responded, "Yeah! From under the car seat!"

~Elaine Stallman
Chicken Soup for the Nurse's Soul

A Child's Blessing

Children seldom misquote.
In fact, they usually repeat word for word
what you shouldn't have said.
~Author Unknown

A couple invited some people to dinner. At the table, the mother turned to her six-year-old daughter and asked her to say the blessing. "I wouldn't know what to say," she replied. "Just say what you hear Mommy say," the mother said. The little girl bowed her head and prayed, "Dear Lord, why on Earth did I invite all these people to dinner?"

~Richard Lederer
Chicken Soup for the Christian Family Soul

Breakdown of Family Traced to Psych. 1 Student

You can learn many things from your children.
How much patience you have, for instance.
~Franklin P. Jones

There is no joy quite like a visit from your college kid after he's taken half a semester of Psychology 1.

Nosirree.

Suddenly you're living with Little Freud, and he's got your number. With all this education, he now knows that a) your habit of washing the dishes after each meal is obsessive-compulsive, b) you smoke because you're orally fixated, and c) you're making terrible mistakes raising his younger brother.

No behavior escapes Little Freud's scrutiny. The simplest conversations take on profound and incomprehensible meaning.

Getting Little Freud out of bed in the morning, for example, suddenly becomes a control issue:

"It's past noon," says the simple-minded mother. "Why don't you get up?"

"Mom," says Little Freud in a voice fraught with meaningful implication, "you're obsessing. You shouldn't disempower me this way. Why allow my behavior to affect your own sense of self? Besides,

I have to stay in bed for a while to experience the consciousness of my being when my being is in nothingness."

"That's easy for you to say," says the simple-minded mother. "But I say you're sleeping. Now get up and help rake the leaves."

"Classic transference," says Little Freud in such a way that the simple-minded mother can only conclude she must have a psychic ailment as repulsive as fungus.

Little Freud also knows now that nothing is as simple as it might seem. Calling him to dinner can set off an analysis of your childhood:

"Dinner's ready," says Simple Mind.

"Don't you think it's time you stopped taking your Oedipal rage out on me?" asks Little Freud. "Just because you could never lure your father away from your mother is no reason to resent me."

"What are you talking about?" asks Simple Mind. "I said it's time to eat. What does that have to do with Oedipus?"

"In your unconscious, you associate food with pre-Oedipal gratification, which sets off a chain of associative thoughts leading straight to your rage, which you cannot acknowledge and, therefore, you transfer your hostility to me."

"Be quiet and eat your dinner before it gets cold," says Simple Mind.

"Aha!" says Little Freud, triumphant. "You see? Classic regression."

Little Freud is also a skilled marriage counselor now that he's done so much studying:

"I think it's time you two confronted your feelings," Little Freud tells his parents, who are simple-mindedly enjoying a bottle of wine in front of the fireplace.

"We can't. We're playing cards," says Mr. Simple Mind. "Your mother and I have a policy against confronting our feelings and play-ing cards at the same time."

"Classic avoidance," declares Little Freud.

Little Freud is at his most eloquent, though, when he points out how wrong his simple-minded parents are about their method of raising kids:

"You're not parenting him properly," says Little Freud of his younger brother. "You're too permissive, probably because you're projecting your desire to be free of the shackles of your own stifled childhood."

"What are you talking about?" says the simple-minded mother, who is getting pretty tired of asking Little Freud what he's talking about.

"And he also seems to have a lot of rage," says Little Freud, plunging on. "His id has taken over, and his superego has collapsed. He seems to be entertaining some classic primordial fixations. In fact, I think he wants to kill me."

"He doesn't really want to kill you, dear," says Simple Mind. "I've hired him to do it for me."

"Classic projection," says Little Freud, disgustedly.

~Beth Mullally
Chicken Soup for the College Soul

The Concession Stand

Things could be worse.
Suppose your errors were counted and published every day,
like those of a baseball player.
~Author Unknown

The sign on the door read, "No Admittance to the Concession Stand Unless You Are Scheduled to Help." I smiled. That was me—volunteer parent—contributing to the good of Little League baseball worldwide. I knocked. The door opened narrowly.

"Yeah?"

"I am a concession-stand volunteer," I said proudly.

"Where's your wife?"

"She couldn't make it," I said. "I'm filling in for her."

The door opened just wide enough for me to slip through. It took a moment for my eyes to adjust. As they did, three women in aprons—Rose, Juanita and Theresa—came into focus.

"Hi," I said cheerily. I grabbed a French fry from the infrared warming machine and popped it into my mouth. "So this is the concession stand," I said. "It looks bigger from outside." I swung my arms in a grandiose gesture, knocking over a rack and sending bags of potato chips skidding across the linoleum floor.

"You've never done this before, have you?" Rose asked.

"Well... no... But hey. How hard can it be?"

"Can you make change?" Juanita asked.

"Change? Sure."

"You're on window duty," Rose said.

"Window duty, huh?" I grabbed another French fry. "Don't need me to cook?"

"No," they said in unison.

They scurried about the small building, preparing for a big evening. Rose skillfully pushed hot dogs onto a rotating rotisserie. Juanita filled cups with soda. Theresa started the popcorn machine and poured purple and green syrup into the slushy maker. There was a knock on the window. I slid it open.

"Hot dog, Coke, fries, and Reese's Pieces."

I looked into a smiling retainer, surrounded by round rosy cheeks and the beginning of a second chin.

I shut the window. "How do I know how much to charge?"

"Candy's a buck. Popcorn's fifty cents. Hot dogs and drinks are seventy-five. Fries are fifty cents. Slushies are a quarter." Rose took a breath.

"Chips are seventy-five and coffee is fifty. Refills on coffee are free," said Juanita. Frantically I looked for a pen.

"And we do not allow any credit," said Rose.

"So how much?"

"Three bucks," they sang out.

"Of course," I said.

Faces came and French fries left. I got into a rhythm — repeating the orders loudly and waiting for the magical amount to sound out from behind me. I had several minor mishaps, including two hot dogs that now rolled about beneath my feet and an order of fries that I was sharing with a group of ambitious ants.

The fat kid with the retainer returned for a third time.

"More Reese's Pieces." He slid a couple of sticky dollar bills through the window.

"I'm out of Reese's Pieces."

"No way. What else ya got?"

I scanned the candy rack for inspiration. "Got some imitation-strawberry-flavored taffy."

"Cool. Gimme two."

I beamed with salesmanship. But the others did not seem pleased. I shrugged, skillfully sliding two sodas to a small girl and a hot dog to her friend. Then I served a party of three, but I slid one Coke a little too hard, right off the counter onto the ground. I rebounded, though, with two trouble-free slushies.

A woman appeared.

I bent down and displayed my smiling face. She grabbed me by my shirt collar and pulled me halfway through the small window.

"You ever buy a retainer?"

"Ahhh... no...."

"I've bought two of them in the last six months. They ain't cheap."

"I'm sure they're not...."

"You know what kills retainers?"

"Ahhh... no...."

"Taffy kills retainers."

Suddenly I saw the resemblance. Before I could comment another mother appeared.

"This the guy?" she asked a small girl with one very large cheek. I remembered her. Only had a quarter. I gave her a deal on jawbreakers.

"You a dentist?" the second mother asked.

"No, I...."

"Fronting for a dentist?"

"Of course not. I just...."

Behind me I heard a knock on the door.

"We once caught a dentist giving out all-day suckers at the mall. We ran him out of town."

The first mother let go of my throat.

"I was only doing my duty as a concession-stand volunteer...." I felt a familiar hand on my shoulder.

"What are you doing here?" I asked my wife. "I thought you were sick."

"They...." She lowered her voice. "They called me at home."

"But...."

"It's okay, honey. I'm feeling much better. Besides, it turns out they need an umpire for the seven o'clock game."

I bent over and took one more look at the angry women at the window. I hugged my wife. Then I quickly made my way to the back door, released the bolt and grabbed the doorknob.

"You ever umpired before?" Rose asked.

I smiled. "Well, no.... But hey. How hard can it be?"

~Ernie Witham
Chicken Soup for the Sports Fan's Soul

On, Being a Parent

Moms Really Do Know Best

A mother is the truest friend we have, when trials heavy and sudden,
fall upon us; when adversity takes the place of prosperity;
when friends who rejoice with us in our sunshine desert us;
when trouble thickens around us, still will she cling to us, and endeavor
by her kind precepts and counsels to dissipate the clouds of darkness,
and cause peace to return to our hearts.
~Washington Irving

The Nicest Thing My Mother Ever Said to Me

The other day a man asked me what I thought was the best time of life.
"Why," I answered without a thought, "now."
~David Grayson

When I was about twelve my mother was recounting some clever thing I did when I was three. Her memories, undoubtedly edited by the years, painted me as the perfect preschooler. I compared myself unfavorably with the golden-haired charmer she recalled. Not quite a teenager, I was awkward, with horn-rimmed glasses and hair frizzed from home permanents. (Frizz was not the style then.)

Other girls were teased by the "obnoxious" boys at school and clustered in happy groups. My romances were all imaginary, my friends few. "When was I the best age?" I asked a trifle hesitantly.

Mother looked at me in surprise. "Right now," she told me. "You're the best age you've ever been."

At a luncheon the day before my college graduation, Mother was talking about how fast time flies. It seemed only a month ago she was a Brownie leader, and I was a Brownie. In college, I hadn't been a cheerleader. The hairstyles were now bouffant, but my hair was in a skinny ponytail.

Most nights I'd been at the dorm desk ringing the rooms of other girls as their dates arrived. I had no grad school or Peace Corps applications in the mail. I commented to my mother that I supposed she missed her little girl.

"Heavens, no," she said emphatically. "You're the best age now you've ever been."

Three years later, I was living with my parents again, this time with two babies in the spare room. I'd married my high school sweetheart, and he'd left me. Only for two months until we could join him at the air base in Okinawa, it's true, but there I was with diapers and rattles and baby powder.

Coping with infants who woke at dawn, spurned their oatmeal, then nibbled on the newspapers, I turned my parents' well-ordered home into a nursery.

I ate a bit too much, slept a bit too much and crabbed a bit too much. Apologetically I told my mother I was sure she'd be glad to get back to normal—kids were fine, but I was a bit old to be her child.

"Oh, no," she said. "I enjoy those baby boys, but right now you are the best age you've ever been."

Suddenly my "babies" were teenagers with vacuum-cleaner appetites. My house was never entirely clean, and I was all too inclined to start planning dinner at 4:45. "Frizz" was finally in style, but my hair was straight as a string. Nevertheless, during a holiday visit, my mother said, "You're the best age ever."

The very next week my sixteen-year-old son and I were having a discussion. Although I've forgotten the subject, I remember it was somewhat, um, heated.

We often held heated discussions since we held vastly differing views on the redeeming benefits of TV, the definition of a clean room and whether the just-under-a-quarter-full gas tank he left me had quite a bit left or was darn near empty.

"Brother," he finally said in exasperation. "I bet you wish I was two years old again and you could boss me."

But looking up (!) at him, I only paused a moment before saying honestly, "No, Dan, that's not true at all. Right now you are the best age you've ever been."

And with those words I passed on a gift of acceptance, a feeling of worth and worthiness and security. I handed on my mother's gift of love.

~Marilyn Pribus
Chicken Soup for the Mother & Daughter Soul

Homecoming

As a teenager during World War II, my mother had the unpleasant experience of watching her young friends go off to war, with some never coming home. Twenty-five years later, when the U.S. Army sent me to fight in the Vietnam War, her memories of those days returned with added anxiety, because this time it was her son who was being sent into the unknown. Since I was in the infantry, Mom knew that combat duty would often be dangerous, but her frequent letters never once hinted that she was not coping with my absence. In fact, Mom's ability to keep up my spirits while I was so far from home made it easier for me to deal with the uncertainty of the war.

As my yearlong tour was coming to an end, the Army gave me an eleven-day early release. I decided not to tell my parents I was leaving Vietnam ahead of schedule because I thought it would be more memorable to surprise them by me unexpectedly walking through the front door. As it turned out, we all got a surprise.

My cousin Donald secretly picked me up from the airport, and on the way home we fantasized about how I would make my entrance. When we arrived at the house, we were amazed to find it locked up tight and no one at home. My family had taken a trip out of state and was not expected back until late that evening!

Unsure of what to do next, I decided to get out of my uniform and change into civilian clothes. I did not have a key, so the only way I could get into the house was by crawling through an unlocked window. Once inside, a warm and inviting feeling rushed over me; I was really home! I fondly inspected the familiar surroundings and was happy to see that nothing had changed; even the clothes in my closet were just as I had left them. The only thing different was a map of South Vietnam hanging on the kitchen wall identifying all the places I had written home about. I still wanted to keep my arrival secret, so I decided to spend the night at Donald's. I was careful not to disturb anything or leave any evidence that someone had been in the house.

Shortly after midnight, my tired parents shuffled into the house, and my mother suddenly proclaimed, "Artie is here! He's home!"

Whether or not there is such a thing as mothers' intuition, Mom had somehow detected my presence. Knowing that I was not due home for at least a week, my father laughed at the notion, claiming that Mom was simply tired from the road trip. Yet she insisted that I was hiding in the house and called for me to come out. When there was no response, she began searching. After checking the closets, under the beds and in the attic, Mom finally gave up but could not shake the sensation that I was near.

Her antics put the family on edge, and although no one said anything, they shared the eerie feeling that perhaps I had come home but not in the flesh. They worried that I might have been killed in the war and that my spirit returned to say goodbye. Needless to say, they had a restless night.

Early the next morning, Donald called my parents to make sure everyone was awake because he wanted "to drop something off." When I triumphantly walked through the door, my father, sister and brother gawked at me without speaking a word.

"Hi, everyone," I cheerfully sang out, only to be confused by their silence and darting glances as they suddenly recalled Mom's announcement that I was home.

"What's the matter with you guys?" I asked, noticing that my mother was not in the room. "Hey, where's Mom?"

"Still sleeping," my father sputtered, choking on the words as his eyes followed me down the hall.

The moment I stepped into my mother's room, her eyes opened, and she tilted her head back as if she was expecting me. When I said, "I'm home," Mom gently replied, "I know, you were here last night." Before I could ask how she knew, Mom leaped from the bed and crushed me with a giant hug to make sure I was real. Tears rolled down our faces as she cried, "I knew you were safe. I knew it all along."

For my mother, the war and the waiting were over.

~Arthur Wiknik, Jr.
Chicken Soup for the Mother and Son Soul

19

Potato Salad and Picnics

Kids spell love T-I-M-E.
~John Crudele

Life is like potato salad; when it's shared it becomes a picnic.

When my three children were young, my husband Roy and I were very busy. He was working on his master's degree while working three jobs, and I had three jobs of my own. There was very little time that wasn't crammed with stress, busyness and term papers.

"Can we go on a picnic, Mama?" my six-year-old daughter, Becky begged. "Please."

I had said no so many times in recent months, I decided the usual Saturday morning chores could wait. To her surprise, I agreed. I prepared a few sandwiches and filled a cooler with ice and drinks and called Roy at work. "Meet us at the college pond for a picnic at twelve o'clock sharp," I said excitedly. My eleven-year-old twin sons loaded the cooler and the picnic basket in the trunk, and off we went to spend some quality time together as a family. I glanced at the kitchen counter just before heading to the car and spied a package of stale hamburger buns. I thought about the family of ducks living at the pond. We stopped and picked up a bucket of fried chicken at a fast-food restaurant on the way.

Becky and I spread the tablecloth on the cement picnic table while Brad and Chad tossed a football back and forth. In no time flat, the ducks joined us. Becky squealed with delight as the ducks begged for breadcrumbs. About the time I got the lunch spread out on the table, Roy arrived on the scene. We joined hands and bowed our heads. As the wind blew and the ducks quacked, he thanked God not only for the food but for our family.

That was one of the happiest meals we ever shared together. The gentle breeze God sent our way caressed my face, as the sunshine warmed my heart. The meal was graced with giggles and laughter. We felt a closeness that had been hidden by work and school-related responsibilities for so many months. Once the food was consumed, Roy and the boys skipped rocks on the lake. Becky continued to feed the ducks, and I sat quietly on the picnic table, thanking God for blessing me with such a wonderful family.

Too soon, Roy had to go back to work. The kids continued to play together while I watched. I put the many things that I needed to do on the back burner of my life and simply enjoyed sharing the day with my children. Seeing the joy on each of their faces made me smile.

When we got into the car to return home, Becky crawled in the front seat with me. "Here Mama!" she exclaimed. She was holding a tiny yellow wildflower. Happy tears came to my eyes as I reached out and took it from her. When we arrived home, I put the tiny flower in a toothpick holder and placed the remaining food into the refrigerator.

That night as I tucked our children under their covers, I kissed their cheeks and realized what a wonderful life I had.

"Thank you for the picnic," one of the boys whispered.

"My pleasure," I whispered back.

As I walked out of the room, it dawned on me that even the busiest lifestyle could become a picnic when it's shared with the ones you love.

Even though the kids have now grown up and moved away from home, I can still remember how I felt that day while sitting on the picnic table.

Maybe today would be a good time to cook potato salad, call all of my grown kids, feed some hungry ducks and throw a few rocks into the lake. Since life is like potato salad, let's make it a picnic.

~Nancy B. Gibbs
Chicken Soup for the Christian Soul 2

20

Wishing Away

There are people whom one loves immediately and forever.
Even to know they are alive in the world with one is quite enough.
~Nancy Spain

D o you believe that some people are sent into your life to teach you an important lesson? I do! One such special person in my life was Katherine.

At the time I met Katherine, I was an extremely busy single mother, raising three rambunctious children. Life seemed to be a continual merry-go-round of work, home, schedules and activities. My fondest wish involved a deserted island with warm sunny days, an inexhaustible supply of romance novels, and quiet peace.

I became aware that Katherine had moved into my apartment complex when my seven-year-old daughter, Amber, asked if her new friend could spend the night. "Please? Her name is Joy, and she just moved into number 18 with her mommy."

I stopped making hamburger patties long enough to gaze at my child. Standing next to her was a blue-eyed, blond-haired, gap-toothed little girl, waiting anxiously for my response. Issuing a resigned sigh, I agreed. "Go get Joy's things. We'll be eating in a half-hour." With big grins, the two pint-sized whirlwinds were gone. I continued dinner preparations, wishing that I could be ordering steak in a fine restaurant.

Within minutes, the phone rang. Katherine was calling to introduce herself and to confirm the invitation to spend the night. As we chatted, I noted that her words slurred occasionally, and wondered if she had a speech impediment. I had little time to ponder Katherine's speech, however. I had children to feed, laundry to do, and evening rituals to perform. With a hurried goodbye, I began peeling potatoes as I wished for the late-evening hours when I could retreat to my personal oasis called "my time."

From that beginning, Joy and Amber were inseparable. I spoke to Katherine on the phone occasionally, but never found the time to meet her. I would glimpse her sitting on a bench by the apartment playground, talking to the children, and wonder how she managed to find the time to spend on such frivolous activity. Didn't she have a job to go to? Housework to do? Schedules to keep? How I wished I knew the secret of finding time to play. What fun it would be to toss a ball and laugh in the summer sun.

As time passed, I began to notice that Katherine had problems. At times her speech was difficult to understand. She seemed to stagger and lose her balance. She dropped things. I wondered if she had an alcohol problem, and if the girls were safe with her. I decided the time had come to get to know this woman better, and invited her to a family dinner.

The evening that Katherine and Joy came to dinner proved to be a pivotal point in my life. I watched her closely as she sat at the table surrounded by children. Her speech was muffled in spots; her movements measured and slow. But, I could not detect alcohol on her breath, and she declined the glass of wine I offered.

She seemed happy to focus on the children, listening intently to their stories. She asked them questions and considered their answers seriously. She flittered from topic to topic, keeping pace with their rapid thoughts. She entertained them with amusing stories of her own childhood.

After our meal, the children raced outside to play in what was left of the summer sunshine. Katherine and I followed at a more sedate pace. She walked slowly and carefully while she revealed her past life as a budding executive married to an active, high profile man. She told me of a lifestyle filled with social activity, vacations, and diverse people and settings. She had lived the life I'd always wished for and never achieved.

We settled on a bench beside the playground, and quietly watched the children at their games. I thought of how predictable and unexciting my life was compared to the picture Katherine had painted. With a sigh I told her how I wished the children were older. Then I would have more time to do some things for myself.

A small smile crossed her face as Katherine replied, "My only wish is to be able to stay out of a nursing home until Joy is grown. You see, I have multiple sclerosis. It's slowly taking over my body. It's changed my entire life. My husband couldn't deal with being married to an invalid, and I couldn't keep up with my career. Now, all I want is to be able to raise my daughter. I want to share as much of her world as I can for as long as I can. I've learned to treasure every minute of every day with her, because I don't know how many more of those there are left."

Katherine turned to me, and with another smile, she continued, "Don't spend your life wishing away what you have. You never know when it will be gone."

Approaching darkness ended our conversation, as we became involved with herding our children to their baths and beds. But later that evening, in that quiet time between wakefulness and sleep, her words floated through my head and heart, as I resolved to appreciate my world, instead of wishing for something different.

Time passed quickly, as it always does. Joy and Amber progressed through childhood and adolescence. I spent as much time as I could with them and Katherine. Life was a kaleidoscope of excitement and joy, pain and sorrow. For each stage of development the girls experienced, it seemed Katherine's body claimed a price as she slowly deteriorated physically and mentally.

Katherine's wish was granted: She was able to watch Joy receive her high school diploma, go on to further her education and start a rewarding career.

Some of my many wishes were also granted. The children are now raised and on their own, and I have time to pursue my interests.

I have precious grandchildren to keep me focused on the wonders of the world, and friends and family to love and enjoy. And I carry with me the knowledge that I was granted something for which I never wished... the rewards of knowing Katherine and learning from her wisdom.

~Lana Brookman
Chicken Soup for the Soul Celebrates Mothers

21

Ruby's Roses

Bread feeds the body, indeed, but flowers feed also the soul.
~The Koran

The neighborhood kids nicknamed the cranky old couple Crazy Jack and Ruby Rednose. Rumor was that they sat inside and drank whiskey all day. It was true that Jack and Ruby Jones preferred to keep to themselves. About the only words we ever heard from them were "Keep out of our rosebushes!"

The rosebushes were seventy beautiful floribunda shrubs that served as a fence between our house and theirs. The rose fence took quite a bit of abuse, since our house was the neighborhood hangout. I was eleven at the time and the oldest of six active girls. We should have played our softball games elsewhere to avoid hurting the roses, but we secretly enjoyed irritating Crazy Jack and Ruby Rednose.

Jack and Ruby had a son whom we nicknamed Crazy Jack Junior. He was due to come home from Vietnam. We heard he had been discharged because of a nervous breakdown. The neighborhood had thrown a big party for Jimmy Brown when he came home from the war, but no one offered to have a party for Crazy Jack Junior.

The day Crazy Jack Junior was scheduled to come home, we had a neighborhood softball game in our yard. Johnny McGrath was trying to catch a fly ball. He stumbled over one of Ruby Rednose's thorny rosebushes and fell on top of several more. Boy, did he yell, but the roses were the ones that really suffered. From my vantage point at second base, it looked like about ten of them were damaged pretty badly. Johnny's timing was terrible, because as he lay there swearing at the roses, the Joneses' pickup rolled into the driveway. The truck screeched to a halt and Crazy Jack Junior sprang out. He ran full speed toward Johnny.

"You little punk!" he screamed. "Look what you've done to our family's roses! You've always been trouble. I'm going to fetch my gun and shoot you!"

The next few minutes were a blur. The neighborhood kids ran for their lives. Ruby and Jack tried to restrain their son. He continued to yell threats and profanities. Ruby wasn't my favorite person, but I felt sorry for her when I saw her tearfully pleading with Crazy Jack Junior. Finally, they coaxed him inside.

Meanwhile, my sisters and I tore into our house. Breathlessly, we told Mom what had happened. She put down her sewing and scolded, "Girls, I have told you not to play softball near those bushes. Come outside right now and help me fix them."

"Mom, we thought you didn't like the Joneses," we protested. "They're mean to us. Besides, Crazy Jack Junior might shoot us."

Mom just glared at us. We followed her outside to help mend the rose fence.

While Mom examined the damaged roses, my sisters and I hung back, plotting how to get out of the thorny job. As we whispered back and forth, the Joneses' garage door opened and Ruby slowly walked out. She looked sad. And it wasn't her nose that was red, it was her eyes.

Ruby walked over to my mother. The two women stood looking at each other through the new gap in the rose fence. We girls held our breath, waiting to see who would shout first and what terrible things would be said. How much trouble would we be in when it was all over?

Suddenly my mother stepped forward and hugged Ruby. "I'm glad your son came back home," she said gently. "It must have been a horrible experience in Vietnam. We're sorry about the flowers. The girls will replace them if we can't fix them. In return for all the bother, they'll help you weed the roses this summer."

My sisters and I looked at each other in horror, but Ruby smiled at my mother through her tears. "I know we're particular about these roses," she said, "but they're very special to us. When my mother came from England, she brought one tiny part of her favorite rosebush. That was her reminder of home."

She paused a minute, then said sadly, "My mother had a magic touch with flowers. Over the years that one plant multiplied into all these bushes. Since she died, I've tried to keep them up, but I just don't have her magic touch."

Her voice was all choked up. "Mom died while Jack Junior was in Vietnam. He just found out about her death today. When he saw her rosebushes damaged, it was the last straw."

Ruby mopped at her tears. "Once we got him inside and calmed down, he admitted he's out of control. Jack just drove him to Clinton Valley to be admitted to a treatment program."

By now I felt really bad for the Jones family—what a sorrowful homecoming! I could tell my mother and sisters felt the same.

"We all enjoy the roses as much as you do. We'll be happy to help you care for them," my mother said. "You know, some people say I have a magic touch with flowers, too."

Soon both women were down on their knees talking and examining the damaged bushes together. A few weeks later, the plants all returned with vigor.

My mother and Ruby worked together on the roses all summer long and many summers to follow. So did my sisters and I. A friendship formed between the families that would include countless birthdays, graduations and weddings—including Jack Junior's.

Years later, when her son left home and her husband died, Ruby became part of our family, spending many happy hours at our house.

She wasn't Ruby Rednose anymore; she was Aunt Ruby. And the rose fence wasn't a fence any longer. My mother had turned it into a bridge.

~Donna Gundle-Krieg
Chicken Soup for the Gardener's Soul

22

Getting My Priorities Straight

What a grand thing, to be loved!
What a grander thing still, to love!
~Victor Hugo

One of today's most precious commodities is time. No matter how many gadgets we buy, books we read or classes we take, there is no quick fix to busyness.

As a working mother, I constantly juggle the demands of work, personal interests, household errands and my children's school activities—games, practices, music lessons, rehearsals and performances. These activities are designed to enrich my children's lives and develop their skills, talents and values.

However, mothers can be so busy juggling that they lose sight of the true purposes for the child's participation in these activities. From infancy, children seek parental approval and attention. Parents heap tons of encouragement and praise as the baby learns to crawl, pull up, walk, speak, hit the ball—the list goes on and on. As the child grows older, simple learning tasks are replaced with other activities such as sports, cheerleading or music. Parents are always on the sidelines or in the audience cheering, cajoling, clapping and encouraging.

However, sooner or later, a working mother is faced with a major conflict between some personal or business commitment and her child's game, play, concert or other event. She can't be in two places at once. Her heart is ripped into pieces trying to decide what to do; what is best for her child; what would a good mother do; how to make a bad situation into a win-win for everyone.

I experienced one of those decisive situations when my daughter's school district hosted its annual "String Fest," where five school orchestras are packed into a gymnasium along with a sea of family and friends. The participants were to arrive about forty-five minutes earlier than the event's start time so that the musicians could tune and warm up their instruments. As often happens, the event occurred during a crunch period for both my husband's and my jobs. We arranged for my teenage son to drop off his sister at the appointed time.

My daughter, who was very much aware of my time-management efforts, attempted to cut me some slack by saying, "Mom, you don't have to come tonight. Just be there on time to take me home." I couldn't have asked for a better solution. I wouldn't have to fight the rush-hour traffic for my thirty-two mile commute. I could work a couple more hours. By then the traffic would be light, and I could make it to the gymnasium in record time. Besides, how many concerts had I already attended? I could afford to miss this one, right?

After pondering my choices, I decided it was not okay with me if I was absent. Even though my daughter had given me her permission to miss the concert, it did not justify my absence. I felt guilty enough for my not taking her to the concert. I left work and arrived just before the concert began. I found a seat in the bleachers several rows directly across from my daughter's orchestra. I had her in my line of sight, but in the ocean of faces, she would never see me.

As I watched, the warm-up session ended and my daughter put her violin aside. I saw my daughter's eyes as they began to scan the audience row by row, looking for a familiar face. When her eyes found me, I was waving my arms in that embarrassing way mothers do, and we exchanged smiles. Her body language said it all. I had "made her night." No promotion, raise, bonus or anything could ever pay for that moment. It was an image that is forever etched in our hearts and memories and could never be recorded with a camera or camcorder. It was just two hearts exchanging love across the gymnasium.

~Sybella V. Ferguson Patten
Chicken Soup for the Working Woman's Soul

23

Apron Time

My daughter walked into the kitchen and asked, "Mom, what are you doing?"

"Having my quiet time," I calmly replied, as I stood there, surrounded by dirty dishes, with an apron over my head. Crazy as it sounds, I had gotten the idea from a very reliable source.

At the turn of the eighteenth century, an Englishwoman named Susanna Wesley gave birth to nineteen children, ten of whom survived infancy. It is said that when she needed time alone with God, she simply stood in her kitchen and pulled her apron over her head!

In addition to finding time for God, she also spent thirty minutes of one-on-one time with each of her ten children, every week. She taught all of them to read using the Bible as her only textbook. Two of her sons, Charles and John Wesley, were key leaders in the great spiritual awakening of the eighteenth century. We still sing hymns today that they wrote: "O for a Thousand Tongues to Sing," "Hark! The Herald Angels Sing," and many more.

Many historians believe that this great spiritual awakening was the primary reason England was spared a bloody revolution like the one that occurred in France. Susanna Wesley's children literally changed the course of a nation and influenced the destiny of countless thousands.

A man named John Taylor was among the men John Wesley led to the Lord. He heard John Wesley preach on the morning he was to be married and was so moved he ended up late for his own wedding!

John Taylor became a lay Methodist preacher and raised several sons who also became lay preachers. Those sons had several sons who became—you guessed it—lay Methodist preachers.

One of those men had a little boy who listened to his daddy pray every day: "O Lord, please send missionaries to China." When that little boy was six years old, he said, "God, I will go to China." J. Hudson Taylor grew up to become the founder of the China Inland Mission (CIM) and the father of the modern faith mission movement. In his lifetime, more than eight hundred missionaries served with CIM and it continued to grow in the decades after he died.

So far, there are nine generations of preachers in the Taylor family, one who is currently serving as a missionary in Thailand.

And it all started where? In the kitchen of Susanna Wesley, one woman who had a vision that mothering could make a difference for eternity.

So, if you ever stop by my house and discover me standing in the kitchen with an apron over my head, don't ask me what I'm doing. I'm changing the world!

~Donna Partow
Chicken Soup for the Christian Woman's Soul

24

In the Sack

"You want to go where, Grandma?"

"You heard me. Here. Right here." She pointed.

"Here? Are you sure?"

"Here." Grandma Vic was adamant.

With a sigh, Jenna shrugged the strap of her purse higher on her shoulder as she steered the wheelchair up the mall ramp and turned towards the store Grandma indicated. But she paused at the entrance.

"Grandma, you do understand what they sell here, don't you?"

"I'm neither blind nor stupid, dear. And, contrary to what you might be thinking, I still have all my marbles. I know exactly what I'm doing." Victoria—Grandma Vic—took a deep, audible breath, cocked her silvered head even higher, and ordered, "Now, push me in."

Jenna shook her head in dismay. In all the years she'd cared for her grandparents, run their errands, and taken them on excursions, nothing had prepared her for this demand. Nothing. It was downright embarrassing. Grandma Vic was asking too much of her this time. What would people think? What if they saw someone they knew? This was... awkward.

She sighed again, then wheeled her stubborn grandma right into... Frederick's of Hollywood. But Jenna stalled just inside the door... she had to... after all, her own jaw was dragging the floor.

While her arms hung limp at her sides, Jenna absorbed the

displays of intimate apparel. She hadn't been in Frederick's in a few years herself. A lot had changed. A lot. Everything was skimpier. More transparent. More daring. Why, some might even call it obscene! She should never have agreed to escort an elderly....

It was several moments before she realized that Grandma Vic had impatiently self-propelled the wheelchair to a mannequin. She studied the risqué lingerie.

"Hmmph. That's the new-fangled underwear? Why, I've got Band-Aids that cover more," Grandma Vic tsked with an ornery grin into Jenna's stunned face. "I want to see it all—everything in the store."

"Grandma Vic...." Jenna was amazed to find a blush staining her own thirty-three-year-old cheeks.

"All of it, dear."

Row after sexy row, rack after sensuous rack, the two toured the store with Grandma delivering more spicy one-liners than a standup comic.

"You say it's called a 'thong?' How odd. We used to wear those on our feet!"

"They're 'bustiers?' They look as painful as my mother's corset. Of course, hers didn't come in leather... or leopard skin."

"Why would they call it a 'teddy?' The trim doesn't look like bear fur to me."

"Flavored lotions and edible undies? Why don't they just print up a menu?"

Jenna flinched. Customers grinned. Sales clerks eyed them doubtfully. At last, Jenna leaned into Grandma's face and looked her squarely in the eyes. "Now, are you ready to tell me what this is all about?"

"Jenna, you've always been so good to tend to our needs. Shopping, chauffeuring, even putting up the Christmas tree so we can celebrate the holidays. You're the only one in the family I could trust with this errand."

Grandma's chin sank a little further onto her ample bosom and she sighed. After a thoughtful silence, she spoke low and falteringly into her lap.

"Our sixty-fifth wedding anniversary is just around the corner. I want to surprise your grampa. For just a few hours, I want to be young and whole again. Or, at least, look that way. For Grampa. For... me."

Grandma glanced up with new determination. "I might be old and... broken... but I'm not dead. I need a new nightie, something... suggestive... and I want to buy it here. At Frederick's."

Jenna bit her lip. Not in vexation. Not in embarrassment. Certainly not to stifle a giggle. She bit her lip to prevent it from trembling and hinting at the tears that threatened.

"Why, you old romantic!" She hugged Grandma. "I guess it's never too late to re-invent love."

Without hesitation, Jenna pushed the chrome wheelchair to a display of naughty nightwear and watched a pair of aged, corded hands lovingly caress diaphanous baby-dolls, sheer chemises, and velvet camisoles.

"This one." Grandma's dove-gray eyes sparkled over the easy decision.

With a conspiratorial smile, the middle-aged salesclerk folded the full-length spaghetti-strapped nightgown, rang up the sale, and complimented them on their choice. As Jenna steered her out the door and through the mall, Grandma Vic wore a smug look. And she made certain the sack from Frederick's of Hollywood — that cosseted her lacy, racy-red purchase — perched prominently on her lap.

When shopper after shopper turned to stare after her, she looked up at Jenna. "Let 'em guess!" she winked devilishly. "This Victoria's not keeping anything secret!"

~Carol McAdoo Rehme
Chicken Soup for the Caregiver's Soul

On, Being a Parent

Wise Dads

Wisdom begins at the end.
~Daniel Webster

25

Ballerina Dog

One April afternoon a few days after my twenty-first birthday, my parents announced that they were ready to give me—their live-at-home, frazzled, college-student daughter—a belated birthday present.

Wheelchair-bound since birth, I propelled myself from my bedroom into the living room where my parents anxiously waited.

"Bring it on! Good things come to those who wait," I joked, as I closed my eyes and extended my hands waiting to feel the weight of a beautifully wrapped gift.

"Why are you holding out your hands?" my dad laughed. "Your gift isn't coming in a box this year."

"Huh?" I opened my eyes to study the glee stamped on both of their usually calm faces. "I know! It must be that handicapped-accessible van I've been praying for!"

"No, it's not a van, but it's almost as good," my mom chuckled. Then she said more seriously, "Jackie, we know you were devastated when Buck passed last year. We all were. He was a great dog. But we think our house has been devoid of doggy joy long enough. It's time to hear puppy noises again."

"So today, right now, in fact," my dad broke in, "we're going to a place where you'll be able to select the puppy of your choice."

There was no time for protest as he scooped me out of my chair and into our car. My parents chatted to each other while I sat in the back, desperately trying to quell overwhelming waves of sadness.

Sadness because not so long ago, this trip would have seemed incomprehensible—a betrayal. After all, it had been only seven months since Buck lay on my cold bathroom floor drawing his last breaths. Seven months since I slid from my chair onto the floor, gently caressing his gray-streaked black-and-white fur, as his spirit passed from this world to the next. Sobbing, I vowed to him and to myself that I would never get another dog... but now here I was, about to break that promise.

Finally, my father turned to me and asked, "It'll be nice to hear the pitter-patter of paws again, won't it?"

"Yeah," I said flatly, trying to conjure up the excitement he'd expected. But I couldn't. Tears began to roll down my cheeks. I wiped them away quickly as my father, unaware of my tenuous emotional state, continued.

"When we get there, should we make a beeline to the shih tzu puppies? I know they're your favorites."

My favorite was Buck, I thought, not his breed. Buck, my constant companion, who climbed up on my lap and, like a salve, soothed my spastic, palsied muscles in a way that no drug ever could.

"Buck is irreplaceable!" I wanted to scream, but I held back, opting for something kinder. "Breeds don't really matter. It's their heart that counts. I'll look at them all." I paused, then continued as we pulled into the parking lot, "Who knows? I may not find any and walk out empty-handed." I wanted to prepare my parents for this possibility.

"I doubt that," Dad smiled at me, as he plopped me in my chair and headed toward the building, "but we'll see."

A chorus of barks and howls heralded our arrival, as a friendly employee offered to show us the available puppies. My parents accepted, but I lagged behind, gazing at the other dogs, shimmying and shaking, pleading to be released from their four-walled prisons. I smiled, but held myself in check, determined to keep my vow. Until...

Until I saw my father's face shining like the noonday sun. "Over here," he called to me.

Intrigued, my heart began to race, as I pushed toward the pen where my parents stood. Struggling to get a better look, I hoisted myself up, my legs tightening with the effort. There, nestled in the pen, were two angelic shih tzus. The male, a fluffy caramel and white pup, was gregarious and charged right at me. His smaller sister, a beautiful midnight-black-and-white puppy, was more demure, waiting for me to lean in a bit, before licking my nose. Aww, she looks like Buck, I said silently, my heart beginning to soften. Then suddenly, before I knew what was happening, my resolve toppled. I was hooked.

"Well, it looks like we won't be going home empty-handed," my mother said, as if voicing my thoughts.

"Wonderful." My father was pleased. "Which one?"

I was leaning toward the male; he was obviously the alpha and far more playful. Yet the girl was so tiny, her ebony eyes captivating and sweet.

I held them both, the male against the center of my chest, while the female lay curled in the warmth of my lap. It was nearly closing time as the male nibbled the ends of my hair, and the female slept serenely against my atrophied legs. Still, I was hopelessly undecided.

The employee, observing my deadlock, lowered his voice to a whisper and said, "Look, if I were you, I'd take the boy because the female's disabled. Her legs are deformed; she stands like a ballerina in first position."

Stunned at his insensitivity, my eyes widened. Hadn't he seen my legs or the wheelchair I sat in?

Noticing my expression, the employee continued, "I don't mean to upset you, but she'll need constant care. And the last thing you probably need is another pile of doctor bills."

Wanting to prove him wrong, I placed her on her feet. Instantly, her two bowed legs scissored, as she strained to keep her balance. Yet, despite her valiant effort, her tiny disabled legs faltered and she tumbled onto her side.

"See her legs cross?" he said quietly. "She's our little ballerina dog."

My eyes glistened as I listened to her tiny panting. I knew her struggle far too well. I recalled those times when I had used all my strength to stand upright—and that glorious second when I stood tall—only to come crashing down. I wanted to take her, but the employee was right: could I really afford her care?

"Okay... I'll take him," I said sadly.

As we were saying our goodbyes to the little female, she struggled back up. Her eyes bursting with determination, she pushed her brother out of the way and then carefully placed one foot in front of the other, as she began her slow, steady ascent across my lap and up my shirt. She wobbled and stumbled but didn't stop until she rested against my heart.

Laughing and crying at the same time, I whispered, "I hear you, ballerina dog. You're coming home with me." Contented, she closed her eyes, knowing her mission was complete. We would manage whatever care she needed; it would all work out.

"Excuse me, sir," I announced loudly, "there's been a change of plans. I'm taking Ballerina Dog."

~Jackie Tortoriello
Chicken Soup for the Dog Lover's Soul

26

Once the Son, Now the Father

When you teach your son, you teach your son's son.
~The Talmud

One winter evening as I sat reading, my young son, Luke, approached my chair in shy silence. He stood just outside the half-moon of light made by an old brass student lamp I cherish. It once lighted my doctor father's office desk.

In those days, Luke liked to approach me with his most serious problems when I was reading. The year before, he did this whenever I was working in the garden. Perhaps, he felt most at ease with difficulties when I was doing what he was getting ready to do. When he was interested in growing things, he learned to plant seeds and leave them in the ground instead of digging them up the very next morning to see if they had grown. Now he was beginning to read to himself—although he wouldn't admit to me that he could do that.

I looked up from my paper, and he gave me his wide-open grin. Then his expression turned abruptly serious, a not-too-flattering imitation of me. "I broke my saw," he said, withdrawing the toy from behind his back. "Here."

He didn't ask if I could fix it. His trust that I could was a compliment from a small boy to the miracle fixer of tricycles, wagons and assorted toys. The saw's blue plastic handle had snapped. My father, who treasured the tools of all professions, would not have approved of a plastic-handled saw.

I said, "There are pieces missing. Do you have them?"

He opened his clenched fist to reveal the remaining fragments. I did not see how the saw could be properly mended.

He watched me intently, his expression revealing absolute confidence that I could do anything. That look stirred memories. I examined the saw with great care, turning over the broken pieces in my hands as I turned over the past in my mind.

When I was seven, I'd gone to my father's office after school one November day. My father was clearly the best doctor within a thousand miles of the small Ohio River town where we lived. He always astonished me—and his patients—by the things he could do. He could not only heal whatever was the matter with anyone, but he could also break a horse, carve a top and slide down Long Hill on my sled, standing up! I liked to hang around his waiting room and hear people call me "little Doc," and I liked the way his patients always looked better when they left his office.

But on this day, when I was seven, my purpose was to see my best friend, Jimmy Hardesty. He hadn't been in school for three days, and his mother had sent word to my father's nurse that she just might bring Jimmy in to see the doctor today.

When the last of the afternoon's patients had gone, Jimmy had still not arrived. My father and I then went off to make house calls. He liked to have me with him, because he liked to tell stories when he drove. It was nearly seven when we finished. As we started home, my father said suddenly, "Let's go up and check on old Jimmy." I felt squirmy with gratitude, certain that my father was doing this just to please me. But when we came in sight of the old gray stone house, there was a light in the upstairs back window and another on the back porch—the ancient beacons of trouble.

My father pulled the car right into the dooryard. Alice, Jimmy's older sister, came running out of the house and threw her arms around my father, crying and shaking and trying to talk. "Oh, Doc.

Jimmy's dying! Dad's chasing all over the county looking for you. Thank goodness you're here."

My father never ran. He used to say there was no good reason to hurry. If you had to hurry, it was too late. But he told Alice to let go of him, and he ran then. I followed them through the yeasty-smelling kitchen and up the narrow, dark hall stairs. Jimmy was breathing very fast and made a high, airy sound. He had mounds of quilts piled over him, so that I could barely see his face in the flickering light of the kerosene lamps. He looked all worn out and his skin glistened.

His mother said, "Oh, Doc. Help us. It was just a little cold, then this afternoon he started this terrible sweat."

I had never seen Jimmy's mother without an apron on before. She stood behind me, both her hands on my shoulders, as my father listened to Jimmy's chest. He fixed a hypodermic and held the needle up to the light. I was certain that it was the miracle we all must have. My father gave Jimmy the shot. He then got a gauze pad from his black case and put it over Jimmy's mouth. He bent over him and began to breathe with him. No one moved in that room and there was no other sound except the steady pushing of my father's breath and Jimmy's high, wheezing response.

Then suddenly as lightning, there was the awful sound of my father's breathing alone. I felt his mother's hands tighten on my shoulders and knew, as she knew, that something had snapped. But my father kept on breathing into Jimmy's lungs. After a long time, Mrs. Hardesty went over to the bed, put her hand on my father's arm and said, very quietly, "He's gone, Doc. Come away. My boy's not with us anymore." But my father would not move.

Mrs. Hardesty took me by the hand then, and we went down to the kitchen. She sat in a rocker and Alice, looking as forlorn as I've ever seen anybody look, threw herself on her mother's lap. I went out onto the porch and sat down on the top step in the cold darkness. I wanted no one to see or hear me.

When Mr. Hardesty came back and saw our car, he went into the house and in a while I could hear voices. Then silence, then voices again. At last my father came outside, and I followed him to the car.

All the lonely way into town, he said nothing to me. And I could not risk saying anything to him. The world I thought I knew lay sundered in my heart. We didn't go home. We went to his office instead. He began going through his books, looking for something he might have done. I wanted to stop him, but I didn't know how. I couldn't imagine how the night would end. From time to time, all unwilling, I would begin to cry again. Finally, I heard someone at the door and went out through the reception room, grateful to whomever it might be. News of the beginnings and endings of life traveled far and fast in a community like ours. My mother had come for us.

She knelt down, hugged me, rubbed the back of my head, and I clung to her, as I had not done since I was a baby. "Oh, Mama, why couldn't he, why couldn't he?" I wept and lay my head against her shoulder. She rubbed my back until I was quiet. Then she said, "Your father is bigger than you are, but he's smaller than life. We love him for what he can do; we don't love him less for what he can't. Love accepts what it finds, no matter what."

Even though I'm not certain I understood what she meant, I know I felt the importance of what she said. Then she went in to get my father. That winter seemed to have gone on forever when I lived through it long ago, but the memory played it out in seconds.

I sat turning over the pieces of Luke's broken toy. I said to him, "I can't fix it."

"Sure you can."

"No, I can't. I'm sorry."

He looked at me, and the expression of awesome confidence faded. His lower lip trembled, and he fought his tears even as they came.

I pulled him on my lap, and comforted him as best I could in his sorrow over his broken toy and his fallen idol. Gradually his crying subsided. I was certain he sensed my melancholy at seeing myself only an ordinary mortal in his eyes, because he stayed nestled against me for quite a time, his arm about my neck.

As he left the room, giving me a direct and friendly look, I could hear my mother's voice telling me in her certain way that love was not conditional. Once the son, now the father. I knew absolutely that out of the anguish of that discovery came the first faint light of understanding.

~W. W. Meade
Chicken Soup for the Father's Soul

27

A Veteran's Garden

The best proof of love is trust.
~Dr. Joyce Brothers

My uncle was with the 8th Air Force in World War II. After the war, he got into growing gladiolas. My dad was a Marine in Korea. When he got out, fruit trees were his thing. I was a Marine in Vietnam from 1968 to 1969. When I came home, it took me years to realize what plants can do for you.

I never could talk about the war. Neither could Dad or Uncle Louie. But I was worse. I couldn't talk about anything. My wife said over and over, "You never say anything!" I couldn't. I didn't know how. I lost that skill in Vietnam. I don't know how or why I lost it. I had it when I got there. But it was gone when I came back. I just stuffed things inside and let them eat at me.

A lot of the Vietnam vets I know have a problem getting close to people. When you're in combat, you form fierce bonds with your squad members. You get closer than you were with your own brothers. After a few of these people get killed, the loss is so great, you're afraid to get close to other people. You love your wife and children, but you're so afraid you might lose them you can't express it. At the same time, you get protective, very protective, maybe controlling at times. You can't relax and be normal.

That's how I was: wound-up, tight, silent, a mess. Then one day I heard my dad talking to his apple trees. Well, I want you to know it is very impolite to listen to a man talking to his plants. So I didn't. But it got me to thinking. I started my garden the very next day.

The first year I didn't talk to my plants like my dad. I yelled at them. "How can you be so dumb?" I'd shout at the tomatoes. "What's wrong with you?" I'd rant at the sunflowers. "Lighten up, would you?!" "It's over, okay?!" "Who do you think you are?!" I was like a drill instructor swearing at his recruits. Only when I was yelling at the plants, I was really yelling at myself.

Those days of yelling at my poor plants let me sort out the things that were bottled up in me. Sometimes I watered my plants with tears. Going to war isn't nice. It's a time where, on one hand you are a god, and on the other you are a scared high school kid. Then, when I got back from 'Nam, some people spat on me and called me a "baby killer." I was so mad, so frustrated, so empty inside I didn't know what to do. So I yelled at my plants.

It's hard for a combat vet to ask for help. But my plants gave it to me. My garden became my community. I cared for my plants. I brought them things like water and compost. I protected them from weeds and insects. I read about gardening and learned how you could plant flowers to attract "good" insects that would help with the "bad" ones. And they responded. They grew—wonderfully.

After that first season, I got so I could talk to my plants. I could even sing to them, stuff like show tunes and the Marine Corps Hymn. I would say things like, "How's it going?" "You need anything?" "You look good today." I learned patience from plants—you can't hurry a carrot. I got to feel pride again—I have the best Early Girl tomato you ever tasted! And I wanted to talk to people again—to tell them about my garden and share my harvest!

Then I started to think about communicating my inner feelings with my three children. By this time my wife was gone, and I deeply wanted a real relationship with my kids, one where we could talk about life and ideas and feelings, not just school and the weather. So I practiced with my plants. "I want you to know how important you are to me," I'd say. "I'm trying." "Sometimes I get so mad I just want to shout and I don't know why." "I want you to read this book. I think it would explain how I feel about this."

That made all the difference in the world. Today I am friends with all my children. We can talk in an equal person-to-person way. My oldest, Nikki, is an adult now. We talk each week. She and I can talk about anything. Garrett, my son, will finish college this spring. We are good friends. Whitney, my baby, just got back from a ten-city concert tour with her college singing group. She called on her first day back to tell me all about it.

After I was able to connect with my children, I met Charmaine, the woman I want to spend the rest of my life with. And the garden was right there waiting for me when I wanted to practice what I'd say to her.

I'm proud now to be a Vietnam vet. I wasn't a baby killer. I was a guy like my dad or Uncle Louie who got his country's call and answered it. And I can talk to people now. I've learned that people are just like plants. You treat them nicely, and they will do the same for you.

The Marines sent me overseas. But it took gardening to bring me home.

~James P. Glaser
Chicken Soup for the Gardener's Soul

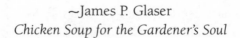

The Halfway Point

I glance at my daughter in the rearview mirror. What does Denise think, I wonder, when she looks at the four of us—two sets of parents, each of a different race? What does she see when she looks at us from the back seat? Does it mean anything to her that her father is white and her stepmother is Chinese-American? In a few moments, she will see her mother, who is Filipino, and her stepfather, who is African-American.

I sense that it doesn't mean nearly as much to her as it would to a social scientist, or maybe even a politician. To her, we are just four adults who are in charge of raising her and making sure she is safe.

The highway between Monterey and Salinas is so familiar. I know every turn, every pothole and how long each red light lasts along the way. I drive it every week. I once looked at my car's odometer several years ago and wondered if our meeting point truly was exactly halfway between my ex-wife's house and mine. Am I driving a little more than I should have to?

"Denise," my second wife says, "next week when school is out, I'll bring you to my office and you can help out. I have a big mailing you can do; a lot of envelopes to stuff, okay?"

"Cool! I can't wait."

My wife could say that she needed Denise to help out with nearly anything at her office and Denise's response would be the same. The girl just wants to spend time with her stepmother. They effortlessly took to each other from day one.

"Denise, do you have your karate outfit packed? Mom will bring you to your class next Saturday, and I'll pick you up there."

"It's packed, Dad."

Her duffel bag and backpack are full for her week with her mom and stepfather. One week with one set of parents, the next week with the other. Same school. The schedule is very finely tuned. Same meeting place in the same park for the past five years.

I exit the highway. There they are. I pull alongside their car and we all get out. Denise's mother and I look at each other with more than just a look. We accept each other. We each see someone we didn't know when we were married to each other, although we thought we did. Long gone are the anger and the threats to keep one another from seeing our daughter. We see someone we have forgiven, someone we stopped being vindictive toward and someone we still have a hard time feeling comfortable with. But most importantly, we see someone we have learned to work with for our child's best interest.

I get Denise's bag while she, my wife and my ex-wife all make goo-goo ga-ga noises over Denise's half-sister, now almost two years old. I give Denise's bag to her stepfather. We nod and say "Hi." Not too much in common, but a certain respect. I respect him for being a good father and stepfather. I am fully aware that this man is in charge of my daughter's safety for exactly half the year, every year.

I finally realize that it takes more of a man to accept that than to be intimidated by it.

"Is she starting to walk yet?" my wife asks Denise's mom, speaking of the baby.

"She kind of bounces from sofa to chair to me, falling the whole way." More laughter.

I walk over, pinch the baby's cheek in an obligatory manner and then stand back and watch, wondering if I should be surprised. Denise's stepfather is African-American. Her stepmother is Chinese-American. Her mother is Filipino and I am white. This doesn't really matter, I say to myself, but I know just how much it truly matters. Four different races. Four different personalities and temperaments. The most that we have in common is that we have a child to raise.

Denise is now kissing her stepmother goodbye. They each say "I love you" and "See you next week." She comes over to me and kisses me goodbye.

I am extremely proud of my daughter. She's testimony to the resiliency of kids. She knows the schedule by heart. She's always packing a backpack or duffel bag and often forgets things in the other house—a book for school, a friend's telephone number or her clarinet. Nobody complains, least of all her. She will get what she needs the next day. One of her four parents will drive the distance to deliver it. I'm reminded of her school play, which we all attended a few weeks earlier. After the curtain call, she came out beaming, eager to see her two sets of parents who all sat at the same table. Suddenly she hesitated, wondering which set she should hug first. A look of relief then shot across her face. She knew that it didn't matter. She would hug the other set precisely a second later.

They get in their car and we get in ours. As I start the engine, I put my hand on my wife's shoulder and ask her if it's really all that hard. She fully understands what I'm asking.

"No, it isn't," she says, "it isn't at all." She's right, I think. It's not that hard if you know your priorities and know how to love.

We follow them out of the park, and I think of all the children who don't know where one or both of their parents are, who receive, at most, a card once or twice a year. I think of the many ugly custody battles and can't help but wonder what those warring parents could find if they just reached a little deeper inside themselves. I think of Denise's friend who slept over a few months ago, who hasn't seen her father in years and doesn't seem to care.

Just before reaching the highway, Denise turns around and waves at us through the back window. She blows us a kiss and we blow one back. She then turns around and talks to her mom and stepfather. I wonder if she'll think of us this coming week, although it doesn't matter, since before we know it, we'll be driving this same road again.

There's so much ahead yet: adolescence, boyfriends, failure, rejection and triumph. There are so many bumps and bruises yet to be had. So many life experiences still to come. I ask myself how long we can keep on making life secure for her. I know it's a redundant question since it's the best it can be, and we can only do our best right now. A step at a time and a day at a time.

As we reach the highway, I put my signal on to turn left towards Monterey, and they put theirs on to turn right towards Salinas. When we have gotten up to speed, I look at my odometer and wonder if it really is halfway. Am I driving more than I should be? I suddenly look back at the road, realizing it doesn't really matter.

~Dennis J. Alexander
Chicken Soup for the Unsinkable Soul

Baseball Game Plan

When you realize you want to spend the rest of your life with somebody,
you want the rest of your life to start as soon as possible.
~Nora Ephron

When her father died of a heart attack, Kelli was a nine-year-old little girl with blond hair and hazel eyes. She first came into my life when I met her mother in 1986. Carolyn and I were married that same year. I had one son, Kevin, from my previous marriage, and Kelli was the daughter I never thought I'd have. I never tried to replace her father, only to be her dad and a good friend. Over the years, she and I gained a closeness few step-relationships ever hope to attain. She and Kevin were by my side through the good times and the not-so-good. I watched her with pride through dance recitals and volleyball games, through high school proms and college graduation. I saw her grow from a little kid in pigtails to a beautiful, mature and successful woman. Even when she was twenty-five years old, living in Texas and in a serious relationship, she and I were best friends.

That summer of 2002, I fulfilled a childhood dream—going to historic Fenway Park in Boston. A young man sitting next to my wife and me leaned over and politely asked if he could get us something from the concession stand. As a Texas sportswriter for over thirty years, I'd been to hundreds of games and never had a total stranger be so considerate. I was struck by the thoughtfulness of this twenty-five-year-old man from Maine. I liked Dave the moment we met. We visited throughout the game about sports, our families and my grandkids. Afterward, we continued to keep in contact through e-mails and phone calls. When Carolyn and I were in New England to visit our grandchildren, Dave and I got together again and became close friends.

In October the following year, Dave and I drove to Boston to watch the Yankees and the Red Sox in an exciting playoff game. After the game, I telephoned Kelli in Texas just to say "hi." During my conversation, for no reason, I handed my cell phone to Dave to say "hello" to her. It was the first time they'd spoken. Although he spent only a few minutes on the phone with her, he told me he felt like he had known her for years and remarked how he wished she wasn't married.

To his disbelief, I told him she wasn't. Two days later, he called her in Texas, and their relationship took off. Over the next three weeks they talked for hours late into the night, learning more about each other in a month than some married couples know in years. Dave and Kelli admitted then that they had finally found the person they had been looking for all their lives. We didn't take them seriously at first. But it didn't take long to see it was the real thing. Kelli eventually moved to Maine, and she and Dave got engaged on Valentine's Day 2004. One of the proudest moments of my life was when I walked her down the aisle of St. Patrick's Catholic Church in Portland, Maine, and placed her hand firmly in the hands of Dave Walton for what I know will be a lifetime of happiness.

I know I'm not the reason they fell in love. God just used me and baseball to fulfill his game plan.

~Larry Bodin
Chicken Soup for the Father & Daughter Soul

30

Papa's Best Lesson

A thousand words will not leave so deep an impression as one deed.
~Henrik Ibsen

From kindergarten through high-school graduation, I went to a Catholic convent school, Ursuline Academy, in the old border town known as Laredo, Texas. My parents were not wealthy, but they sacrificed many things to keep me in a parochial school.

Many of my friends were Anglos, but the majority of them were Latinas like myself. We played, sang and studied together, had slumber parties, picnics and sock hops in those carefree days of the fifties. We grew up eating tacos, enchiladas and tamales, but we couldn't resist burgers, Cokes and apple pie either.

We were raised in a city where the great Rio Grande divides Mexico and the United States, but we loved to cross the bridge that gave us the flavor of both. Sometimes I felt torn between the two, tangled together like badly cast fishing lines. For example, my parents spoke Spanish to me at home, reminding me often: "Never forget where you came from, your roots, your culture, your language and Mexico, the land where your grandparents were born." But at school we were fined a quarter if we were caught speaking Spanish! That confused and upset me. I surrendered many quarters to the nuns because I was always speaking what came naturally. But eventually, after being punished so many times for speaking Spanish, I began to see our native language as something to be ashamed of.

I have fair skin and honey-colored eyes. My grandfather used to call me Blanca Nieves (Snow White)! Once, the pep squad went to an out-of-town football game, and afterwards we stopped at a burger place for a bite to eat. It took forever for someone to wait on us, and when someone finally came, it was the manager telling us to leave the restaurant because they did not serve Mexicans there. Talk about discrimination! Then he had the nerve to look at me, the Mexican Snow White, and say, "Oh, but you can stay."

We stormed out, but not before I confronted him and asked, "What makes you think you're superior to us?"

He just pointed at his sign that said they had a right to refuse service to anyone.

The next day, with tears running down my face, I told my father how I felt about our experience at the restaurant. His emerald green eyes betrayed his anger, and tears welled up in them like hot lava. He asked me, "Are you ashamed of your race?" I replied that people were beginning to make me feel like we were of a lower class because of the color of our skin, because we spoke Spanish or because of our accented English. I told him that I liked being called Snow White, and that I was beginning to resent being labeled Chicana, Mexican or Latina. I had come to believe that it was better to be Anglo than Latina, since Anglos aren't fined for speaking their language, and all the heroes and heroines that I saw in the movies or read about in the history books were definitely Anglos with blonde hair and blue or green eyes.

That night my father made a promise that changed my life. He promised to take us to Mexico City on a vacation where we could learn more about the beauty, history, art, culture and people of our ancestral country.

What a delightful time we spent—visiting our relatives, going to museums and palaces, learning the names of mountains. At the museums, my father made me read each historical caption and all the facts about the great heroes of Mexican history, the generals, soldiers and troops from the revolution. The evenings were filled with fiestas in Garibaldi Plaza with mariachis dressed in their beautiful charro costumes. We saw the gorgeous folklórico dancers and singers at the Palacio de Bellas Artes, and we climbed the famous pyramids at Teotihuacán. I was intrigued and inspired by the majestic architecture of the buildings of Mexico City, especially the Basilica of Our Lady of Guadalupe.

But most of all, I was impressed by the kindness and charm of the people we met and the way they welcomed us back to our ancestral land.

Since that memorable journey, I have been so proud to tell people who ask me that I am a Latina, Chicana or Mexican-American, whichever name they decide to use. I am no longer insulted. I speak up for both of my countries, and I speak the two languages every day.

I will always be grateful to my papá for the wonderful lesson he taught me during those visits to Mexico, where I was enlightened to see beyond color or accents, labels or stereotypes.

Today, I don't mind being called Blanca Nieves, but I am 100 percent proud to be Latina.

~Olga Valle-Herr
Chicken Soup for the Latino Soul

31

A Moment Can Last Forever

Loading the car with the paraphernalia of our youngsters, ages three to nine, was hardly my idea of fun. But precisely on schedule—and at a very early hour—I had performed that miracle. With our vacation stay on Lake Michigan now over, I hurried back into the cottage to find my wife Evie sweeping the last of the sand from the floor.

"It's six-thirty—time to leave," I said. "Where are the kids?"

Evie put away the broom. "I let them run down to the beach for one last look."

I shook my head, annoyed by this encroachment on my carefully planned schedule. Why had we bothered to rise at dawn if we weren't to get rolling before the worst of the traffic hit? After all, the children had already spent two carefree weeks building sand castles and ambling for miles along the lakeside in search of magic rocks. And today they had only to relax in the car—sleep if they liked—while I alone fought the long road home.

I strode across the porch and out the screen door. There, down past the rolling dunes, I spotted my four youngsters on the beach. They had discarded their shoes and were tiptoeing into the water, laughing and leaping each time a wave broke over their legs, the point obviously being to see how far into the lake they could wade without drenching their clothes. It only riled me more to realize that all their dry garments were locked, heaven knew where, in the over-stuffed car trunk.

With the firmness of a master sergeant, I cupped my hands to my mouth to order my children up to the car at once. But somehow the scolding words stopped short of my lips. The sun, still low in the morning sky, etched a gold silhouette around each of the four young figures at play. For them there was left only this tiny fragment of time for draining the last drop of joy from the sun and the water and the sky.

The longer I watched, the more the scene before me assumed a magic aura, for it would never be duplicated again. What changes might we expect in our lives after the passing of another year, another ten years? The only reality was this moment, this glistening beach and these children—my children—with the sunlight trapped in their hair and the sound of their laughter mixing with the wind and the waves.

Why, I asked myself, had I been so intent on leaving at six-thirty that I had rushed from the cottage to scold them? Did I have constructive discipline in mind, or was I simply in the mood to nag because a long day's drive lay ahead? After all, no prizes were to be won by leaving precisely on the dot. If we arrived at our motel an hour later than planned, no forty-piece band was going to be kept waiting. And how could I hope to maintain communication with my children, now and in later years, if I failed to keep my own youthful memory alive?

At the water's edge far below, my oldest daughter was motioning for me to join them. Then the others began waving, too, calling for Evie and me to share their fun. I hesitated for only a moment, then ran to the cottage to grab my wife's hand. Half running, half sliding down the dunes, we were soon at the beach, kicking off our shoes. With gleeful bravado, we waded far out past our youngsters, Evie holding up her skirt and I my trouser cuffs, until Evie's foot slipped and she plunged squealing into the water, purposely dragging me with her.

Today, years later, my heart still warms to recall our young

children's laughter that day—how full-bellied and gloriously com-
panionable it was. And not infrequently, when they air their fondest
memories, those few long-ago moments—all but denied them—are
among their most precious.

~Graham Porter
Chicken Soup for the Father's Soul

32

A Letter to Santa

My five-year-old scribbled out his Christmas list. It's there by the fireplace. The Coke and chocolates are from him, in case you're hungry. You know five-year-olds these days. The Cheez-Its are from me.

Santa, if you don't mind, I thought I'd go ahead and leave my list, too. It's long, but do what you can.

It's all I want for Christmas.

- Santa, let my little boy grow up still believing that he has the funniest dad in the neighborhood.

- Give him many close friends, both boys and girls. May they fill his days with adventure, security and dirty fingernails.

- Leave his mom and me some magic dust that will keep him just the size he is now. We'd just as soon he stayed five years old and three feet, four inches tall.

- If he must grow up, Santa, make sure he still wants to sit on my lap at bedtime and read *Frog & Toad* together.

- If you can help it, Santa, never let him be sent into war. His mother and I love our country, but we love our five-year-old boy more.

- While you're at it, give our world leaders a copy of *The Killer Angels*, Michael Shaara's retelling of the Battle of Gettysburg. May it remind them that too many moms and dads have wept at Christmas for soldiers who died in battles that needn't have been fought.

- Let our house always be filled with slamming doors and toilet seats, which are the official sounds of little boys.

- Break it to him gently, Santa, that his dad won't always be able to carry him to bed at night or brush his teeth for him. Teach him courage in the face of such change.

- Let him understand that no matter how nice you are to everyone, the world will sometimes break your heart. As you know, Santa, child's feelings are as fragile as moth wings.

- Let him become a piano player, a soccer star or a clergyman. Or all three. Anything but a politician.

- Give him a hunger for books, music and geography. May he be the first kid in kindergarten to be able to find Madagascar on a map.

- The kid's a born artist, Santa, so send more crayons. May our kitchen window and refrigerator doors be ever plastered with his sketches of surreal rainbows and horses with big ears.

- Steer him oh-so-carefully to that little girl destined to be his bride. Let his mother and me still be around when he walks her down the aisle. If there is a just God, let her daddy be obscenely rich.

- Grant him a heart that will cherish what his parents did

right, and forgive us for the mistakes we surely will have made over a lifetime of raising him.

- Let him not hold it against us that he was born with my chin and his mother's ears. Time will teach him that these are God's ways of girding him for life's adversities.

- While you're flying around the heavens, Santa, make sure God has heard our prayer for this child: Lead our little boy not into temptation; deliver him from evil.

Be careful out there, Santa. And close the flue on your way up.

~David V. Chartrand
Chicken Soup for the Soul Christmas Treasury

On, Being a Parent

They Grow Too Fast

Childhood is a short season. Enjoy it while you can!
~Helen Hayes

33

Lost and Found

This is how it begins: One night in early September, while watching TV, you decide to make some popcorn. So you go into your kitchen to dig out the old popcorn machine, but it's nowhere to be found.

Then, a week or so later, you feel a chill in the air and decide it's time to get out the portable space heater. But after an hour or two of searching you turn up nothing. Nada. Zilch. Zero.

The pace begins to quicken.

Over the next fortnight, you search for, and fail to find, such items as your hair dryer, Mr. Coffee machine, tea kettle, kitchen shears, assorted luggage, extra-large bath towels, hair mousse, Chinese wok, sewing kit, desk lamp, portable phone, electric blanket, transistor radio and electric blender.

As the mystery deepens—and the list of missing items grows—all kinds of scenarios run through your head. A cat burglar. Early senility. A friend who borrowed your luggage. A blanket deposited at the cleaners. The phone left at the beach house.

Then, before you know it, it's the middle of October—the time when parents of college freshmen traditionally visit their kids on campus—and suddenly the Mystery of the Missing Household Items is solved: They are all residing in a room on a distant college campus—the one occupied by your college-age son or daughter.

Why is it, I wonder, that nobody warns parents that when your kids go away to college, so do all your small appliances?

And why is it that none of the child experts—not even Dr. T. Berry Brazelton—sees fit to include this developmental phase in their books on raising children: "At approximately the age of eighteen, the average, college-bound teenager goes through a period of relocating household appliances. A general rule of thumb is that after each visit home, the student takes at least four additional appliances and/or household items back to college."

My own first encounter with this developmental phenomenon occurred while walking across a campus on freshmen parents' weekend. From a distance, I spotted my son. I recognized him, in fact, by the sweater he was wearing—an intricately patterned ski sweater I purchased for him in Norway.

However, upon closer inspection, I confirmed that while it was, indeed, the aforementioned sweater, it was not my son.

"He lent it to me," said the young man who was not my son. He then directed me to my son's dormitory.

And what a pleasant surprise it was, upon arriving at the entry to my son's room, to be greeted by an old familiar friend—the "Welcome" mat that had disappeared from my very own front door just a month before.

Inside, I was made to feel equally at home. There, reclining among the batik-covered pillows from my den, I sipped a pineapple frappe from my blender and marveled at how many wonderful patterns could be formed just by stacking up assorted pieces of my luggage in an interesting way.

And the climate control in the room was excellent. My space heater going full blast in the bathroom produced, I thought, just the right temperature, even on a day when it was eighty-five degrees outside. Another plus about the bathroom was that I got to use my own towels again—the monogrammed ones that had been given to me as a wedding gift.

I also enjoyed seeing my white, pearlized wastebasket and matching soap dish again. I'd forgotten how attractive they were.

To my surprise, I felt equally at home in the room across the hall. Invited there by my son's friend, I noted how attractive my desk lamp looked sitting next to my portable phone. And what good reception my radio got, even up here in the hills of the Berkshires.

From there, it was a movable feast over to a room occupied by another of my son's friends. The popcorn made in my popper never tasted better, and I must say that my old patchwork quilt looked mighty good thrown across the back of his friend's futon.

In fact, I was so impressed with this recycling of household goods that at Thanksgiving I scarcely minded when the sleds disappeared from the garage, or after Christmas break the disappearance of an Edward Hopper poster, a small side table and a bedside reading lamp.

At spring break I minded even less when a number of sheets, pillowcases and pillows—along with a small desk chair—vanished. Actually, the house was beginning to look more spacious, less cluttered, somehow.

What I did mind, however, was that awful day at the end of the school year when the son arrived home with a U-Haul trailer. I think you know what was inside.

~Alice Steinbach
Chicken Soup for Every Mom's Soul

34

When Did She Really Grow Up?

A daughter may outgrow your lap,
but she will never outgrow your heart.
~Author Unknown

Every night after I tucked her into bed, I sang to her, a silly song, a made-up song, our song. "Stay little, stay little, little little stay; little stay little stay little."

She would giggle and I would smile. The next morning I would say: "Look at you. You grew. The song didn't work."

I sang that song for years, and every time I finished, she crossed her heart and promised she wouldn't grow any more.

Then one night, I stopped singing it. Who knows why. Maybe her door was closed. Maybe she was studying. Maybe she was on the phone talking to someone. Or maybe I realized it was time to give her permission to grow.

It seems to me now that our song must have had some magic because all the nights I sang it, she remained a baby... four, five, six, seven, eight, nine, ten. They felt the same. They even looked the same. She got taller and her feet got bigger and some teeth fell out and new ones grew in, but she still had to be reminded to brush them and her hair and to take a shower every now and then.

She played with dolls and Play-Doh. Though Candy Land was abandoned for Monopoly and Clue, across a table, there she still was.

For years, she was like those wooden dolls that nest one inside the other, identical in everything but size.

Or at least that's how I saw her. She roller-skated and ice-skated and did cartwheels in shopping malls and blew bubbles and drew pictures, which we hung on the refrigerator. She devoured Yodels and slushes and woke early on Sunday mornings to watch *Davey and Goliath*.

She never slept through the night, not at ten months, not at ten years. When she was small, she'd wake and cry and I'd take her into bed with me. When she got bigger, she'd wake and make her way down the hall, and in the morning, I would find her lying beside me.

She used to put notes under my pillow before she went to bed. I used to put notes in her bologna sandwiches before she went to school. She used to wait by the phone when I was away. I used to wait at the bus stop for her to come home.

The song, the notes, the waking up to find her next to me, the waiting at the bus stop—all these things ended a long time ago. Upstairs now is a young woman, a grown-up. She has been grown up for a while. Everyone else has seen this—everyone but me.

I look at her today, one week before she graduates from high school, and I am proud of her, proud of the person she has become. But I'm sad, too—not for her, but for me. There has been a child in this house for twenty-five years. First one grew up, then the other, but there was always this one... the baby.

Now the baby is grown. And despite what people tell me—you don't lose them, they go away but they come home again, you'll like the quiet when she's gone, the next part of life is the best—I know that what lies ahead won't be like what was.

I loved what was. I loved it when she toddled into my office and set up her toy typewriter next to mine. I loved watching her run down the hall at nursery school straight into my arms, after a separation of just two-and-a-half hours. I loved taking her to buy stickers and for walks and to movies. I loved driving her to gymnastics and listening to her friends. I loved being the one she raced to when she was happy or frightened or sad. I loved being the center of her world.

"Mommy, come play with me."

"Mommy, I'm home."

"Mommy, I love you the bestest and the widest."

What replaces these things?

"Want to see my cap and gown?" she says now, peeking into my office. She holds it up. She smiles. She's happy. I'm happy for her. She kisses me on the cheek and says, "I love you, Mom." And then she walks upstairs.

I sit at my desk and though my heart hurts, I smile. I think what a privilege motherhood is, and how very lucky I am.

~Beverly Beckham
A Second Chicken Soup for the Woman's Soul

35

Sending Kids Off to School

I could see how the scene was going to play itself out as clearly as if it had been written in a movie script.

"Five more minutes, honey, then we have to leave," I called to my five-year-old daughter, who had been frolicking in the Pacific Ocean for the past hour. It was a partial truth. Although I did have a million things to do that day, I decided to collect my child when I saw that she had found some older kids to frolic with. They were bigger and stronger, and the waves didn't knock them down as easily as they did my daughter. With exuberant five-year-old confidence, she kept following them out farther and farther toward the breaking waves. She was a proficient pool swimmer, but the deep blue sea was a different matter.

Maybe she didn't hear me calling her name above the roar of the ocean; maybe she did hear and was just ignoring me — it was impossible to tell. It had been an impromptu trip to the beach, so I wasn't wearing my swimsuit. Reluctantly, I hiked up my shorts and plunged into the ocean. Even in August I drew in a sharp breath as the water came in contact with my thighs.

"Hey, time's up, we have to go now." She turned, gave me a "see ya, Mom" look and headed farther into the surf. I splashed out and grabbed her arm. My shorts were soaked. I wondered if anyone was watching our little drama unfold.

"No!" she screamed, "I don't want to leave!" (Why is it that kids never want to get out of the water?) She jerked her arm away from me and pushed her defiant little body closer to Tokyo. I could see the headline now: "Child drowns while pursued by irate mother."

Now she was in over her head. Overcome with fear and rage I grabbed her, firmly this time, and began to drag her out. She did not come willingly. She screamed more intensely with every breath. It didn't stop when we got on shore. She wriggled and kicked, struggling violently in the sand to rid herself of me and charge back into the water. Now people were staring. I didn't care. I had to get her far enough away so that she couldn't plunge back into the powerful waves. She screamed and thrashed about like a wild animal caught in a trap, growling and scratching. The gritty sand clung to our wet skin.

By now I was shaking. I could hardly believe what happened next. A firm believer in nonviolent discipline—until now, that is—I smacked her on the bottom, hard.

It stunned her enough to make her freeze and stop her hysterical ravings. She stood there almost completely covered in sand and with her mouth wide open, unable to take a breath.

"Come on!" I said through clenched teeth as I pulled her along toward the path that would lead us away from the beach. She hopped alongside of me, seething and jibbering. I realized she was trying to tell me something. Her unintelligible words alternated with jagged sobs as she shifted her weight from one foot to another. Her feet! Now that we were out of the surf, the sand was scalding hot. I had been clutching her thongs all along. "I'm so sorry, sweetie. Put these on." I slipped her thongs on her trembling feet, then we climbed the path toward the car and headed home.

That was weeks ago. Now it was September, and I was back on the beach, alone. This time the sand was cool. It yielded softly beneath my feet as I walked along the edge of the receding water line. The morning sun had not been up long enough to work its magic. As I walked the beach, tears welled up in my eyes. I could see the image of my daughter earlier that morning, heading into her freshly painted kindergarten classroom for her first day of school. Her new day pack was slung proudly over her shoulder. The design of yellow and purple puppies and kittens verified her tender years.

I'd driven straight to the beach after dropping her off. There was something so reassuring in the never-ending cresting and breaking of the waves. I hoped the pounding surf would soothe my anxious thoughts.

"I love you, Mommy!" she had called out cheerfully from the window as I walked back to my car.

"I'll pick you up after school," I called back. I turned to blow her a kiss, but she had already turned from the window.

I had dreamed of this day for years—five to be exact. I dreamed of this day soon after I brought her home from the hospital. I tried holding her, rocking her, and singing to her. When all that failed, I would give her a bottle, her "binky," her bear... anything.

I dreamed of this day when she was only a year old and she spent her days lurching through the house unsteadily, learning to walk. I was so concerned that she might maim herself, I followed her around, hovering with arms outstretched like a giant bear. There was the time she ran smack into the corner of a door at full toddler speed. The blood gushed like a fountain from above her eye, but she was much more calm and brave about having it stitched than I was.

When she was two, I needed a break from full-time mommy-hood badly. I had never been away from her for even one night. But there I was, halfway around the world in Austria. I had left her with my parents and had finally taken my break. But when I heard her tiny little voice over the long-distance phone lines, my voice cracked so badly that I could hardly answer her back.

And this past summer, our days on end of being constantly together caused her to demand my unfailing attention. As the summer's heat grew more oppressive, I got listless but she became more spirited. She wanted more of everything—more pool time, more ice cream, more Popsicles, more playtime, more of me. Every day I heard, "Mom, let's go to the park, let's go to the beach, let's go to the Wild Animal Park, let's go, let's go, let's go!"

Why the tears then? I stopped walking and sat on a rough out-cropping of rocks, on a lovely beach on a glorious day feeling miserable. I watched the seagulls wheel and dive, their constant motion distracting the thoughts running through my mind.

I should be happy, I thought. No more incessant chatter bombarding me twelve hours a day. Now I could think free, uncluttered thoughts in a stream of connected ideas. I would be free to go back to school or start the business I'd been thinking about. I could have lunch with friends at restaurants that didn't hand out crayons and coloring menus as you were seated. I could go shopping by myself, without having my daughter stand in the middle of the clothing carousels spinning the rack, perilously close to tipping it over while the sales clerk glared with disapproval. I could roll up the windows in my car, pick a CD that wasn't Raffi or Barney and sing at the top of my lungs without hearing her say, "Don't sing, Mommy! Don't sing!" I could even go to the grocery store without having to deal with bribery and blackmail.

The truth is, I'd miss having her by my side. I'd become used to having a constant companion for the past five years. "Don't worry, Mom, we'll still have our afternoons together," she had reassured me at the breakfast table that morning.

With that thought in mind, I collected my things off the beach and headed for my car. It was time to go pick up my baby — oh, my kindergartner — from her first day of school. I was looking forward to spending the afternoon together.

~Susan Union
A 5th Portion of Chicken Soup for the Soul

36

Here and Now

Don't look back unless you intend to go that way.
~Marc Holm

If there's one word that describes the life of a single parent, it's hectic. Even though my kids are older now, it doesn't take much for me to remember the feeling of having too much to do and far too little time to do it. I thought I'd never have a moment of rest again. But here I sit in a quiet house, wondering how time could have possibly passed by so quickly.

I remember one particular week when I thought I'd lose what little remained of my sanity.

"Mom, you went to Noel's stuff last week. You have to go to my pom-squad performance this Friday."

"No way, Serena!" argued Nik. "Mom is going to my gymnastics meet."

With my head spinning, I told all three kids to sit down. I walked to the living room, dreading what was sure to become one of our Schiller showdowns. Why does it always have to be so overwhelming? Why does it always have to be so difficult? I steadied myself for the onslaught. Each child tried to persuade me to attend his or her activity, leaving me feeling pulled in too many directions. Finally, I managed to coordinate our schedules so that I could attend all three events. Everyone seemed satisfied with the results, but I was emotionally exhausted. That was Sunday.

The rest of the week was nonstop activity. Monday, I managed to get myself to one meeting and the kids to another. Tuesday was Nik's gymnastics meet. I arrived in time to see him compete in the vault event, his favorite. Wednesday night meant school for me and a quick dinner for the kids. Thursday night was Noel's ballet practice, and Friday night brought Serena's halftime performance with the pom squad.

As I drove home from work on Friday, I hit heavy traffic. All I could hear was Serena's reminder to me that morning: "Mom, you can't be late! I need your help with my hair!" Pulling into the garage, I raced upstairs to see the panic on her face. We made it on time — barely.

By Sunday night, I needed another weekend to recover. Lord, I prayed, I'm not ready to start again. When will I ever have time to myself? I am tired of this routine. I'm tired of hurrying. I'm tired of scheduling. Please help me get through the week ahead.

Now the days of rushing are behind me. And the truth is, I miss them terribly. Three months ago, I watched Serena walk across the stage to receive her college diploma. Waves of precious memories (and, yes, the not-so-precious memories, too) flooded my soul — gymnastics meets, ballet recitals, pom-pom performances. I reflected back to the daily grind of what felt like the tedious and overwhelming pace of our lives. But those days really were precious. They were filled with tender moments and simple pleasures, like sharing my son's pride in his accomplishment, watching my daughter shine on a stage and helping my teenager get her hair just right. Those are the parts of being a parent that make all the chaos worthwhile.

Yes, life with children can be difficult, especially when you're on your own. Yet very soon, sooner than you think, you'll be asking, "Where has the time gone?" And the house will be quiet. Too quiet.

~Barbara Schiller
Chicken Soup for the Single Parent's Soul

37

Who Called the Sheriff?

*Today could be the day that my mom realizes I'm growing up
and gives me some more responsibility.*
~Jenny Gleason

When my twin sons, Chad and Brad, were born, I was concerned about everything. Was the formula too hot or too cold? Was I doing everything right? Could I actually be the mother that two little boys needed? I wanted the world to be perfect for them.

Five years later, our little girl, Becky, completed our family. Would she get enough of my undivided attention? Would the boys feel neglected by the amount of time a new baby required? I wanted everybody to be healthy and happy. I worked hard to see that they were.

As the kids grew older, I worried about tonsils, earaches, throat infections and many other common childhood illnesses. I worried about their future heartaches. I didn't want anybody to make them sad. I wanted to protect them with all the strength I had.

I didn't like it when the boys spent time "warming the bench" during Little League and midget-football games. I wondered if they felt inferior because of their smaller size. I worried about Becky when she missed the ball when she played softball. I was afraid she wouldn't make it during flag tryouts.

Many times the kids told me not worry. "Everything will be fine," they constantly reminded me. But like most moms, I worried anyway.

Before long, the teen years were upon us. I sat up late at night waiting for the boys to return home. I worried about drunk drivers on the road. I worried about how the boys would react if one of their friends did something wrong. If they were five minutes late, I panicked. Many times the thought crossed my mind that I would call the sheriff if they weren't home on time. Luckily, they always arrived home safe and sound before I had to resort to such measures.

"Please don't ever call the sheriff," one of the boys said when I threatened him after a late arrival.

The day the boys moved away to attend college was a sad day indeed. I worried about the kinds of professors they would have. Would they make good grades in school? Would they ever graduate? I worried about them being able to take care of themselves and actually cook their own meals. Would they starve?

A few months after the boys left for college, our doorbell rang in the middle of the night. It startled us when we looked at the clock and saw that it was three o'clock in the morning. "Something must be wrong," I shouted to my husband, Roy, as we both jumped up. We ran to the door, opened it and there stood a deputy sheriff.

"You need to call your sons," he sternly announced. I picked up the telephone, but unfortunately, it was dead. A line outside had been accidentally cut. Roy and I jumped into the car and took off to the nearest telephone. My stomach ached with middle-aged worry. My husband was shaking so badly that he could barely dial the number.

On the first ring, Chad answered the telephone. "What's wrong?" Roy shouted into the receiver.

"We were worried about you," Chad told him. "We've been trying to call you all night, and you didn't answer. We called the sheriff's office and asked them to go check on you."

Chad then asked to speak to me. "I was so worried, Mama," he confessed.

"Don't worry, son," I said. "Everything will be fine." For the first time in their lives, the table was turned and the boys were worried about us. And to top it off, they were the ones who actually resorted to calling the sheriff.

~Nancy B. Gibbs
Chicken Soup to Inspire a Woman's Soul

38

The Bus Doesn't Stop Here Anymore

I remember leading my older child to the big yellow school bus, name tag pinned to his striped shirt, which was tucked in and matched perfectly with his cotton pants. With a new backpack over his shoulders, he turned to glance at me before heading up the steps.

"It'll be fine," I said. "You'll make lots of new friends, learn wonderful things and have lots of fun." As I gave him a hug, he looked up at me and asked what time he would be back. I tried to assure him as I sent him up the steps. "You'll be home at lunchtime. The bus will bring you right back here, and I'll be waiting for you, and you can tell me everything." It happened just that way. Not long after that I sent my younger child on the big yellow bus, and when it brought her back, I was there waiting for her, too.

As our lives changed, I acquired a full-time job and could no longer wait for them as they arrived home, but the big yellow bus still stopped in front of my house each and every day to bring them safely back. In the evening as we sat for dinner, they were anxious to share their day with me. We talked about friends and recess, teachers and books. My refrigerator became a gallery full of "star" papers, pictures and report cards. Every Mother's Day, they planted marigolds in milk cartons decorated with crayons and construction paper and carefully carried them home accompanied with the most beautiful cards. I wore priceless macaroni jewelry and paper corsages. As my children grew over the years, I still counted on the bus to bring them safely home each and every day, and it continued to do so school year after school year.

Before I knew it, they were talking about driver's licenses and part-time jobs, dances and dates. They no longer made Mother's Day cards; instead they borrowed the car and drove to the store to purchase them. Marigolds in milk cartons turned into hanging planters or small bouquets, which they purchased with the money they had earned. They wore what they wanted whether it matched or not, and the macaroni jewelry found a permanent home as a decoration on our Christmas tree.

Their backpacks grew heavier as the books they carried got thicker. The refrigerator now held a calendar, which was necessary to keep track of their busier schedules, and a dry-erase board so that we could communicate our whereabouts to each other when we weren't at home-which by now was most of the time. They were once small children, and now they were young adults who were quickly becoming more and more independent. The big yellow bus no longer stopped each day in front of my house.

High school had gone by quickly; and before I could turn around, my daughter, was investigating colleges, and my son had graduated. He pondered his future and opted to join the military. He was ordered to report to his station one sunny, August morning to be sworn in. I went along with other proud parents to witness the beginning of their new lives. I caught a glance of him when I was leaving, just as he was swinging his backpack over his shoulders. Although I had seen him do this hundreds of times, it was somehow different this time. I looked around at all of them, these fine young men and women lined up, one foot over the threshold of their bright futures, backpacks over their shoulders and waiting for—what else—a bus! I walked over to my son and reached up to give him a hug, and he looked down at me. I had done this before, I thought, but where had the years gone?

He was suddenly five years old again, and I asked him if he was nervous. "A little," he said.

"Don't be nervous," I assured him. "It will be fine. Think of all the opportunities you'll have and all the new people you'll meet."

I hugged him again and sent him on his way. I could barely get the words out of my mouth as he walked forward, but I did manage to whisper, "When you come home, I'll be here waiting for you, and you can tell me everything."

~Denise Syman
A 6h Bowl of Chicken Soup for the Soul

39

I Am My Mother and Proud of It

I looked in the big bay window,
And, surprise, what did I see.
I swear I saw my mom,
looking back at me.

Although she's been in heaven,
for over fourteen years,
I know I saw her smiling at me,
while I was wiping off my tears.

I had just come back from taking
my oldest sons to school.
I was having second thoughts about
the whole darn college rule.

Where moms are not allowed to stay,
in the dorms with them safe and sound.
Oh, no, they send us home to wonder,
what the heck kind of home they've found.

I was standing in my living room,
with tears running down my face,
And I thought of how my mom had felt,
when I joined that college race.

I don't remember tears that were cried,
or sad little messages sent.
I remember the freedom and life was so good,
But for Mom, I never knew what it meant.

But for now, as I look in the window,
at the face that I see as my own,
I see Mom and the smile she had given,
and I know that somehow I have grown.

Into a mom I know she is proud of,
A mom who is almost like her,
And I know that she cried, but she hid it from me,
on that day that I left on my own.

~Teresa Tyma Helie
Chicken Soup to Inspire a Woman's Soul

On, Being a Parent

Loss and Lessons

There are things that we don't want to happen but have to accept, things we don't want to know but have to learn, and people we can't live without but have to let go.
~*Author Unknown*

40

An Even Greater Lesson

How you and those dear to you live earns your reputation;
how you and those dear to you face death reveals your character.
~John William Russell III

Warm, friendly, attractive, gifted. That described Julie, one of my all-time favorite students from human development courses I taught at the University of Nebraska. She was a delightful person and an ideal student.

I remember Julie coming to the front of the classroom after class one autumn day in September 1976. While most of the other students hurriedly left to enjoy the balmy weather or to relax at the student union, Julie remained to ask questions about the next week's exam. She had obviously already done some serious studying. Several other students overheard her questions and joined our conversation. Julie's winsome personality drew people to her.

Julie never made it to the exam. The day after our conversation, she was tragically struck by a large concrete truck as she biked through an intersection near campus. I was stunned to hear that Julie lay unconscious and motionless in a hospital across town from the campus where only hours before she was talking with friends, laughing, making plans for the future.

Only minutes before the accident, Julie and her mother had enjoyed one of their customary daily telephone conversations. Her mother recalls their last conversation. "Julie was so bubbly. At a store near the campus, she had seen an outfit she wanted to wear on a special date the next day. I told her to go ahead and buy it. She didn't take her car because she would lose her parking place on campus. Instead, she jumped on her bike to go buy the new outfit. The accident happened just a short distance from the sorority house where she lived." My thoughts cried out to Julie—You cannot die, Julie! You're every professor's dream—and every parent's. You have so much to offer. So much to live for.

Nurses silently came and went from Julie's room. Her parents stood nearby in quiet desperation. Then the attending physician entered the room, cleared his throat, and said to Julie's parents and two brothers, "Your Julie has only a few hours to live." He felt the freedom to ask, "Would you consider donating some of Julie's organs?"

At that same hour in a neighboring state, Mary leaned forward, struggling to see better in her small, cluttered living room. Her eyes followed every movement of her lively two-year-old. This devoted mother was storing up memories to savor when she could no longer see her child. Mary was going blind.

Several states away, John had almost finished six hours on the dialysis machine. This young father was reading to his two sons while his immobilized body was connected to a life-giving "artificial kidney." Doctors had given him a grim prognosis of only weeks to live. His only hope was a kidney transplant.

At the same time in the Lincoln, Nebraska, hospital, Julie's grief-stricken parents pondered the finality of the physician's question. Their pretty brunette, brown-eyed daughter had once said she wanted to be an organ donor in the event of her death. The two parents looked at each other briefly, the anguish in their hearts reflected in their eyes. Then they turned to the physician and responded, "Yes. Julie always gave to others while she was alive. She would want to give in death."

Within twenty-four hours, Mary was notified that she would receive one of Julie's eyes, and John was told to start preparing for a kidney transplant. Julie's other organs would give life and sight to other waiting recipients.

"Julie died right after her twentieth birthday — twenty-four years ago. She left us with very happy memories," says Julie's mother, now in her seventies. "Nothing — absolutely nothing — could possibly be as heartbreaking as the death of your child," she emphasizes, "for your heart breaks again and again. At each birthday. At each holiday. At each milestone: when she would've graduated; when she might've married; when she might've been having children." Taking a slow and deliberate breath, Julie's mother says, "But Julie's life was a gift to us. Knowing that in her death, she gave the gift of life and sight to others is comforting to us, and remembering that we carried out her wishes has helped us cope with her death more than anything else."

Her voice softening, Julie's mother says, "You and Julie's other friends and teachers were an important part of her life. Your teaching influenced her life tremendously, and you remind us that our love for Julie and Julie's love for others are alive today."

As one of Julie's professors, I hold dear the thought that I may have had a small part in teaching Julie how to live. But she — and her family — are still teaching me an even greater lesson. How to die.

~Barbara Russell Chesser
Chicken Soup for the Golden Soul

41

Blessed

Love cures people—
both the ones who give it and the ones who receive it.
~Dr. Karl Menninger

A friend and I were standing in line at the grocery store the other day, and I was telling her how lazy my children were. I had come in from work that morning, and like most times, my house was wrecked.

"I believe children nowadays are just out for what they can get. I bend over backwards for them, and they can't even help keep our house clean. It wouldn't bother me so, but it's the woman who looks bad if the house is a mess."

"Do you know how blessed you are?" a woman behind us asked. "I would love to go home and find my house a mess. I wouldn't mind my carpet being ruined or the dishes left everywhere. I wouldn't mind the dirty clothes being piled high or the many socks to match. I wouldn't even mind anyone talking about my dirty home. Matter of fact, I would love it. I would dearly love to kick my way through the house just to get to my kids and be able to hug them, kiss them and tell them how much I love them. You see, my two children were killed in an auto accident, and now it's just my husband and me. My house stays clean, my clothes stay put up, the dishes are done. There are no fingerprints on my walls, no mysterious spots on my carpets. There are no sounds of arguing, no slamming doors, no laughter, no 'I love you Mom.' So you see, you are very blessed. What I would give to be going through what you are right now. How I would love to be able to hold my kids, wipe away their tears, share their dreams. Just to watch them play. If I had my children, I wouldn't care how my house looked. I would be happy just to have them."

Now if you come into my house and see a big old mess, you can think bad thoughts if you want, but I feel greatly blessed.

~Tammy Laws Lawson
Chicken Soup for the Christian Family Soul

42

Cassie

I knew a little girl with copper hair.

She loved her family, her cat, red-tailed hawks and watching squirrels from her grandmother's kitchen window. Most of all, she loved horses.

Cassie was a redheaded ball of fire. Even as a child, she would spend endless hours in the kitchen jumping broom handles and chairs as "Cassie the Wonder Horse."

My route to and from my office takes me by the stable where Cassie started her riding. The morning always seemed to be a quick rush with little time to reminisce. But as I drive past, I can hear echoes of days spent in a dusty arena watching Cassie practicing yet another jump. "Just one more, Dad, and then I'll stop!" I recall the hours it took to get her to leave the barn to head home. Every horse had to be touched, stroked, talked to, fed, stared at, admired, loved.

She had an awesome rapport with her animals. Her most beloved horse, Elmo, would follow her around the arena right by her side as if being led, when in fact there wasn't a lead attached to his halter. She wanted him to do it that way, and so he did.

Her eighth grade graduation in June 1995 was an exciting time for all of us. She was sad to leave Whitchurch Highlands, but welcomed her next years in high school.

Two months later, in August, Cassie was preparing for her riding lesson, and as usual she planned to spend the afternoon at the barn doing all the horsey things she loved to do. After unloading a large bag of horse feed, she complained that her shoulder was sore. During her lesson, Cassie rode over to her mom to tell her that her shoulder was worse, and she was feeling very tired. Sandra suggested that maybe she should end the lesson early.

Undeterred, Cassie finished the lesson, put her horse away and then agreed to see a doctor about the pain.

After many tests, we found out that Cassie's sore shoulder was in fact a collapsed lung caused by malignant tumors. Before we knew what hit us, we were swept up into a cruel surreal fog of chemotherapy, surgery and fear.

To make matters worse, we had to put Elmo down that Christmas of 1995 because of medical problems. Cassie, just home from three days of chemotherapy, wept for her friend and thanked him for the wonderful times they had shared.

Cassie fought the disease with every bit of strength she had, but the cancer did not retreat. The next months were filled with endless radiation treatments, major surgery and, finally, high-dose chemotherapy followed by a bone-marrow transplant. Sandra and I were devastated to watch our daughter, once so fit and strong, who could maneuver an 1,100-pound animal four feet into the air over a jump, become unable to pick up even a cup because the chemotherapy had left her fingers completely numb.

In August the following year, we brought Cassie home from isolation after her transplant, a frail shadow of the hair-flying, "no time to talk, gotta get to the barn, don't touch that phone it's for me!" teenager she was just twelve months before.

Holding her cat again, her joy returned. Soon, she was heading down the lane to have a heart-to-heart with Red, our family quarter horse.

Cass started back to high school that fall—just for one or two periods a week—taking the rest of her classes at home with a tutor. Her hair was growing back, not as much she had before, but it was that same beautiful copper red. Cassie started to plan again for the life ahead of her.

In October, a woman named Laura from a local wish-granting

organization offered Cassie the chance to have anything she wanted for the hardship she had gone through.

Cassie turned to her. "I don't think I should have a wish," she said. "They should save it for a child who isn't going to make it. They need it more than I do."

But Laura convinced Cass that she also deserved a wish.

Within a few weeks, Cassie had picked her wish—to go to the Master's Cup at Spruce Meadows as a VIP. We had just missed the competition for that year, so the date was set for September 1997.

She was very excited and started planning her trip—who she would meet, who would be there, where she would like to go... a wish is a wonderful thing.

But by January our world was rocked again. The tumors had returned with a vengeance and, because of the amount of chemotherapy Cassie had already received, our options had run out.

Cassie's health was failing fast, and she was placed on morphine to reduce the pain. She celebrated her sixteenth birthday on February 19th, and a couple of weeks later I took her to get her driver's permit. She was so proud of herself. We laughed at the thought of Cassie being pulled over for speeding and having to explain the morphine pack attached to her arm!

As the days passed, we realized it was becoming more unlikely that Cass would be able to make it to Spruce Meadows in September. Laura made it clear that the Spruce Meadows trip would not be canceled and, in the meantime, she offered Cass the chance to meet Rosie O'Donnell, the second choice on her wish list. It was a wish that could be organized fairly quickly.

Meeting Rosie in New York was wonderful for Cassie. After all the turmoil and fear and pain of the past months, reality was in some far-off place. There were no doctors to see, no blood tests to wait for, no radiation, no reminders of situations and conditions. The city was lit that weekend by the glow of a sixteen-year-old girl's smile.

Despite the tenacity of her disease, our daughter remained in charge right to the very end of her life. One morning a few months later, Cassie sat up in her bed, took off her oxygen mask and very quietly lay back down in her mother's arms, finally free of the pain she had lived with for so long. Her favorite horse was waiting for her in her new life, and she had some riding to catch up on. We understood.

Cassie will not be sitting under the maple tree this winter holding out her hand to feed the birds, and never again will she stroke that soft spot at the end of a horse's nose. But the Cassie we knew, loved and still love is with us every day. She's with us in the whispered memories of the rockers on our front porch, the smell of a well-worn saddle and the snicker of a contented horse roaming in our front pasture.

~Blaine Bonnar
Chicken Soup for the Nature Lover's Soul

Ryan's Hope

The day started out normally enough. It was May 1, 1997. Ryan was upstairs preparing to leave for school, while his six-year-old sister, Jamie, waited for him at the front door. Suddenly Ryan started to tell us all about Albert Einstein with such enthusiasm and excitement, it was as if a light had gone on in this head. He said, "E=mc2 — I understand what Einstein was saying: the theory of relativity. I understand now!"

I said, "That's wonderful," but thought, "How odd." It wasn't his thinking about Einstein — Ryan was so intelligent — but rather the timing that seemed peculiar.

At ten years old, Ryan loved knowledge and seemed to have an abundance of it, far beyond his years. The possibilities of the universe were boundless to him. When he was in first grade, the children in his class were asked to draw a picture and answer the question, "If you could be anyone, who would you be?" Ryan wrote: "If I could be anyone, I'd want to be God." At age seven, while sitting in church one day, he wrote:

The tree of Life, O, the tree of Glory,
The tree of God of the World, O, the tree of me.

Somehow I think Ryan just "got it."

In the midst of his strange outburst about Einstein, Ryan suddenly called out that he had a headache. I went upstairs and found him lying on his bed. He looked at me and said, "Oh, Mommy, my head hurts so bad. I don't know what's happening to me. You've got to get me to the hospital."

By the time we arrived at the hospital in Newmarket he was unconscious. We stood by helplessly as the doctors fought to save his life, and then they transferred him by ambulance to Toronto's Hospital for Sick Children.

A couple of hours later, we were finally allowed to see him. He was hooked up to a life support system. When the doctor told us our son had suffered a massive cerebral hemorrhage and was "legally and clinically brain dead," it felt like a terrible nightmare. We went into shock. Nothing more could be done, the doctor said, and asked if we would consider organ donation. Astonishingly, we had discussed this with Ryan only recently. We looked at each other and simultaneously replied, "Oh yes, Ryan would have wanted that."

In April, Ryan had seen his dad filling out the organ donor card on the back of his driver's license. His dad had explained to him about organ donation and how you could help save another's life by agreeing to donate your organs when you die. When Ryan wondered if you needed a driver's license to do this, his dad replied that anyone could donate their organs.

Organ donation made such perfect sense to Ryan, he went on his own campaign persuading the entire family to sign donor cards. We had no doubt that donating Ryan's organs was the right thing to do.

After a small bedside service, we said our goodbyes to our son. When we left the hospital, we left a part of ourselves behind. Driving home, I could feel a thick fog roll in and surround me, crushing me. We were in total disbelief. My husband, Dale, and I cried in each other's arms all that night and for many nights after. It was as if part of me had died with my son.

Grief consumed me for a long time. We kept waiting for Ryan to walk in the door. We grieved for the loss of today, and also for the loss of our hopes and dreams. I realize now you never get over the death of your child. With time you heal, but you are forever changed.

It was our daughter Jamie who gave us a reason to get up in the morning and carry on.

Then, on a beautiful morning four months after Ryan's death, the first letter arrived, addressed to my husband and me. As we read it, we both began to weep. It was from a twenty-year-old university student thanking us for our "gift of sight." He had received one of Ryan's corneas and could now see again. It is difficult to describe our emotions—we wept, but at the same time, we felt wonderful.

Sometime later we received a second letter from a young woman of thirty who had received one of Ryan's kidneys and his pancreas. She'd had diabetes since she was five, spending much of her recent years hooked up to a dialysis machine. She told us that because of Ryan, she was now free from insulin and dialysis, able to work again and return to a normal life.

Early May brought the painful first anniversary of our son's death. Then we received our third letter. A young boy of sixteen, born with cystic fibrosis, had received Ryan's lungs. Without the double lung transplant he received, he would have died. Besides being able to return to school, he was now doing things he had never done before—running, playing hockey and roller blading with his friends. Knowing this boy's life had been renewed lifted our spirits immensely.

Due to confidentiality laws, organ donation is completely anonymous in Canada. However, organ recipients and their donor families can communicate through the organ transplant organization. Although we didn't know the identities of the individuals who had received Ryan's organs, we were given updates about their health.

We learned about a six-year-old girl who had received Ryan's other kidney and was now healthy, free from dialysis and attending school full time. We also learned that the forty-two-year-old woman who had received Ryan's liver was doing well and was able to again spend time with her young family.

Such joy seemed to come from our sorrow, so much happiness from our loss.

Although nothing could take away our pain, we took great

comfort and peace in knowing that Ryan had done something most of us will never do — he had saved lives!

That summer, while on vacation in Haliburton, we met a young man — by sheer coincidence — who had had a kidney and pancreas transplant at the same hospital where some of Ryan's organs had been transplanted. He knew the young woman who had received her kidney and pancreas on May 2nd from a ten-year-old boy he believed to be our son. Her name was Lisa, and she was doing great. Afraid to ask her last name, I later wondered if I might have passed up my only chance to meet one of Ryan's organ recipients.

This chance meeting inspired me, and the following spring I decided to share our experiences with others. I'm not a writer, so it was a challenge to write a story and send it to the newspapers for National Organ Donor Week. I faxed my article to three papers, and to my astonishment, all three wanted to feature it! A flurry of interviews and photo sessions followed, and we experienced an excitement we thought we were no longer capable of.

When the first article appeared, Dale and I were totally overwhelmed when we opened the paper to find that Ryan's story of hope was the banner story — right on the front page! Included in the article was the poem Ryan had written when he was seven, just as we had it inscribed on his tombstone. We wept tears of joy and sadness as we read it over and over. In his brief ten years on this earth, our son Ryan had made a difference.

A few days later, the article appeared in the other two papers, and for a few weeks we received calls from people all across Canada. Surprised but delighted, we hoped the story would help raise awareness about organ donation and perhaps inspire others to donate.

Apparently Lisa also read the article. When she saw Ryan's poem, she recognized it from a letter we had sent her and realized he was her organ donor. The article said we would be at the Gift of Life medal presentation in Toronto two weeks later, so she decided to attend. Once there, she was unsure about introducing herself. We all wore name tags, and when Lisa found herself standing next to my husband Dale she just couldn't hold back. You can imagine the emotional scene of hugs and tears that followed! It was truly a miraculous, unforgettable moment! It felt so wonderful to see her standing there alive and healthy, knowing that our son had helped make that possible. Ryan's kidney and pancreas had apparently been a perfect match. And part of him now lives on in her.

Moments later, a woman approached us with her eight-year-old daughter. "I think my daughter has your son's kidney," she said. Kasia was just four when both of her kidneys had shut down and she had gone on dialysis. The details of her transplant matched, and we all felt certain it must have been Ryan's kidney that had given this lovely girl a new life. A few weeks later when we visited Ryan's grave, we wept tears of joy when we found a beautiful drawing left there, signed "Kasia."

Due to the Canadian confidentiality laws, meetings such as these are very rare, and it is impossible to describe the intense emotions that result. When Ryan died, I thought I would never again feel joy. But meeting Lisa and Kasia was a kind of miracle, opening my heart to those feelings I thought had been forever buried with my son.

Today, I now know I will always be the mother of two children. Ryan is, and always will be, part of our family and our lives. Although the pain of losing him will never completely leave me, I have begun putting the pieces of my life back together, though it now takes a different shape. Part of our healing came from our experience of donating Ryan's organs. I am so grateful that God allowed me to meet Lisa and Kasia so my heart and soul could reopen. Meeting them allowed me to experience that "once in a lifetime" kind of feeling again, the one I thought was gone forever.

~Nancy Lee Doige
Chicken Soup for the Canadian Soul

One So Young

In the night of death, hope sees a star,
and listening love can hear the rustle of a wing.
~Robert Ingersoll

Grieving over the death of my newborn twin sons taught me many lessons. The most important was, whatever the challenge, we all have enough strength within us, as long as we have enough support around us. I resolved to do my part in providing that support to as many grieving parents as possible, including gentle encouragement of the family to take advantage of every opportunity that would help them heal. Since the luxury of time for decision making is not allowed in the days following a death, time was of the essence. I never heard a grieving parent express regret for something they had done, but many times I'd heard, "I wish I had...."

On a late winter evening, a mutual friend informed me that a young couple's baby had died the day before, apparently of sudden infant death syndrome (SIDS). She told me that the mother especially was having a very difficult time and asked if I would visit them.

Armed with photos of my own babies, I was met by the grieving father as I walked up the driveway.

"I'm so sorry," I said. He nodded and showed me into the house.

At the table, seemingly oblivious to my entrance, sat the baby's mom, Rhonda. She stared at her hands with swollen eyes. Our mutual friend and her daughter were with her, looking sad and feeling very helpless.

We were introduced, and Rhonda barely tipped her head in acknowledgment. I sat next to her and waited. When she offered no conversation, I started talking about my own experience with my twins. Although I was aware that in no way could I know what she was going through, I did want her to know that I had endured a similar situation, and yet I was still here, whole and alive.

Finally, Rhonda spoke about how she had found her daughter. Rhonda had picked the infant up and handed her to her husband, hoping beyond hope that Barry would be able to revive their baby. Automatically, he tried, but it soon became apparent that Sarah was dead.

When the coroner arrived, he placed baby Sarah on her parents' bed while he made his preliminary examination. Rhonda shivered, "How could I ever sleep there again?" Now it was clear. Not only did she detest death because it had separated her from her baby, but also because it had contaminated her home and family. Rhonda had little energy left, and she was spending the remainder on loathing her vile enemy.

I brought out the photos of my little boys. "When Josh and Cole died, we kept them with us for several hours," I said quietly.

For the first time, Rhonda looked at me, her eyes penetrating, searching my face for answers to questions she didn't even want to ask. I continued, "We took locks of hair, had our babies footprinted and just held them close."

"But they were dead!" Rhonda had stumbled into a territory so foreign to her that she couldn't even believe she was saying the words.

"Yeah. They were dead. But we had to make the transition from loving them as earthly bodies to loving them as spirits. It's one of the hardest things to learn to do, but it can be done. Even though the spark of who they were, their soul, was no longer in those little bodies, nonetheless, the bodies were there for us to hold. And for that, I will be eternally grateful."

She looked back at her hands. "Barry wants to go see her. He wants to say goodbye," she whispered. "I don't want to, though..."

I knew that Rhonda was reliving all the feelings of horror that she felt when she found her still daughter. "She won't look the same as when you discovered her. She will be more peaceful," I offered.

After a good hour of mild persuasion, this young, frightened mother murmured, "Well, maybe I'll just take a peek...."

Now I had to convince the staff at the small town hospital.

A phone call had me discussing the situation with an administrator, the head nurse and a social worker, until finally I was connected to the pathologist. I explained the scenario to a shocked and very reluctant doctor. "But I've already autopsied that baby!" he exclaimed.

"That's okay. It just means she has some stitches. We can deal with that."

"But I wouldn't want to see my kid that way!" He was incredulous.

I wanted to say that he wouldn't want to see his child dead either, but this family had to work around that reality.

Persistently, I told him about my own sons, and how we had held them for hours. I could feel him starting to bend.

"Well, all right. But you have to come, too."

"Absolutely! I'll be there."

We parked our cars and as we walked toward the hospital entrance, I talked to Rhonda and Barry about the fact that men and women grieve differently. "After the initial phase, when you both support each other beautifully, men tend to not want to talk much about it. They want to get on with life and don't feel that they can do so when they think about their child constantly. So they put it aside. Now women, on the other hand, will talk to anyone who will listen, and sometimes even if they won't. They bring it all out, over and over, and heal from the inside out. The problem is, the mom thinks that the dad didn't really love the child since he doesn't seem to care. Whereas the dad thinks his partner has gone crazy because she is dwelling so much on it.

The thing is, if you understand each other's method of grieving, you can get through it intact, as a couple. Just realize that Mom needs to get her support elsewhere for awhile, probably from another woman. But you must be aware that you both loved the baby just as much, and you both will miss her terribly." They walked in silence.

When we arrived at the room where Sarah was, we were met by the pathologist. He was obviously anxious, seemingly nervous that this young woman would pass out, or sue him, or maybe both. I left Rhonda and Barry in the hall. "I'll go in first."

I looked at the sweet baby in the bassinet. A bonnet covered the stitches on her head, and she was wrapped in a blanket. I noticed the area on her face where the blood had pooled after she died. I returned to the couple.

"She has some mottling on her cheek. It just looks like a bit of a bruise. And you'll notice that her lips look different—not as full. But that's all normal," I told them.

Rhonda reached inside herself and gathered every ounce of strength she could find. She marched into the room, like a soldier to war, the pathologist close behind. The attending nurse picked up little Sarah, and Rhonda immediately reached for and cuddled her daughter.

The doctor held his breath as Sarah's mom looked her over carefully and then glanced up at me, her eyes shining with emotion. "I told you she was beautiful, didn't I?" she beamed. The anger, fear and disgust visibly drained from the young mother. The transformation was miraculous, and the only adjective that could truly describe Rhonda now was peaceful.

I left her and Barry alone with their little girl and walked into the hall with the doctor. He nodded at me, smiled and returned to his duties. After a while Rhonda realized that Barry needed private time with Sarah, and she joined me, closing the door behind her.

As we left the hospital, a noticeably calmer Rhonda walked with us. She began to plan her baby's funeral, even including an open casket viewing. Later, when Barry lifted their eighteen-month-old son to see his little sister in the casket, Mathew pointed to her and declared, "Baby!"

And it was a serene, brave mom who stood at the front of the congregation and, with a steady voice, read a poem for her daughter.

Rhonda and Barry brought another baby girl into the world and named her Kathreen. She and her brother are much loved and appreciated in a way that only parents who have lost children can understand. Every moment, including the difficult ones, is experienced with gratitude, thankful for being able to nurture the gifts that are their children.

As is the way of the world, the events surrounding Sarah's death turned what could be viewed as a tragedy into an extraordinary formation of hope. Rhonda began facilitating grief support for bereaved parents, even accompanying some while seeing their dead babies. As she learned more about bereavement, she started to perceive a correlation between poverty and infant mortality. Eventually, her journey led her to work for a large antipoverty group in British Columbia.

Baby Sarah's impact on the world in which she lived so briefly is profound. Although I had never met her in life, she touched my heart in the way of an old, wise soul. The love that she brought to this Earth has grown with its own momentum, and it's spreading still, a gentle, healing wave, helping to wash away sorrow.

It's quite an accomplishment for one so young.

~Diane C. Nicholson
Chicken Soup for the Grieving Soul

On Top of the World

The snow glistened like sparkling diamonds in the sun as Blain came zipping around the moguls at the base of lower Treasure. His bright yellow ski parka was easy to spot among the children coming down the same run. This was Blain's second year of skiing, and like many other twelve-year-olds in his sixth-grade class, he had taken to it like a duck to water.

As my husband Judd and I ran up the gentle slope calling out to our son, the snow crunched under our footsteps. Hearing his name and turning around, Blain was delighted to see us and to think we had seen him skiing down the mountain so expertly that cold, crisp morning. His expression changed to one of concern as he realized that something must be wrong.

It had been only twenty-four hours since the hospital conducted the tests and only a couple of weeks since his teacher noticed him putting his head on his desk when his work was completed. Then we spotted his enlarged spleen. When the doctors wanted to keep him overnight, Blain got teary-eyed and was very upset. He really wanted to be with his buddies from school on their special ski day. And then the doctor called: If we didn't get him off the mountain, our son might fall, rupture his spleen and die. They didn't tell us about the leukemia until later.

On the way down from the mountain, Blain slept with his head in my lap. He knew we were headed to the hospital, but he was exhausted. In his present condition, he was operating on pure guts, refusing to give up anything, even if he really didn't feel up to it.

Ever the outdoorsman, at ten years of age, Blain had become the youngest member of an exclusive group known as "The Circle of the Gobbler," after he called in and brought home his own spring turkey. He had nearly driven us out of the house with his endless clucks and gobbles as he spent all of his spare time practicing, trying to get just the right sound.

When he was only six, he and Judd went on a pack-in fishing trip with some friends, including a boy around Blain's age. They all rode into the high country on horseback, and Blain and his little buddy were flying high as they bounced along the mountain trail, astride their respective mounts. After setting up camp, they took out their fishing gear and headed down to the picturesque lake. It wasn't long before Blain and his dad had a stringer full of pan-perfect trout. They had caught their supper, and I'm certain that fish never tasted better to the two little novices. Alongside his day's catch, Blain looked like Huckleberry Finn as he posed for his proud father on the other side of the camera.

One weekend after Blain's radiation treatments were completed, some friends invited us to a picnic extravaganza. After eating our lunch, our fifteen-year-old daughter Lisa and a couple of other teenagers decided to climb the peak that was looming before us like a giant challenge. It wasn't long before others decided that it would be a great way to work off the delicious meal we had all just devoured.

I made sure Blain was busy throwing a Frisbee with someone and told him where I was going. Then I began my ascent along with some other hardy souls. It was a beautiful climb and not particularly easy. Along the way, we all had to stop periodically to catch our breath. As we reached the top, there was a great sense of accomplishment in having made the climb. The view from the summit was spectacular! The vehicles and those people remaining at the picnic site were as tiny as toys moving around below us. I looked for Blain, but couldn't see him anywhere. Then I spotted Judd making the climb; he was already about halfway up.

Suddenly, I recognized Blain's colorful shirt. He had decided he wasn't going to be left behind. If the rest of us had made the climb, so would he.

I prayed that he wouldn't fall and hurt himself. He was wearing western boots, hardly the best thing for climbing. Everyone began to cheer Blain on as he headed closer and closer. He crossed over a rockslide area, and I held my breath as he eased his feet over those slippery rocks. Slowly and confidently, he took his next step, one by one, with the same determination that had always marked his spirit. We were so proud of him.

No matter how demanding the challenge was or how badly he felt, our precious Blain had been through fourteen months of treatment, but he wouldn't give up. And slowly but surely, he made his way up the mountain — to be with his family and friends.

When our courageous son passed away eight days short of his thirteenth birthday, he was still on top of the world! And we're still right there with him.

~Diane Graff Cooney
Chicken Soup for the Nature Lover's Soul

On, Being a Parent

Parents by Choice

Making the decision to have a child is momentous. It is to decide forever to have your heart go walking around outside your body.
~Elizabeth Stone

The Question

Joyfully, our adoption process was nearing the finale! In the beginning, I had supplied, verified and simplified every question and every fill-in-the-blank. But even then, amidst the facts and figures, one lone and very specific uncertainty tugged at my heart. I thought about it when we attended our first welcoming seminar. I tried not to be obvious as I searched the faces of the other prospective parents—were they feeling the same uncertainty?

Finally, we received the long-awaited "call," and the next day a tiny baby was placed into my arms. That one nagging little fear was overshadowed by the sheer joy of holding my newborn son and naming him Eric. I considered it once again in the courtroom the day the paperwork became final. He was six months old, able to coo and giggle, oblivious to legalities or titles. Yet all the while I wondered. Where and when and how would he ask me the inevitable question: Are you my real mother?

I knew there were books and pamphlets explaining all the "right" answers to be given at all the "appropriate" age levels. I told myself I would read the scholarly information and wait my turn to recite the correct reply.

So I read and reread, but the security never came with the knowledge. Now I knew what to say, but would I say it right, say it so he could understand? What if the question came on the freeway while the two of us maneuvered in and out of traffic? Would I pull the car to the side? Would I ask that he wait till we got home and we'd talk?

After all, a question so important could hardly be addressed between Thirty-second and Thirty-fourth Street.

Maybe he would ask me in the playroom of a golden-arched restaurant or as we exited his favorite movie. I would be prepared, I told myself. I would briefly, very briefly touch on conception and then even more briefly on pregnancy and then deal with the who and why of what came after that.

Would there ever be words that could explain it all? How could I make him understand that he grew in one woman's womb and another woman's heart? How could he know the anguish his birth mother felt on placement day as she held him one last time or the breathless joy I felt the second he was placed in the warmth of my arms?

One night, as I was preparing dinner, tired from the day's lack of accomplishment and frustrated by the lateness of the hour, a small-framed three-year-old boy came and stood beside me as I stirred the mashed potatoes.

"Mommy," he said. "I have a question for you."

"Uh-hum," I mumbled out of habit.

"Mommy," he tugged at my shirt. "Mommy, I said I have a question."

"Okay, okay." I stopped and turned to see two bright eyes staring up at me. I knew something was wrong. He blinked, trying to hold back the tears, but they fell nevertheless. I bent down to him, forgetting the potatoes and the day. What mattered more than anything was the little boy before me. I held his chin in the cup of my hand and asked him softly. "What's wrong? What is so important to ask me that it would make you cry?"

No sooner had the last word left my lips than I knew. We were here. The moment had arrived, and I was as unprepared as the minute it had first crossed my thoughts.

"Mommy, Sarah says you aren't my real mommy. I told her she was wrong. She was wrong, right, Mommy?"

All the days of guessing and planning and memorizing, and I was speechless. I pulled him closer to me and wrapped my arms tightly around his little body. My son. My precious son. I wiped away the tears continuing to fall against his cheek. Then with a calmness I'd never before possessed, I held out my hand.

"Sweetheart, do you see Mommy's hand?"

"Uh huh," he replied as he bobbed his head up and down.

"Well," I slowly said, "go ahead and touch it. Touch my hand." His tiny fingers stroked across my palm.

"Do I feel real to you?" I asked.

"You do!" he said as a smile broke across his face. He ran his fingers along my arms and then against my face and through my hair.

"Then I am your real mother, and my love for you is real. But there is another lady who loves you and is very real, too. She loved you so much she gave you life and let you grow inside her until it was time for you to be born and join Mommy and Daddy. She's called your birth mother, and one day we'll get to meet her.

"How does that sound?" I asked. I wasn't sure who the question was for, him or me.

He grabbed my neck and began to cover my cheek with kisses. I pulled him closer, the tears rolling down my cheeks. And then before I was ready to let go, he pulled away and off he ran to the living room, ready to play once more.

It had happened. I had seen tears that needed to be wiped away, and they had left with the stroke of my hand. I had seen a little boy who needed to be hugged, and I had given him the warmest, softest hug I could give. The question had been asked. And I had answered.

I knew, in another time and another place, there would be other, harder questions but for now, I knew... I had done well.

~Mary Chavoustie
Chicken Soup for the Mother's Soul 2

47

Fostering Memories

*A memory is what is left when something happens
and does not completely unhappen.*
~Edward de Bono

Kate was six years old when we first became her "holiday people." She lived in a children's home in our South African city, where she had been since the age of two. Her mother was an infrequent visitor whom Kate barely remembered, and no one knew the whereabouts of her father.

The children were allowed outings two Sundays a month. My husband and I didn't have children of our own, and we felt that sharing a couple of Sundays with Kate would not be much of a sacrifice if we could bring some pleasure into her life.

Kate was a thoughtful, sensible and well-behaved child with a ready giggle. Soon, we planned every alternate Sunday with her in mind. We found ourselves at places we'd never previously visited—mini-town, the fun fair, the bird park—and doing things we'd never done, like riding model trains and ponies. Sharing in her enjoyment brought us an enormous amount of pleasure.

We would arrive at the home at nine in the morning to find a cluster of excited girls waiting on the veranda for their parents, or "holiday people." Soon, there were only a handful of "leftovers" to wave a wistful goodbye. There was never jealousy from those left behind, who willingly shared their best clothes with the girls going out. Sometimes, we would add a couple of leftovers to our threesome.

At the end of the day, when it was time for home, we gave Kate pocket money to buy sweets. She took great care to be sure everything was shareable, and she took into account the likes and dislikes of the other girls. Lollipops could not be shared; packets and tubes of sweets could.

When we arrived back at the home, she hugged us and gave cheery goodbye kisses, then off she went to share her carefully selected goodies.

On one occasion, after we had given Kate her money, she went skipping ahead of us to the shop. We saw her stop and talk to a beggar. Then she turned and slowly walked back to us, admitting she had given all her money to the beggar.

"But what about your sweets?" we asked.

"That's all right, it doesn't matter," she assured us.

On holidays and special weekends, she was allowed to stay over with us. At first, we wondered how to keep her entertained. I asked if she would like to help with the chores of everyday family life. We did the dusting and washing-up together, hung out the washing and bathed the dogs. Then we swam, took the dogs for a walk or played games.

We had an old cash register that she used for playing shop. "Have you got a jar or tin?" she asked, placing the jar on top of the cash register.

"What is it for?"

"For people to give donations to the poor."

We obviously had a lot to learn from Kate.

We tried to cram as much as we could into the time she had with us, and at bedtime, she was often tired but "not sleepy." Yet, within half an hour, her eyes closed and we carried her to bed. Sometimes, we would find hidden under her pillow presents for us fashioned from scraps of paper and material, and touching thank-you cards.

Over the next six or seven years, we tried to enrich her life by taking her to as many places and doing as much as we could—the aquarium, feeding pigeons in the town square, a children's Christmas party, shopping for new clothes, a niece's wedding, ballet lessons, visits to restaurants, learning to ride a bicycle, the botanical gardens. When we ran out of ideas, we asked parents where they took their children for a treat. That's when we discovered the historical village, the model-yacht pond, the mini-zoo, and a rowing boat on the river.

When she entered her teenage years she moved to another home and we gradually lost touch. Ten years went by.

One day, there was a knock on the door. A young man in his twenties stood there with an air of apprehensive excitement. "Are you the couple who were Kate's 'holiday people?'"

His name was Peter. Kate was in a nearby maternity home after giving birth to their first child. He hadn't told her he was coming to look for us, but hoped we would come and see her and the baby. She would be so excited.

I invited him in, anxious to catch up on all the news.

"Kate often spoke about her times with you." He looked around. "Is that the same dining table that Kate sat under to dust the legs? Is that the kitchen stool she sat on to help with the washing-up? Are these the same cats and dogs?" He knew all their names.

I showed him "Kate's bedroom" and the swimming pool where she had learned to swim. I even found the old photograph album. He pored over the photos, exclaiming, "Kate told me about that! I remember her talking about this. She's going to be so excited to see you."

The following afternoon, I set off for the maternity home armed with gifts. Kate and I immediately hugged and wiped away the tears. Then I had to see the baby, a daughter who looked just like Kate. Was this how a grandmother felt?

And then began the 'remember-whens.' Kate rattled on. "Remember when I was little and helped you to dust the legs of the dining table, because I was small enough to fit underneath? Remember when Uncle Neil used to play tricks on me? Remember how we used to wash the dishes together? Remember how we bathed the dogs? Remember how you taught me to swim and to read Roman numerals? Remember how the cat slept on my bed?"

I recalled all the special places and events we had so diligently planned. "Remember the aquarium, the children's Christmas party, shopping for new clothes, the ballet lesson, riding model trains and touring the botanical gardens?"

Kate sat pensively. "Yes, those were all nice, but my fondest and most vivid memories, the ones I really treasure..." she kissed her baby, "...are the ones of everyday family life."

~Janet Nicholson
Chicken Soup for the Caregiver's Soul

Behind Blue Eyes

Children have more need of models than of critics.
~Joseph Joubert

amantha stood in the center of the shabby social services office wearing a threadbare pink sweatsuit. The flickery fluorescent lighting illuminated shaggy boy-cut blond hair, dirty fingernails, a runny nose and huge blue eyes ringed with dark, tired circles. Around the thumb jammed between her teeth, she stared up at me and asked, "Are you my new mom?"

My husband, Dan, and I had gone through all the usual contortions to have a second child. His and hers surgeries, artificial insemination. Nothing happened. I had always envisioned adopting, but my husband was unconvinced. Dan's initial reservation about adoption was understandable given that, at the time, the evening news was filled with terrifying stories of anguished biological and adoptive parents fighting for the rights to be some little one's "real" mom and dad. Still, we decided to move forward.

Our ten-year-old son, Matthew, was also a little slow to jump on the adoption bandwagon. He had been the center of our universe for a long time, and he liked it that way. He was also a typical kid in that he wanted to fit in and not be "different" in any way. We planned to adopt a baby from China, which especially concerned him; he feared that an Asian baby in our Caucasian midst might invite dreaded attention.

As part of the adoption agency screening process, a social

worker came to interview Matthew, and we encouraged him to "just be honest." So, with prepubescent eloquence, our son explained to the attentive social worker that he loved being an only child, that he didn't want a sibling from another country, that he didn't like Chinese rice, that people would stare at us if we had a Chinese baby, and that basically a little brother or sister would pretty much ruin his life. He was evangelistic in his passion, Galilean in his logic. Brilliant. When he was through, my husband and I watched the social worker back out of the driveway, wondering if she would even make it back to the office before setting fire to our application.

Miraculously, when the whole screening process was finished (references, fingerprints, credit and criminal checks, etc.) my husband and I were approved. My son remained skeptical, and my husband was still a bit nervous even as we settled down to wait. Then, on a bitter January morning we got the call.

The social worker told us about a little girl, suddenly available—a four-year-old white girl from New York—who had come into this world with cocaine humming in her veins. "How soon can you be here?" the social worker asked.

Our preliminary visit was to last about an hour or so. Taking Samantha's hand in mine, I led her down the steps and out the door. We walked though a winter-bare park with Samantha on my shoulders. She got shy around Dan and wouldn't accept a "pony ride" from him. She had no mittens and her icy little fingers squeezed my hands. Her chatter was nonstop and more than a little desperate. Her blue gaze focused over my shoulder, or off in the distance, but never settled on my face. Her eyes were both blank and wild, like a wary captive.

In the park, we stumbled upon a dry fountain and pitched our pennies in, making silent wishes. I wished for the chance to quell the quiet panic in her eyes.

After the visit, we took Samantha back to the social worker. We were told to think about the adoption and to let them know. There was little discussion in our car on the way home. Our fears were too numerous and too ethereal to put into words, but our commitment was already rock solid. The next morning we brought our daughter home.

From the very first day, Samantha called me "Mom." I had waited years for this moment, anxious to be privileged again with that most singular title. But there was no epiphany when she said it, no fireworks, no choir of angels. I knew that to Samantha, "Mom" was just the lady who was taking care of her at the moment. No more intimate than "Waiter" or "Stewardess." All the meaning had been drained from that word the night her "real mom" took the garbage out and never came back.

After her biological mother left, Samantha lived with a steady succession of mothers. Some were just temporary care for a night or two; others were longer "trial visits." One, Samantha's mother for five months, told Samantha they were going to adopt her into their family soon, that the other children were her "sister" and her "brother." When Samantha came to us, one of her few possessions was a little purple sweatshirt, hand decorated with craft paint spelling out the words "Little Sister." But, one night, when Samantha had said something inappropriate in front of the biological kids, she was abruptly stripped of her title and sent away. A dishonorable discharge for the littlest soldier.

Now at our house, Samantha was somebody else's daughter, somebody else's little sister. Matthew's initial fears about a new sibling thrusting him into the limelight were replaced with relief; his new sister looked remarkably like him and the rest of the family. There would be no undue attention, no compulsory rice.

At first he treated Samantha like a cute new pet. "Want to come in and see my new sister? Look what she can do!" After a few days the novelty wore off, and routine set in.

But Sam remained enthralled with Matthew. She lingered over the many pictures of him that covered the walls of our house: Matthew in a soccer uniform, Matthew at the beach, Matthew with Grandpa. On her third day with us, Samantha found some old catalogues and asked for scissors. Patiently she cut out pictures of two dolls, a boy and a girl. She turned over one of the silver frames and lifted the back. With great care she arranged her boy and girl on the mat and replaced the frame, beaming. "Look, Mom! Look at the picture of me and Matthew!"

For reassurance, or maybe just to remind herself who he was, Samantha had taken to calling our son "Matthewmybrother." When she had been with us about a week, she called to him at bedtime. With her wide blue eyes shining up at him, she said, "Matthewmybrother, I'm glad your room is next to mine so that you can protect me from the monsters." For a boy of ten, not that far removed from believing in monsters himself, this was high praise. He swaggered out of her room like he had just been knighted.

My husband, too, had bonded with Sam. The little blondie who wrapped around his legs was just as tightly wrapped around his heart. He did not need to fear a parental tug-of-war over this child. Her biological parents had neglected and abandoned her, having fallen so deep into their dark, destructive world that there was no hope—or risk—of them climbing out.

We saw glimpses of their lives through Samantha. One day, she deftly took a rubber plastic blood-pressure hose from a play doctor's set and tied it around her forearm, pulling it tight with her teeth. Then she tapped on her veins as though feeling for "a good one." The father who had shot up in front of Samantha never once came looking for her.

As the weeks passed, Samantha worked hard to learn the names of all of her new relatives. "Is it Uncle Dale and Aunt Kelly, or Uncle Kale and Aunt Delly?" She knew Grandma and Poppa and numerous cousins. And I was Mom.

She called me "Mommy," "Mama," and sometimes, "Mumsy," because Matthewmybrother did too. I knew that if Samantha were to draw a picture of her mom it would be my face she would draw, my stick hand holding her stick hand. But I had been a mother for ten years. I knew the difference between the word and the relationship it represented. Once, when I left Samantha with my parents for an evening, she asked my mother, "If she doesn't come back, are you my new mom?"

Weeks turned into months. We were progressing as quickly as

legally possible from foster parents to adoptive parents. Samantha nestled down into family life, preferring hand-me-downs from her new cousins to store-bought clothes, getting crushes on the same Montessori teachers as her brother had a few years before. She danced around the living room with my old rhinestone earrings clipped to her ears. She smiled at herself smiling back at herself from the silver frames on the piano... and the desk... and the walls.

And we were friends, she and I. We baked cookies. We shopped together—a lot, once I discovered the "pink aisle" at the toy store. She put on my lipstick and gave me elaborate, fanciful hairstyles. And during all this time, she called me "Mom." But it still felt more like "Aunt," or "teacher" or "pal." During all of our mother-daughter moments, Samantha's big blue eyes checked me out, looked me up and down, kept me at a distance.

Once, in the middle of the night, I went into Samantha's room to check on her. She was sitting up in bed. She hadn't called out to us, and she wasn't crying, but when I came close to the bed her eyes registered fear. "I dreamed you were a witch, and you were going to kill me." I held her, whispering that I would never hurt her. She was safe now. That night she told me about violence she had witnessed, about playing with rats, about being locked in the trunk of a car. Other times, only late at night, only in the dark, and only when I wasn't looking at her, she told me of many horrible experiences she had lived through in her four short years.

Therapists had warned me that of all the hurts that Sam had endured in her short little life, the cruelest blow was from her biological mom. I should be patient, they said. She needs to learn to trust again.

When a tiny brain is growing, a circuitry network of neurotransmitters and jumpy dendrites branch out, creating a blueprint for the future. Through experience, children lay down patterns in their brain, designed to keep them safe and help them thrive. Children learn to recoil from big dogs, or scary clowns, or weird Uncle Max with fermenting breath, but they don't usually recoil from mom.

Moms are supposed to be the soft lap, the gentle hands that

soothe away the nightmares. They are supposed to be the big warm blanket you wrap up in when the world is too cold and too rainy. But what happens when Mom is the stinging rain? When it is Mom who is the monster under the bed?

Samantha did not trust me. Nothing I said was accepted as truth. She had to see things with her own eyes. "Don't touch that knife; it's sharp," led to bloody fingers. "Wait on the curb; a car is coming" sent her running into the street to see for herself.

Samantha had come into our home with a "colorful" vocabulary. Once I overheard Barbie and Ken arguing in language that could make a hard-core rapper blush. I explained to my angel-faced daughter that those were not nice words; they make people uncomfortable. That night, at a restaurant with friends, she spewed profanity throughout the dinner, all the while gauging their reaction. Our son was highly entertained. Our friends were not.

Samantha challenged me in a thousand different ways, calculating the results, evaluating the extent of my affection. How far could she go before I'd be gone? She broke treasured heirlooms, defied rules, lied, hoarded, stole. She did not scare us off, but still she refused to depend on me, to believe in me. When I tucked her in at night, and whispered, "I love you," she squirmed. When her runaway mind kept her up at night, restless and anxious, I massaged her hands and feet, but her muscles stayed taut and tense beneath my fingers. I ached to relieve her from her post of hypervigilance, to loosen her grip on her emotions, to hear her genuine laugh, to help her just let go and resume her rightful role as innocent child.

Intellectually, I knew her therapists were right. I would nod my head. Yes, yes, I know. But secretly my gut clenched. I wavered between self-disgust and self-pity. What arrogance had me thinking that my house, my family, my love, could reach this broken little girl? If, in the end, she could not love me back, but she was safe and content, surrounded by health and hope, shouldn't that be enough? Perhaps there would be no sacred bond or whispered trust between us. But if she could live without pain and in relative peace, shouldn't I just be thankful, and let the rest go?

One night, about a year after Samantha arrived, I was awakened by a choked cry. I hurried in and found Samantha sitting up in bed, her white nightgown a mess. She had gotten sick all over herself and her bed linens. Cleaning up throw-up was my domain, so my husband helped Samantha to the bathroom as I began to strip her sheets. I could hear Dan speaking quietly to Sam as he knelt with her in front of the toilet bowl. I was filling up a bucket when suddenly she let out an anguished cry. Her words were loud and distinct, "I WANT MY MOMMY!"

She was hurting and needing help, scared and needing comfort. She was a child who needed her mom. And not her biological mom, or her foster moms, or the social workers. She wanted me! What kind of a mother rejoices when her daughter is sick and in distress? I couldn't help it — my heart sang.

I cradled my daughter's head while her little body heaved. It wasn't pretty, but it was real. I knew then that although I wouldn't be Samantha's first mom... or her second or third, nothing could keep me from being her last. And that was more than enough.

~Jenny Graham
Chicken Soup for Every Mom's Soul

EDITORS' NOTE: Sam became a healthy, happy teenager who loves music, horseback riding, and her family.

George and Gracie's Babies

Adopting babies was a popular thing to do among show business people in the 1930s. I was agreeable; Gracie wanted to have children and I wanted to make Gracie happy. But we just kept putting it off. We were on the road too much, the apartment wasn't big enough, we had a picture coming up, there was always something. Then one afternoon we had lunch with another actor and he brought along his adopted daughter. The kid did all the right things—she smiled at Gracie and laughed at my cigar. As soon as we got home, we called The Cradle, a Catholic foundling home in Evanston, Illinois.

Months passed before we heard from The Cradle. Finally, they called and told us that we could have a baby if we came to Evanston immediately. Gracie and her friend Mary were on a train to Chicago three hours later. I stayed in New York.

They showed Gracie three babies to select from. How do you pick out a kid? How do you know which one is going to be tall and attractive and smart? How do you know which one is going to have a good disposition? How do you know which one is going to laugh at her father's jokes? The answer is, you don't, you can't. It's exactly the same chance you take as having a child naturally.

Gracie picked the smallest baby, a tiny five-week-old with great big blue eyes, and named her Sandra Jean. Sandra Jean Burns.

The Cradle offered to provide a nurse to accompany Gracie and Mary back to New York, but Gracie figured two grown women should be able to take care of one small baby. And the two of them felt very confident — until the baby sneezed. That's when Gracie realized they were outnumbered. Neither one of them knew what to do, so Gracie covered the baby's body with her fur coat. Sometime during the night, the coat slipped down and covered the baby's head. When Gracie woke up and saw that, she thought she'd smothered her daughter. Making a lopsided cake was one thing, but smothering your daughter a few hours after you've had her? She grabbed the coat and watched helplessly to see if the baby was breathing. The baby was fine — it was Gracie who was having trouble breathing. So she sat up in the compartment the rest of the trip just watching her daughter breathe.

I didn't get to pace up and down in a waiting room; I had Grand Central Station. Believe me, I was as nervous as any expectant father has ever been, and I knew exactly when my baby was due. The train pulled in on time. That was one of the rare occasions when a train conductor delivered a baby.

The first night we had Sandy at home, Gracie asked me if I wanted to change the baby. "Nah," I said, "let's try this one out first." That was about as close as I ever came to actually eating a cigar. I guess Gracie was a little sensitive. But what did I know about changing a baby's diapers?

The thing about the baby that surprised me most was how much space something so small could take up. Our second bedroom, which had been my den, became her nursery. The kitchen was the operations center — that's where we kept her bottles, her milk, her formula, her jars of baby food, the piles of clean diapers and some of the toys that overflowed from my former den. I don't know, maybe there were some babies who had more toys than Sandy did. Santa Claus's kids, for instance.

As it turned out, Sandy was such a delight that we decided she should have a brother.

Gracie picked out our son Ronnie because he needed her most.

Now, that sounds like a line written by a Hollywood press agent, but it's true. The other babies they showed her were all chubby and healthy, and she knew there was a long list of people waiting to adopt chubby, healthy babies. Ronnie's crib was off by itself in a corner; maybe that's what first attracted Gracie's attention to him. She went over and looked at him. "He was so small," she told me when she finally brought him home, "and he followed me with his eyes when I moved, and I knew I had to take him."

He was premature, a nurse told Gracie, and for several weeks doctors didn't know if he was going to survive.

Since I'm telling the truth, I have to admit that Ronnie was an ugly baby. People say all babies look like Winston Churchill; Ronnie made Winston Churchill look handsome. Ronnie looked like a wrinkled little man with a funny-shaped head. "What do you think, Nattie?"

I thought that if I was smart, I'd keep my mouth shut. "Look, you know I don't mind responsibility," I said, "but, Googie, why'd you pick a sick kid?"

"I just fell in love with his eyes. I know he's not well, but we can make him well. It's the same chance we would have taken if we'd had him, isn't it?"

Ronnie had a tough first year. For a long time he couldn't gain any weight, and his skin was so sensitive that we could only bathe him in oil and we had to wrap him in cotton. Gracie and our nurse spent a lot of time in doctors' offices. Gracie fussed over him like I worked on our scripts. But Ronnie was a smart kid, and once he figured out how to grow, he didn't stop until he was almost 6' 2" tall and much better looking than Winston Churchill.

Gracie had been right.

~George Burns
Chicken Soup for the Mother's Soul 2

50

Son for a Season

If you haven't any charity in your heart,
you have the worst kind of heart trouble.
~Bob Hope

The last Friday in September was supposed to have been Jeremy's "Special Day" at nursery school. That's when he would have brought a favorite toy for show-and-tell and picked the book his teacher would read to the class. His mom would have supplied snacks for all the kids.

"Special Day" came differently for Jeremy. He didn't go to school with his toy and book and snacks. Instead, his day began at 7 A.M., when a man he didn't know arrived in a car he didn't recognize. Imprinted on the car were the words STATE OF NEW JERSEY. Jeremy was still rubbing the sleep from his eyes when the man carried the single bag that contained Jeremy's entire wardrobe to the car and tossed it into the trunk. He returned for two boxes of Jeremy's stuffed animals, miniature cars and other cherished items. Then it was Jeremy's turn.

I will never forget the look on his face as he was taken away. We'd tried to prepare him, telling him he was going to live with his Grandma and Grandpa in Pennsylvania. But he didn't understand. To three-year-old Jeremy, I was "Mommy." My husband was "Daddy." His "sister" and "brother" were our children, Catherine and Michael.

All Jeremy understood was that he was going somewhere in a strange car with a strange person. "I want Daddy," he cried, tears stinging his soft cheeks and hazel eyes. "Where's Catherine?" he wailed as the state worker strapped him into his car seat. "No, no, no!" he screamed. We waved goodbye as the car pulled away and disappeared from sight.

Both my husband and I had tears in our eyes. Finally I was able to comment, "That's more than Jeremy could say when he got here," referring to Jeremy's departing words. And it was true. When he came to live with us, he could barely talk.

Jeremy was our foster son. He stayed with us from June 20 to September 30, 1994. We would have kept him longer—forever, if possible—but the state of New Jersey felt it was better for him if relatives, in this case grandparents in their seventies, raised him. Who are we to judge?

He came into foster care for many reasons, but I'll just generalize and say he was neglected. When he arrived, his vocabulary numbered no more than twenty-five words. He couldn't dress or feed himself, and he wasn't potty-trained. At night, despite all our efforts to calm him, he screamed for hours, unable to sleep without the lights on and someone near him.

By summer's end Jeremy was a different child. He had grown two inches and gained two pounds. We gave him vitamins and a diet of healthful foods, and sent him to nursery school and speech therapy. His vocabulary increased, and he began forming sentences. He was no longer afraid of the dark and went to bed willingly by 8:30 P.M., sometimes earlier, after learning to announce, "I'm tired."

And then, he was gone.

People ask us why we became foster parents. "You have your own children," they say. "Why do you want other people's problems? How can you bear to let these kids go, wondering what will happen to them? Doesn't it break your hearts?"

Yes, it does. But not doing something would make our hearts ache even more.

When Jeremy first came to us, I cried a lot, wondering how we could cope with his many problems while caring for our own children. I asked my husband then, "Why are we doing this?" He didn't reply because neither of us truly knew why.

Months after I posed that desperate question, Mike and I attended church together. We listened to the scripture reading: "He then took a little child whom he set among them and embraced, and he said to them, 'Anyone who welcomes a little child such as this in my name, welcomes me; and anyone who welcomes me, welcomes not me but the one who sent me.'"

Mike nudged me and whispered, "That's why we do this." I suddenly remembered my question—and I'll never forget my husband's answer. And that's why we'll be foster parents for years to come.

~Jo Ann C. Nahirny
Chicken Soup for the Christian Family Soul

51

Hanging On to Hope

I was thrilled to be pregnant within the first year of our marriage. My husband, Russ, and I were so excited, we went out to a department store the night we found out and bought two little shirts. We were certain it was going to be a boy.

But our excitement was short-lived. The pregnancy ended in a miscarriage after three months. Following doctor's orders, we waited six months and tried again. This time, the pregnancy made it past the first trimester. It made it to the second and then the third trimester. It made it all the way to a week before my due date, but then, during a routine examination, the doctor failed to pick up the baby's heartbeat. I was admitted to the hospital where labor was induced, and after spending most of the night in labor, I finally delivered a ten-pound, two-ounce stillborn son.

We named the baby Hugh Leon, and although we received cards, flowers and words of encouragement, unless someone's been there, there's no way to describe the overwhelming disappointment and grief a stillbirth can bring. Realizing that losses like this either make or break a marriage, we leaned on each other. And we leaned on God.

They say time heals all wounds, but being inundated with advertisements for everything from diaper services to baby insurance seemed to slow the healing process. I packed away all the brochures and samples, believing that someday we would use them.

The next several months were spent applying to every adoption agency we could find. They all had waiting lists longer than the Congressional Record, so we did the only thing we could do—we applied and we waited.

After several discouraging years, we decided to take a step of faith. Believing that God would give us a family someday, we moved from our two-bedroom home into a four-bedroom one. We didn't know when God was going to answer our prayers and fill the extra bedrooms, but we knew He would. Someday.

When I called the adoption agencies to give them our new address, several of them informed me that since our move had taken us out of their area, they would drop us from their waiting list. We were stunned. Our hopes crashed and burned before our eyes. Were we going to have to start all over again? Had our giant step of faith turned into a giant step backward?

We had been in our new home one week, and we were still living with wall-to-wall boxes. We decided to start fixing up the nursery first, thinking it would be the easiest room to arrange. We hung baby clothes, moved furniture around and nailed up wall decorations. It seemed a bit futile to spend so much time arranging a room that wasn't being used, but we were driven to finish it. Russ was driven until midnight. Then, because he had to go to work early the next day, I stayed up to complete the job—although I ended up doing more crying than unpacking.

I couldn't understand why God was allowing this ongoing tragedy in our lives. At two o'clock in the morning I finally decided to "give up." I'd been blaming God since the stillbirth, and I was tired of being bitter and hurt and angry. After a few more hours of licking my wounds and being mad at Him, I finally surrendered. I knew I couldn't go on harboring bitterness and resentment. He had a plan for our lives, even if it wasn't our plan. I vowed I would remain faithful to God even if He didn't answer our prayers for a baby. Then I went to bed, feeling at peace for the first time in a long while.

At 6:00 A.M. the phone rang. It was one of the adoption agencies. I thought they were calling to get our new address to update their records, but they told me they had a three-week-old baby boy waiting for us. All I could do was cry and jump up and down on the bed, waking my husband!

We named our son Russ II, after my husband, and within the next few years, we adopted a second son, Matt—when I was six months pregnant. Our third son, Tony Shane, was born three-and-a-half months later. Two years after moving into our new home, God had filled every bedroom.

Our step of faith turned out to be a step forward after all.

~Martha Bolton
Chicken Soup for the Christian Woman's Soul

After the Tears

Be strong and take heart,
all you who hope in the Lord.
~Psalm 31:24

"I'm sorry, Mrs. Coe. The test was negative."

Not that I was surprised. I felt it coming. I'd known I wasn't pregnant for the last week and a half.

What did I do to deserve this?

Sobs broke from my husband first. I was numb. We held each other, but there was no comfort. It had been our last in vitro fertilization attempt, the last we would ever try. We'd spent the last seven years hoping for a baby, undergoing every procedure known to reproductive gynecology — hoping, hoping.

I'd gone home and put on a record — a song wailing about how God sometimes just doesn't come through. Intermittently, I cried. But mostly I was angry and scared. I was at the end of my rope, faith-wise, hope-wise. God, sometimes you just don't come through.

Adoption, I sighed in resignation. There was a meeting for prospective adoptive parents, and Tom wanted to go. He was getting over the infertility issue; he wanted to move forward. Okay, I'd go. I didn't want to go, but I'd listen. I would try to keep an open mind.

Six couples stared across a conference table at each other. Five minutes into the meeting, the woman across from me was sobbing. Finally, I broke down, too. This agency had judged me hopelessly unable to give birth, only able to become a mother by taking someone else's child. I was officially unfixable. This was the pain I'd just begun to face.

The next Sunday was Mother's Day, and all the kids at church were invited up front for a children's homily. The priest told them what blessings they were to their parents. But what about us? Why didn't we get these blessings? What did we ever, ever, do to deserve this?

We went for counseling. We met with a woman who had suffered multiple miscarriages, who could now say, "If those children had lived, I would never have had these other children." We looked into the face of someone who had survived this, someone to whom this all finally made sense.

So we'd adopt. But the agency hadn't placed any babies in the last year. We'd have to advertise and find a baby ourselves. We'd have to get out there on the front lines and leave ourselves open to even more pain, even more disappointment. Worst of all, if someone did agree to give us her baby, she could change her mind, and there would be nothing we could do about it—except grieve again, and ask, why us?

I took a deep breath, and asked a group of women, some I hardly knew, to pray for me. It was something I'd never done before. And I waited.

Then one day while I was hanging around the house, thinking that for once I was actually happy, finally coming out of the funk I'd been in for years, the phone rang. A young woman wanted to give us a baby.

For the next few days, we were in a daze. We were going to become parents. An ultrasound was done. It was a perfect little girl, the doctor said.

Although I knew it was unreasonable, there was a part of me that grieved yet a little more. I had always wanted twins, a boy and a girl the same age. I thought maybe I would get them through all the fertility drugs I had taken. And somehow, I had always thought my first child would be a boy. But I convinced myself that a daughter would be wonderful. Truly a miracle—though not what I had expected or secretly hoped.

Then the most unlikely of unlikelies happened. We got another phone call. Another woman wanted to give us a baby—a boy, born just that morning. We walked into a hospital, and he was placed into my arms. "This is your mommy and your daddy."

The papers were signed within hours. We appeared before a judge, and it was done. We were parents.

But what about the other baby? The girl? We decided to take her, too. Her birth mother was as dazed and joyous as we were. A brother the same age for our little girl! And so, exactly one month later, at another hospital, we were handed another baby—parents again.

As inexperienced parents of two tiny babies, the next few months were harder than we ever imagined. We agonized whether we had done the right thing, whether we had taken on too much. But one day, as I held my beautiful infant son on my knee, he leaned over to smile at his little sister. She had only begun smiling herself in the past few days. But he kept smiling, egging her on, until she burst into a big smile at him. They gazed smiling at each other, held in each of my arms, joyous to be exactly where they were. I felt tears of pure joy fill my eyes. I, too, was exactly where I wanted to be.

Today, a door opens to a nursery school classroom. Two blond heads look up and burst into grins. "Mommy! Mommy!" Two pairs of legs come running toward me. I kneel, my arms open wide.

What did I do to deserve this?

~Cynthia Coe
Chicken Soup for the Mother's Soul 2

The Day I Became a Mother

All things, whatsoever ye shall ask in prayer,
believing, ye shall receive.
~Matthew 21:22

"Y ou'd understand what I'm saying if you were really a mother," my friend said that morning in Sunday school. There it was, out in the open, what she and the others thought.

It was Mother's Day, and our church always recognized the mothers present by having them stand. I had watched this happen year after year as a single woman with no children. I had always sat and clapped along with the rest of the congregation. But this year was different. I was still single, but I was now a foster parent.

I had been thinking of that day as my own first Mother's Day, and now it had been ruined. I looked down at the two little girls sitting next to me. Was I a mother? Did I have the right to be recognized? What dues had I paid to become a member of that elite group? What was a mother, anyway? I wasn't even "Momma" to the kids who passed through my home. I was "Aunt Dorothy."

When the time came to recognize all mothers, I bent down to speak to the child nearest me. I pretended I wasn't aware of what was going on until it was too late. "Darn, I missed it," I whispered aloud as the mothers sat back down. "There's always next year." Who was I fooling?

Foster children came and went that year, each with their own set of problems. I wiped their noses and doctored their scrapes and cuts. I refereed their disagreements and took away privileges when necessary. I was there to wake them up and take them to school, and I was there to tuck them in at night. I comforted those whose sleep was interrupted by nightmares. And when they left my care, I cried.

Shortly before Mother's Day the following year, one of the girls in my care was going through a particularly difficult period. Dealing with her anxiety attacks, coupled with the day-to-day problems of the other three girls in our home, along with my duties as a school librarian and teacher, began to take a toll on me.

I didn't have a husband to share the problems with or to say, "Hey, it's your turn. You deal with it this time." Yes, there was the social worker, but it wasn't the same. I was alone as a parent. Why was I putting myself through this? I wasn't their mother. I was just "Aunt Dorothy," and not really that. What was the use?

One morning when I was feeling very frustrated, I made a decision. I would call my caseworker that afternoon and tell her that I quit. That was when I heard a voice call me by name. "Dorothy, remember all those years ago when I told you that I had a special job for you? Well, these children are it."

Being a mother is a calling. Most mothers have their children delivered by doctors; a few lucky ones, like me, have ours delivered by social workers (and sometimes a deputy or two). Either way, being a mother is far more than giving birth. It's being there through the bad times as well as the good. That was the day I became a real mother.

On Mother's Day, I sat with my four girls in church. When they asked for all mothers to stand, I quickly got to my feet. There was no doubt in my mind as I looked at each of the girls: I was their mother for right now, and they deserved—and were going to get—all the love and attention I could give them.

A few years later, the other mothers in my church were lucky when it was decided not to recognize the mother with the most children. As a single mother whose household now included three adopted daughters, two foster children, two former foster children who had come back to the roost, and one foreign-exchange student, I had them beat by a country mile.

~Dorothy Hill
Chicken Soup for the Single Parent's Soul

A Gift for Robby

ittle Robby, our neighbor's nephew, carefully spooned some of his water ration into a saucer and started for the door. How I hated this water rationing. We were forced to bathe without soap in the deep little pond we shared with Jessie, our cow. She was all we had now. Wells were dry, crops transformed to dust and blew away with our dreams, during the worst drought our small farming community had ever seen.

I held the screen open for Robby and watched, smiling, as he slowly sat on the steps. Dozens of bees circled his tousled brown curls in an angel's halo. He imitated their buzzing, which brought them to the saucer to sip the precious liquid.

His aunt's words echoed in my ears:

"I don't know what I was thinking when I took him in. Doctors say he wasn't hurt in the crash that killed my sister, but he can't talk. Oh, he makes noises all right, but they aren't human. He's in a world all his own, that boy, not like my children at all."

Why couldn't she see the wonderful gifts this four-year-old boy possessed? My heart ached for Robby. He had become the dearest part of our world, eagerly tending the garden with me and riding the tractor or pitching hay with my husband, Tom. He was blessed with a loving nature and a deep admiration for all living things, and I knew he could talk to animals.

We rejoiced in discoveries he joyfully shared with us. His inquisitive and often impish brown eyes mirrored an understanding of everything verbal. I longed to adopt him. His aunt had hinted often enough. We even called ourselves Mom and Dad to Robby, and before the drought had discussed adoption. But times were so bleak now that I couldn't approach the subject with Tom. The job he was forced to take in town to buy feed for Jessie and bare necessities for us had exacted its toll on his spirit.

Robby's aunt eagerly agreed to our request that he live with us for the summer. All his days were spent in our company anyway. I brushed away a tear, remembering how tiny and helpless he looked when she hastily put his hand in mine and gave me a rumpled brown paper bag. It contained two faded T-shirts we had bought him last year at the county fair and a hand-me-down pair of shorts. This and the clothes he wore were his only belongings, with the exception of one prized possession.

On a silken cord around his neck dangled a hand-carved whistle. Tom had made it for him in case he was ever lost or in danger. After all, he could not call out for help. He knew perfectly well that the whistle was not a toy. It was for emergencies only, and to blow on it would bring us both running. I had told him the story of the boy who cried wolf, and I knew he understood me.

I sighed as I dried and put away the last supper dish. Tom came into the kitchen and picked up the dishpan. Every ounce of recycled water was saved for a tiny vegetable garden Robby had planted beside the porch. He was so proud of it, we tried desperately to save it. But without rain soon, it too would be lost. Tom put the pan on the counter and turned to me.

"You know, honey," he started, "I've been thinking a lot about Robby lately."

My heart began to pound in anticipation, but before he could continue, a shrill blast from the yard made us jump. My God! It's Robby's whistle! By the time we reached the door, the whistle was blowing at a feverish pace. Visions of a rattlesnake filled my head as we raced into the yard. When we reached him, Robby was pointing frantically skyward, and we couldn't pry the whistle from his grip.

Looking up, we saw the most magnificent sight.

Rain clouds—gigantic rain clouds with black, ominous bottoms!

"Robby! Help me, quickly! We need all the pots and pans from the kitchen!"

The whistle dropped from his lips and he raced with me to the house. Tom ran for the barn to drag out an old washtub. When all the containers were placed in the yard, Robby ran back to the house. He emerged with three wooden spoons from my kitchen drawer and handed one to each of us. He picked up my big stock pot and sat down cross-legged. Turning it over, he began to beat a rhythm with his spoon. Tom and I each reached for a pot and joined in.

"Rain for Robby! Rain for Robby!" I chanted with each beat.

A drop of water splashed on my pot and then another. Soon the yard was enveloped in soaking, glorious rain. We all stood with faces held upward to feel the absolute luxury of it. Tom picked up Robby and danced about the pots, shouting and whooping. That's when I heard it—softly at first—then louder and louder: the most marvelous, boisterous, giggling laughter. Tom swung about to show me Robby's face. With head tilted back, he was laughing right out loud! I hugged them both, tears of joy mixing with the rain. Robby released his grip from Tom and clutched my neck.

"W-W-Wobby's!" he stammered. Stretching out one tiny cupped hand to catch the downpour, he giggled again. "Wobby's... wain... Mom," he whispered.

~Toni Fulco
A Second Chicken Soup for the Woman's Soul

My Birthday, Her Party

To get the full value of joy,
you must have somebody to divide it with.
~Mark Twain

It was January 1999, and I was a single, successful and totally bored thirty-eight-year-old woman. My life, while fun and full of wonderful friends and family, seemed all too much about me, and I longed to make a difference for others in need. More than a year before, I had started the foster-to-adoption process in the county where I lived. I'd figured that the chances for a single parent to adopt a child would be better if one had fostering-care experience first. I had filled out the exhausting, twenty-plus-page profile, went through the home-study process and began to wait... and wait... and wait.

I had resigned myself to the fact that my goal of becoming a mom to someone who needed one was never going to come true, and found myself telling a co-worker that I intended to begin volunteering at a local senior center. Surely, someone there could use my help and love.

The same morning I made this pronouncement to my co-worker, the phone in my office rang. It was the county, and they had a ten-month-old baby girl who needed a foster home immediately. I went to the agency the following morning for our very first visit. What was to be a preliminary, getting-acquainted visit turned into a three-and-a-half-hour bonding session with a precocious, little dark-haired angel who was already walking. She walked into that room and straight into my arms, and never left.

It was obvious to everyone at the agency that this was a match made in heaven. With emotions whirling like a tornado, I put Jordan, God's little angel, in the car seat I had just installed in the back of my car, and began the journey of a lifetime: motherhood. From the car, I called my entire family and support system and asked them, one by one, to help me get together the necessary items for her immediate arrival since I had no time to go shopping. (Little did I know that, from that day forward, I would never have time for anything; I would have to make time.) They all answered with love and enthusiasm, and within twenty-four hours, her little diaper bag, which had only one shoe in it when it arrived with her, contained thirteen pairs!

The next day was my thirty-ninth birthday, and my sister had asked me to bring the baby over for a quiet, family celebration. When I got to the house, I looked in the window and saw that it was filled with decorations, presents, family and friends. I was overwhelmed with emotion when I went inside and proceeded to celebrate my birthday, but it was really Jordan's party.

A few months later, on a beautiful summer day, God changed the life of two single moms in a beautiful way. It was the first visitation we were to have with Jordan's birth mother. I arrived early at the county office to get settled, only to walk through the front door and right into her. There was no denying who she was: she and Jordan looked like they could be sisters. Both of us moms were apprehensive, but within a short time, we became two women who simply shared love for the same child. Since that time we have formed a unique friendship that is hard to explain and understand.

More than a year later, with a few bumps and dips in the road, Jordan became Jordan Smith, my daughter. We had another party, and this time it really was hers! I couldn't have been happier.

Every so often, my co-worker asks me if I have checked into

volunteering at the senior center. My response: "I'm looking for volunteers to help me!"

~Gerilynn Smith
Chicken Soup for the Single Parent's Soul

56

A Change in Plans

We must be willing to get rid of the life we've planned,
so as to have the life that is waiting for us.
~Joseph Campbell

"Please God, help me. I can't live through another Mother's Day." Heartbroken, Tammy longed to hold a baby and feel its soft skin against hers. She longed to hear a newborn's cry in the middle of the night. She longed to be a mother.

A year ago on Mother's Day, she and Chris were elated because the baby growing inside her was already eleven weeks old. They were hopeful that this time she would go full term. But later that day their dreams were shattered. Waves of nausea and painful cramps overcame Tammy. Fearing the worst, they called the doctor. He confirmed their dreaded thoughts. It was a miscarriage—her third.

Now, a year later, Tammy struggled with memories of fertility drugs, surgery, frustration and disappointment. The verse Jeremiah 29:11 came to her mind: "For I know the plans I have for you, declares the Lord...." She swallowed back tears. "God what is your plan for me? I am forty years old and don't have a lot of time. I pray that a baby is part of Your plan for us."

The emotional ride she had been on for three-and-a-half years came to an end after two attempts at artificial insemination failed. Adoption seemed their next viable choice.

With a renewed sense of hope, Tammy and Chris began the adoption process. Physicals, paperwork, FBI checks, written testimonials, a home study and a profile of them had to be completed before they could be considered. Finally, when it was all done, Tammy breathed a sigh of relief and prayed that God would bless them with a baby soon.

A couple of months passed without any news from the adoption agency. Feelings of doubt crept into Tammy's mind until finally she received a call at work from the caseworker. Would they take a newborn with severe health problems?

Feeling overwhelmed and incompetent, Tammy and Chris tearfully declined, wondering if they'd ever be picked again.

In a few weeks, Tammy received a package in the mail from an old friend of Chris' family whom she'd never met. Inside was a diaper bag filled with necessary baby items and a note:

> When we were planning to adopt our first child, someone gave us a diaper bag. When I heard about your situation, I wanted to do the same thing for you. With each of our children, we were away from home when we received the call saying we were parents, so the diaper bag came in handy. Put this in the trunk of your car and you will always be prepared.

What a gift of hope, Tammy thought. She tucked it away and prayed she would need it soon.

Nearly six months passed; finally they got another call. This time the agency had a pregnant woman due in a few weeks! This time Tammy and Chris said yes, they wanted to be considered. Since they were leaving the next day to spend Mother's Day weekend with her mom and dad, Tammy gave the agency her parent's phone number.

Friday morning, while preparing for their five-hour trek to her parent's house, Tammy remembered the diaper bag. Feeling a little foolish for planning weeks in advance for a baby that might not even become theirs, she tossed it in the truck.

They arrived at her parent's home to find Tammy's dad pacing in the front yard, awaiting their arrival. He raced over and before they got out of the truck, exclaiming, "Get in the house. Get on the phone. Call the adoption agency. You guys are parents!"

Shaking, Tammy called the adoption agency and they all listened in disbelief to the speakerphone. The baby had arrived early and the birth mother had chosen them that morning to be the newborn boy's parents. If they were interested, they had to drive four hours back toward home early the next day to meet the birth mother and get her final approval. There were still no guarantees, but if they were not there by 10:30 A.M., they wouldn't have a chance.

That night Chris and Tammy hardly slept. Was this baby God's plan for them? Were they making the right choice? What would happen to their lives now? Would they be good parents? They held each other and prayed. A peacefulness filled them and they slept soundly for a few hours.

Early the next morning, with the diaper bag in hand, Tammy and Chris headed to the hospital to meet the birth mother and the caseworker. It was hard for Tammy to sit still. She wanted to be considerate of the birth mother's feelings but she wanted so much to see the baby. She could hardly believe that if the birth mother consented, their son would go home with them that day. Finally she heard the words "Would you like to see the baby?"

The caseworker led the happy couple to the room while the birth mother left to shower. They quietly approached the bassinet. Tammy's heart melted when she saw his tiny little face. She gently picked him up and held him close, touching her tear-covered cheek to his soft warm one. Chris embraced them both. She knew at that moment, this was their son.

That evening at home, after their family and friends left, Tammy and Chris lay together with Luke nestled between them. They soaked in the events of the day—it was still so unbelievable. They joked about not having a crib, just a diaper bag. Tammy smiled at Chris, then at Luke. She realized this was God's plan all along. She closed her eyes and knew tomorrow, her dream of a perfect Mother's Day would come true.

~Kerrie Flanagan
Chicken Soup for the Christian Soul 2

57

Love by Choice

Adoption is when a child grew in its mommy's heart instead of her tummy.
~Author Unknown

Solemn brown eyes stared at me through inch-long eyelashes casting spiky shadows on the tiny Native American face. The thickness of his diapers made his legs look short and bowed. At seven months, he walked everywhere. The curiosity of this alert child held my attention. He hesitated at the top of the stairs to my living room.

"This is David," his mother said, pushing him further into the room.

Now that my children were all in school, babysitting was not on my agenda. But my heart overruled my head, and I agreed to babysit for a few days until David's mother could find someone else.

David's sense of security rested in the pacifier hanging around his neck attached to a somewhat soiled string. Once in awhile he popped it in his mouth.

As I talked with his mother, he examined everything with his eyes. I spoke his name in an effort to get acquainted. He looked straight at me but stayed his distance. He was not to be swayed at this early stage.

His mother left us together for the afternoon. He didn't cry or show signs of anxiety but stood his ground in the middle of the living room.

When my daughter, Linda, returned from school, he looked her over, but he did not venture toward her. As she smiled and picked him up, in went the pacifier. She walked quietly to the overstuffed chair. He lay in her arms sucking furiously on the pacifier. Linda cooed and talked to him, tenderly brushing his hair away from his forehead. "I like him, Mom," she said softly, her eyes never leaving his face. The bonding began. And slowly, one by one, David accepted each of us.

As the days turned into weeks, this precocious child stole our affections and captured our attention without any effort on his part. Our only son enjoyed having another boy in the family, even though my son was twelve years older.

Forgotten sounds of babyhood rang throughout the house. Little did we realize then just how much we would be involved in David's life. I could not distance myself from those soul-searching eyes and the smooth way he leaped into my heart. My babysitting went from a few days to several months.

One evening the telephone rang. The voice on the other end was tense. "I won't be needing you to babysit anymore." Then I heard a sudden burst of tears, followed by a rush of words that I couldn't understand.

It was David's mother. "What in the world is the matter?" I asked.

"I just can't handle David anymore. I am going to give him up to the state."

"If I thought you meant that, we'd take him in a heartbeat." My impulsive but sincere words seemed to quiet her down. I convinced her to bring David as usual, and we would talk. I passed the episode off in my mind as an emotional bout of fatigue and frustration.

The next morning the doorbell rang at 6:00 A.M. There stood a disheveled mother, carrying David on her hip, still in his pajamas. He was covered with hives, whining and sucking vigorously on his pacifier. Without hesitation she asked, "Did you really mean it when you said you would take David?"

"Well, I don't know. Do you think it's what you want?"

"I just can't take care of him," she said, obviously exhausted. "He is so hard to handle. He cries all night."

"Honey, you're really going to have to think about this. You just don't give up your baby because he keeps you up at night."

"But I am so tired," she moaned.

"Well, let's both think about it for awhile. I thought you were just upset last night. In the meantime, I will talk to my husband."

After that, she started leaving David for longer and longer periods. Her attitude changed almost overnight... from a concerned mother to an emotional bundle of nerves. One day she gave me a choice. Either I take him or she would turn him over to the state. She had made her decision. I had a week to make mine.

Advice came from all sides. "Don't you think you have enough responsibility?"

"You're probably too old and have too many children."

"Can you really afford another child? You've already got four kids."

Even our pastor and our doctor threw cold water on the idea. And our lawyer didn't encourage such an adventure either. "Let's get the paperwork going and see what happens," he said. "But I don't think any judge is going to go for this."

Within two weeks the court date was set. By now we knew we wanted David—utterly and completely. When the day arrived, I was anxious. So much rested on one man's decision. I hardly heard my lawyer's kind advice as we entered the judge's chambers. "This judge is tough. He might ask a lot of personal questions. Just answer honestly."

The judge greeted us with a warm handshake and began to thumb through the papers before him. Looking over his dark-rimmed glasses, he said, "Do you think you can handle another child?"

"Easily," I chuckled, a little nervously. "He's already been with us for over a year."

He pursed his lips, reading the information in front of him and asked, "Are you concerned about his ethnic background?"

"Judge, to me he is just a baby who needs a family."

The judge rubbed his chin, thinking through my impulsive answers. Then he leaned forward, and after gazing at us intently for a moment, he spoke. "These papers seem to be in order. I think this will be a good move for David."

"You mean we get to keep him, Judge?"

"He's yours." Just like that. Suddenly, the judge grinned from ear to ear and offered his hand in congratulations. My husband sat with his mouth open, and I giggled like a schoolgirl.

Today, over thirty years later, I can still feel the giddy joy of knowing that David was ours. I have never regretted—not even for an instant—the decision to take David into our family. People have told me they thought that David was lucky. Maybe so, but we were lucky, too. For when we left the judge's chambers those many years ago, our lives had expanded—emotionally and officially—to include another child. All at once we had five children to love, four by birth and one by choice.

~Shirley Pease
Chicken Soup for the Mother's Soul 2

On, Being a Parent

Parenting Wisdom

*It's not only children who grow. Parents do too.
As much as we watch to see what our children do with their lives,
they are watching us to see what we do with ours. I can't tell my
children to reach for the sun. All I can do is reach for it, myself.*
~Joyce Maynard

58

Saying Goodbye to Dingo

My daughter Ella had a unique and remarkable relationship with my parents' loving but irascible poodle mix. As a rule, Dingo didn't like children. He would simply move away from them, or, if necessary, growl for them to keep their distance. But he loved Ella. She was always very gentle and kind and he trusted her. She trusted him, too. Trusted him to always be there for ball-fetching, raspberry picking or just for softly stroking his ears.

When Ella was eight years old, Dingo was seventeen and in very poor health. My parents delayed the inevitable as long as they could, but one bright spring morning my mother phoned me to let me know the time had come. I held the phone tightly and looked out the window, my welling eyes making the daffodils and tulips in my garden blur.

"Dingo's in a lot of pain. We've made an appointment with the veterinarian for this afternoon," my mother said, trying to keep the choking emotion out of her voice. "It's against my better judgment to tell you," she said. "But I wanted to let you decide how to handle it with Ella." My mom always wanted to protect her children and grandchildren from any and all heartache; her way to do that was to only tell us about painful events after the fact, or not at all. But for whatever reason, this time she included us. I will be forever grateful to my mother for that phone call. It was a generous gesture, and ultimately, it would have repercussions beyond what any of us could have guessed at that time.

I agonized for a while, thinking that maybe my mother was right, just let it happen and we'll tell Ella afterward and "spare" her the heartache. By phone, I talked at length to my husband and a couple of close friends about whether to offer Ella a chance to say goodbye to Dingo in the comfort of his own home. Was she too young to choose for herself how, or even whether, to say goodbye? I looked at our own aging Wheaten Terrier mix, Petey, sprawled across our kitchen floor, and our spunky Persian cat, Albert, snoozing in the morning sun on the couch. When their time came, we would certainly want to be able to say goodbye. Could I deny that choice to my daughter with her adored Dingo? I decided to trust my mothering instincts, which dictated that we pick out the important "eight-year-old" points of this sad event, and help her to decide for herself.

My husband took the afternoon off from work and we walked to her elementary school. Ella's teacher allowed our daughter to leave the classroom with us. My husband and I sat with Ella on the deserted playground and spoke softly, all holding hands.

"Sweetheart," I said, grateful that I could control my own voice at the moment. "As you know, Dingo is very old. And you know that he often doesn't feel well, right?"

She nodded solemnly, looking from me to my husband and back again.

"Well, the past few days he has felt very bad. He hurts all over and the vet says he's going to die soon. Nana and Da don't want him to hurt anymore, so they are going to take him to the veterinarian and he's going to help Dingo die and not be in pain anymore. Do you understand?"

Ella's eyes welled up with tears but she nodded.

The emotion began to creep into my voice now. "So, even though it's very sad, if we want to, we can go visit Dingo right now and talk to him and tell him we love him and say goodbye. Your teacher and the principal say it's fine. But only if you want to. If you'd rather write Dingo a letter or draw him a picture, we can do that."

Her feelings revealed only by the tears falling down her cheeks, Ella said in a strong, clear voice, "I want to go say goodbye to Dingo."

We took her out of school, with the full support of her principal and second-grade teacher, both of whom knew that this old dog would likely teach Ella a more powerful life lesson than any they could offer that day.

So the three of us went to visit Dingo at Nana and Da's house one last time. My parents graciously arranged to be absent when we arrived. Ella sat next to Dingo on his round, plaid bed. The old guy couldn't lift his head, but when she put her hand near his mouth, his soft pink tongue gently kissed her. Her tender eight-year-old voice and the ticking kitchen clock were the only sounds in the otherwise silent house.

"Remember how I would throw the tennis ball and you used to chase it, Dingo?" she asked him. "Remember when you helped me hunt for Easter eggs?" She held his paw with one hand and stroked his ear with the other. "Remember going up to the cabin and walking across the bridge? I was always afraid to go across that bridge but you waited for me. Remember?" A tiny tip, tip, tip of his tail. She fed him his favorite treats and gently hugged him, told him how much she loved him, her warm tears falling on his gray fur. My husband and I both said our goodbyes and cried, too. The three of us hugged around his bed, Dingo in the center of our love. We all knew together when it was time to leave.

Ella wanted to return to school. As she entered her classroom, several friends rushed to her with comforting words and hugs. Her teacher later told us that she had then read to the class *The Tenth Good Thing About Barney*. Then they had all talked about love and loss and the many different things we learn from our pets. The teacher said it was a remarkable day.

Although I knew then how important and loving that goodbye experience was for all of us, especially Ella, I had no idea what lay ahead for our family in dealing with death. I knew in my heart that we were wisely seizing a "teachable moment," but my head wanted reassurance that we didn't make too big a deal of it. Had I known that in the next twenty months our family would say goodbye to Ella's loving grandfather "Grampi," her wonderful great-uncle "Gruncle," and then our beloved Nana herself, I wouldn't have questioned our response to Dingo's death, not even for a moment.

Saying goodbye to Dingo helped us all to know how important and helpful it is to say goodbye, in any and every way opportunity presents. Grampi died suddenly, with little warning and a thousand miles away. There was no chance to say goodbye before he died, so we wrote letters and drew pictures and put them in the ground with him so he could read them in heaven. Gruncle, too, was far away, but he was able to read our missives of love before he died.

Thankfully, because she lived just three miles from our home, we were able to say goodbye to Nana in person. Over the course of many special visits, we hugged her and kissed her, we talked about special times, we cooked her favorite meals for her. We told her over and over how much we loved her, as she died of cancer in her home. We knew how to do all this because we'd had a wonderful teacher: a little gray poodle mix named Dingo.

~Elizabeth Wrenn
Chicken Soup for the Dog Lover's Soul

Dear Daddy...

The act of putting pen to paper encourages pause for thought,
this in turn makes us think more deeply about life,
which helps us regain our equilibrium.
~Norbet Platt

My father was the gentlest, most loving and caring dad in the world—until we had an argument. During those moments, he transformed into an obstinate, unrelenting ogre who never considered that there could be a side other than his own. My words surely never reached his "open mind" because his ears were sealed. When he spoke, it was with such authority that it was easy to begin to doubt my own point of view. But I, my father's daughter, had inherited his debating skills and argued back with the passion of a courtroom attorney, welcoming the battle of our wills. That was, until the fights became personal and our confrontations charged with emotion. There was no point trying to argue with my dad. He always had the last word. I could never win.

When my father refused to understand that I needed the privacy of a phone in my own room, my frustration turned to tears. When he sensed that I was gaining the upper hand in defending my case for wearing lip gloss to school in junior high, he ended our "discussion," leaving me silently defeated and miserable. So when he refused to budge on letting me go on my senior class trip to Montreal, I could do nothing but race from his room in hysterics. And then came the epiphany. If I couldn't get him to listen to my side of our arguments, maybe I could get him to read it.

With the hope that his eyes would be more open than his ears, I began to plead my case — uninterrupted and uncontested — in a note that began "Dear Daddy" and ended with how much I respected his opinion, how much I hated to fight with him, how much I valued our relationship and, above all, how much I loved him. Following my exhausting catharsis, I folded my note into an envelope, slid it under the door of his bedroom and raced back to my own room where I collapsed on my bed.

It was only minutes before I heard a knock at my door. When I saw the look on my father's face, I knew that my note had melted his temper, softened his stubbornness and touched his heart. After all, there was never any question that I was Daddy's girl.

The victory of winning my dad's permission to go to Montreal was sweet. But even sweeter was the serendipitous discovery of a strategy that enabled me to have an argument with my dad that didn't end in tears, but instead with a hug. My "Dear Daddy" notes became a follow-up to many of our hotheaded confrontations. During our most emotional arguments, when his unyielding final word drove me to tears, when his "I'm your father, that's why!" left me speechless, I knew just how to get through to him. While my notes weren't a guarantee that I'd get my way, they did succeed in defusing the anger between us and paving the way for the truce — and hugs — that always followed.

Years later, when my father died, his memory lived on vibrantly through the many stories about him that friends and family continued to share. One of my favorites was the "Dear Daddy" notes. It always made me smile to remember some of our most passionate arguments and how my dad would become so pig-headed, until he read my notes. He surely must have seen through my calculating strategy, but he never let on; he savored every note that turned him to see my way.

When I first told my own children, then twelve and nine, about my emotional battles with their strong-willed grandpa, they thought that the notes were a silly solution. My daughter, also a recipient of the "skilled debating" genes, responded with, "What a cop-out! Why couldn't you just work out your issues face-to-face?"

But a few months later, when she became a teenager, she finally understood the frustration I had been trying to explain.

During the first major argument, I overheard protests of "Daddy, why can't I take the train to Manhattan? All of my friends are allowed to go — we're thirteen!" As I listened to their shouting match, I suspected that my husband, as stubborn as his father-in-law had been, was not about to give in. My prediction was confirmed when I saw my daughter bound out of our bedroom, sobbing. Knowing the two strong-willed contestants, I prepared to assume my role as mediator. In the privacy of our bedroom, I faced my husband and was all set to begin my speech, when out of the corner of my eye I spotted an envelope sliding under the door.

~Linda Saslow
Chicken Soup for the Father & Daughter Soul

60

Why Monks Sit in the Snow

When you are a mother, you are never really alone in your thoughts.
A mother always has to think twice, once for herself and once for her child.
~Sophia Loren

My six-year-old son and his friend have just left the dining room, where I am writing. The boys were wearing black sweatpants and black turtlenecks that they had pulled from Ryan's dresser. They cinched the pants at the waist with belts, through which they had slipped wooden swords. Then they crept up on me. When I looked up from my computer, they ran squealing from the room.

This stunt was repeated about ten times in eight minutes. The repetition did nothing to diminish the hilarity for the two boys (or increase it for me). The pirate-spy routine had been preceded by attempts to pogo in the family room, in-line skate in the kitchen, dribble a basketball down the stairs, burp the letters in their names (my son has shown genius in this area) and play catch in the stairwell.

I took away the pogo stick, put the skates outside, stored the basketball in a closet, told the boys I'd heard enough burping for one day and guided the game of catch to the driveway. Still ahead: the friend's anguished departure, subtraction homework, spelling flashcards, dinner, dishes, books and a pokey meander into bed. During this time I had to finish my column.

Two nights earlier I had dinner with a friend who was in town on business from Los Angeles. I drove into the city early so we could catch up, and we ended up walking through the shops around Union Square. She has a three-year-old boy and a baby due in three months. At the Banana Republic, she ran her hands over a soft throw blanket.

"Oh, isn't this wonderful?" she asked. Then she found a comforter. "Look at this," she said. At Saks, she found a flannel nightshirt. "Feel this," she said.

I looked at her. "Do you realize everything you've looked at has to do with sleep?" Once upon a time her shopping tastes ran to spike heels and miniskirts.

She laughed. "When I get up in the morning," she said, "all I think about is how many hours until I can get back in."

The next night I sat in a darkened room at a Zen retreat not far from my house. The room was packed with people who had come to meditate, then listen to a lecture on spirituality. The teacher mentioned how he had traveled to Asia as a young man to learn the ways of the monks. He sat in a snowy forest for days with little food, drink or sleep. He sat like a yogi on the bank of the Ganges River for twenty hours at a stretch though his legs burned with pain and his eyes longed for rest. He explained that the effort of his mind to overcome the deprivation and distractions took him to higher states of clarity and vision and taught him patience.

I was thinking about this, and about my L.A. friend, as my son and his pal staged a sword fight in the hallway. The connections of the last few days began to fall into place. I thought about the repeated reminders and admonishments we parents deliver through the day, the noise, the lack of sleep, the long waits for our child to get dressed, clean his room or get out of the car. ("C'mon, we're going into the store now. Put down the soccer ball. No, we can't take the dog. What are you doing? That cookie's probably been under the seat for a month. C'mon. Now. I mean it. Don't worry about the cookie. We'll throw it out in the store. Let's go." The only things children do quickly are go to the bathroom, eat dessert, open gifts and climb fences separating playgrounds from deadly freeways.)

Suddenly it clicked. I understood why monks must sit in snow and on the banks of the Ganges. They don't have children!

It occurred to me that, in my search for self-improvement and spirituality, I had everything I needed in my own home. Every parent does. There are the long painful nights we sit without moving because one twitch might wake the (potentially) very loud baby in our arms. There is the excruciating mind and muscle control to stifle a smile when our child earnestly tells us he didn't pick up his toys because he got hit with a ball at school and suffered brain damage.

There are the tests of concentration when you're talking to a client on the phone and your child appears in the doorway in nothing but boots and a gun belt and acts out the final scene from *High Noon*.

There are the years on end of getting to sleep after midnight because only when the kids are asleep and the phone isn't ringing can you get your chores finished, then you're up at six to make lunches and get breakfast and shuttle them to school before you go, bleary-eyed, to work.

Religious students travel the globe to find tests of will, patience, deprivation and selflessness. Parents live them every day. Anyone looking for a mysterious, contradictory and fulfilling religion couldn't do much better than child-rearing. All the components are there: rituals, generosity, penance, guilt and desperate prayer, all punctuated by moments of transcendent clarity and unmatched joy.

I'm just thinking out loud here, but I'm wondering if we can get tax-exempt status.

~Joan Ryan
A 6th Bowl of Chicken Soup for the Soul

61

It's Only Stuff

Things turn out best for the people who
make the best out of the way things turn out.
~Art Linkletter

On July 18, 1989, I received a frantic call from my sister: Our parents' home was on fire. Fortunately, I learned, no one was home—Mother was at her sister's cabin and Father was "out and about." This meant, however, that no one was able to retrieve irreplaceable family mementos.

During the twenty-mile drive to my parents' house, tears rolled down my cheeks as I thought about the destruction of the only tangible evidence of my youth. Then I heard a voice: It's only stuff, you know. It was not spoken out loud, but it was clear and distinct, and comforting.

When my mother arrived from her sister's cabin, we surrounded her and gently led her to the charred remains of her home. Though she knew she was returning to a disaster, seeing the remains of her home was still a shock.

Fortunately, the firefighters had arrived in time to save the room containing many of our photo albums. When mother saw the albums, she was grateful that she had reacted a few weeks earlier to an inexplicable urge to move them from one room, now completely destroyed, to the only room left untouched by the blaze.

But we had lost many sentimental items, such as our Christmas decorations. Mother had saved the homemade ornaments we children had made throughout grade school, and I had loved showing them to my own children each year.

Among the most treasured possessions were ten Christmas stockings, one for each of us, handmade by our now-deceased grandmother. Each stocking was among the first gifts she would give her newest grandchild. Because I was the oldest in my family and one of the oldest grandchildren, I had often stood next to her, mesmerized, as she carefully stitched each stocking by hand. She decorated them with felt shapes of trains, angels and — my favorite — Christmas trees, which were covered with brightly covered ornaments.

One of my brothers was convinced, against all reason, that these special remembrances of Gram had survived the fiery blaze. He therefore sifted through mound after mound of ashes and burned-out blobs. Finally he found them — in a box under what remained of the basement stairwell. In the box was another treasure, remarkably unscathed: our nativity set. The family rejoiced at this discovery and said a prayer of gratitude.

None of this, though, was a match for what occurred on September 15th, my parents' wedding anniversary. After church, they went out to the homesite for a last look at the remains of their home. By now, it had been bulldozed, and a crew was coming soon to clear away the last traces of the building.

As my parents approached the site, which was still wet from a heavy rain the night before, both spotted something white on the sidewalk. My mother gasped as she bent to pick up the object. It was the prayer book she had carried down the aisle thirty-eight years ago to the day. And it was bone-dry. My father says an angel placed it there.

The fire had destroyed nearly all of the other material possessions my parents had ever owned. But as we reflected on the significance of the items that did survive the fire, we realized each one was symbolic. The wedding prayer book, for example, is tangible proof of my parents' spirituality and religious beliefs, which we, their children, now try to pass on to our children. And every Christmas, as we hang those ten stockings, now lightly browned around the edges, we are reminded of the grandmother who made them. Finally, the photographs help us all recall our youth and remember the importance of family.

The love and happiness contained within the walls of the old house have expanded into ten more households. Those good feelings emerge often, whenever we gather as a clan that now numbers over fifty.

I can still hear my mother's voice calling me as a teenager, as I would back out of the driveway with a carful of my siblings: "Be careful, Honey!" she'd say. "You have my most precious possessions in that car!"

We still are her most precious possessions. The rest, after all, is just "stuff."

~Mary Treacy O'Keefe
Chicken Soup for the Christian Family Soul

62

A Misfortune — Not a Tragedy

I was an ecstatically happy thirteen-year-old riding home for dinner on my new birthday present — a Fleet bicycle made by Schwinn, and it was a dandy. It even had a spring knee-action suspension in front. Better yet, it was the only one of its kind in the neighborhood.

I polished its blue and white frame and fenders to a shiny brightness that could be seen for blocks away. I had been on cloud nine ever since I received it as a gift a few days before. One's first bike is a milestone in any child's life. Like any thirteen-year-old boy there was only one thing on my mind as I pedaled home around four-thirty that afternoon — dinner.

I skidded my bike up to the front porch in a spectacular wheelie and bounded up the steps. As I ran through the hallway toward the kitchen, I began to wonder. I didn't smell any tantalizing aroma coming from Mom's spic-and-span kitchen. Oh well, I thought, smiling to myself, maybe we are having cold cuts with pork and beans — my summer favorite.

I opened the swinging doors to the kitchen, expecting to hear, "Jimmy, wash your hands and help me set the table." Instead, my young eyes focused on my mother, ghostly white, lying in a crumpled heap on the kitchen floor — blood oozing from a deep wound on her forehead. I tried to rouse her but to no avail. All I got were moans.

Beginning to cry, I knelt beside her quiet form on the floor and asked soberly, "Mom, are you okay?" She answered in an almost unintelligible whisper, "Please help me, Jimmy."

Realizing we were alone, like most children would do, I ran to the phone. This was 1944 and there was no such thing as 911, only the operator's friendly voice asking, "Number please." I blurted out my grandmother's phone number between sobs and said, "It's an emergency, operator, please hurry."

I called Grandma because Dad was still at work, and I couldn't remember his office number. The first words out of Grandma's mouth were, "Jimmy why are you crying?" I could hardly speak through the tears by this time. Between sobs I explained to Grandma about Mom on the floor needing help. All she said was, "I'll call the fire department, and I'll be right there. Hang on."

Grandma didn't own a car but lived nearby. True to her word, her running feet hit the porch at the same time the firemen arrived from the neighborhood station. We all converged on the kitchen to help Mom. She was still lying on the floor, not moving or making a sound. As the firemen worked over her in a huddled mass I heard one of the firemen say, "Get a gurney. She has to go to the hospital now."

Once more I began to cry. Grandma immediately swept me into her massive, comforting grandma arms and said soothingly, "Hush child. Your mother is in good hands; she'll be okay. God and the firemen are with her." Grandma always knew just what to say.

Little did we know as we watched the firemen wheel Mom out of the house, our family's life would never be the same. We found out later Mom had slipped on the slick kitchen floor she was mopping. As she fell she hit her head on the sharp edge of the kitchen table, causing severe brain damage — resulting in paralysis to the left side of her body. This misfortune, not a tragedy, changed our lives and lifestyle in a matter of seconds.

After weeks of convalescence in the hospital and extensive therapy, she was still unable to use her left arm or left leg normally. She never would again, and she was only in her late thirties.

I never will forget the day Mom came home. Dad got her settled in a makeshift bedroom downstairs in our two-story house. He then asked all of us children to gather in the living room. Dad, his usual strong voice filled with emotion, said, "Your Mother will never be the same. The fall damaged the right side of her brain. It is like a light bulb that shatters and cannot be put back together—this caused the paralysis. She will never again be like the mom you have known. But she will still be your mom—don't ever forget that." We all nodded our heads in agreement.

There were four of us children: myself, thirteen years old; an older sister, fifteen; a younger brother, eight; and a baby sister, three years old. Struggling with Dad's words, we all reached out and grasped each other's hands as we gathered around him in prayer. We knew then that our family would not be the same, but it would survive—we were all very confident of that fact—Mom and God were still with us.

After more physical therapy Mom soon was able to shuffle about and once again commence her household duties. She only had the use of her right hand and arm. Her left arm hung limply to her side. Her partially paralyzed left leg only allowed her to walk stiff legged.

All of us children, and of course Dad, had increased work to do at home, but none of us really minded. After all, Mom was still with us, along with her happy, perky personality. In spite of this life-changing experience, our family unit soon knitted. If anything, it was stronger than before. Yes, life was good once more for our family.

Dad never faltered in his role as father, husband and part-time mom. They remained together as Mom and Dad, husband and wife for their forty-six remaining years until Mom—who was in a wheel-chair by this time—passed away. We children in the family actually benefited immensely from this misfortune—I won't say tragedy—in many ways for the rest of our lives.

We learned compassion and how to look out for each other. We became a bonded team, working together for the good of the family and, most of all, we learned how to love one another.

At seventy years old I can attest to this fact: No matter how bleak your future can look to you as a child when faced with a family misfortune—I still won't say tragedy—life does get better. Our family found out quickly that even a shattered light bulb can bring brightness to the end of a long, dark tunnel—all we had to do was reach out together, along with God, and turn it on.

~James A. Nelson
Chicken Soup for Every Mom's Soul

Money!

God only looks to the pure,
not to the full hands.
~Laberius

Our family was Christmas shopping in the clothing department of a large department store, when our nine-year-old son, Bradley, shouted, "Money!" Rolled up with a rubber band was a substantial amount of cash, apparently dropped unknowingly by its owner. The money had rolled under a display table and it was by sheer luck that my son saw it at all.

He was so excited about his find that my husband and I hated to rain on his parade with a gentle reminder, "Somewhere, someone else is very sad about losing this much money," his dad told him.

I added, "Yes, and the person who lost it may have saved for a long time and is frantically looking for it now."

After a short discussion of who might have lost it we asked him, "How would you feel if you had lost the money?"

"I think I'd be sad and maybe even sick to my stomach," he admitted.

I asked, "Do you think your should keep the money or turn it in to the store manager?"

It wasn't an easy decision for a nine-year-old. He frowned. "Turn it in."

When the lady behind the desk at Lost and Found asked, "How

can I help you?" I nudged Bradley forward to speak for himself. "But, Mom, what if no one ever comes to claim it?" he asked.

I gave him a smile and stepped forward to explain about the lost money. "Do you think if the money isn't claimed it could be given to our son, who found it?"

The desk clerk had watched Bradley struggle with changing his mind and readily agreed.

We left his name and address and the clerk wrote a quick note. Then using the rubber band she attached the note to the money and placed it in a lock-box.

When we retold this incident to others, many called us naive. "Surely the store manager or some other employee will keep that money," people would say. In fact, the general consensus was that we were "fools" to encourage our son to turn the money in. His neighborhood friends teased Bradley, chanting, "Do gooder! Do gooder! You're nuts!"

He just shrugged it off and said, "It wasn't my money." His dad and I were so proud of him.

Two years later a letter came in the mail addressed to Bradley. It was from the department store, which was now going out of business. The letter stated that they had found a roll of money in their vault with Bradley's name and address on it. A notation said it should be sent to him if not claimed. Attached to the letter was a check made out to Bradley with a note from the manager:

Dear Bradley,

I do admire you so much for making such a grown up decision at age nine. I remember your struggle and know it wasn't easy. It took a person of strong character to turn in that money. There are many adults who would struggle with such a decision. The money was never claimed and so I am pleased to honor your request. The money is now yours!

She made a smiley face with the words "enjoy" and "have a ball" under it.

It would be a wonderful story if it ended right here, but there's more.

Twenty years later Bradley had a son born prematurely. Little Nathan only weighed two pounds and suffered a stroke when two days old. My son was laid off, job searching, and short of money. Times were bad all around for him and his young wife. Bradley left the ICU and went to the hospital chapel and prayed for his son's life. On his way back to ICU, he stopped at a vending machine for a cheap snack. He deposited his coins and retrieved his selection, then coins began to pour out like a slot machine paying off a jackpot! Bradley collected the coins in his shirttail and marveled at his luck. Just when he was thinking about counting his loot he remembered his childhood experience. He knew what he had to do. He had just prayed for a miracle for his son. He knew however, this was not the miracle he needed. Perhaps it was a test from above.

"Well, God" he prayed, "I figure I need all the points I can get right about now. My son's life hangs in the balance and the outcome is in Your hands. This isn't my money. You've seen me through till now and I'm counting on You. Please, God, Give me a strong, healthy son."

Then he walked over to the nurses' desk carrying his shirttail filled with coins and emptied them on the counter. "Can you return this to the vendor, Ma'am?" he asked.

The wide-eyed nurse was astounded. "Are you sure you don't want to just keep this? Most people would."

Bradley just grinned. "I don't know how much money is here... but I'm certain that my reward will be much greater by far."

He was correct...

That was six years ago. Little Nathan is now healthy and happily in kindergarten and the joy of our lives... God's ultimate pay off!

~Christine M. Smith
Chicken Soup for the Christian Soul 2

Anniversary Celebration

Every year, a few weeks before our anniversary, I begin looking at my husband and feeling hopelessly nostalgic. I can't help but miss the people we once were—passionate, carefree, romantic—people who couldn't keep their hands off each other. We used to stay up all night just to see the sunrise. We had midnight picnics in the park, and I would wear sexy lingerie on a regular basis.

But that was before three children (ages ten, seven and two). It was before school-board meetings and budget planning, not to mention diaper disasters. Now, a few weeks before our anniversary, I'm feeling the need to rekindle the passion of days gone by (at least for one night). I plan a romantic anniversary dinner with candles, wine, music, grown-up food and no children. I really wanted to give the evening a special touch, but staying up to see the sunrise won't work when you'll be spending the next twelve to fourteen hours chasing a two-year-old. A midnight picnic sounds too dangerous, considering creeps now overrun the park after dark. I opt instead to cap off our evening with lingerie.

After securing a babysitter I'm encouraged and head to my long-abandoned lingerie drawer. Looking at the ensembles that practically scream sex, I am sure any of these hot little numbers will more than rekindle passion, and I wonder why I ever abandoned them in the first place. I can hardly wait to try them on, and in this spirit I decide my daughter could use an early nap today, leaving me two hours free to contrive an outfit before my boys arrive home from school.

Forty-five minutes and several stories later, my daughter is asleep, and I all but run to the lingerie drawer. My first choice is an emerald and black Wonderbra. I hook the hook and pull the straps over my shoulders, almost giddy with anticipation. Then I look in the mirror and to my utter horror, the full effects of breastfeeding Baby No. 3 are realized as this wonder creation pushes my cleavage to the center of my chest, giving me the appearance of a Cyclops, if you get my drift. The only real wonder is that I can breathe with everything all squeezed together.

Feeling disappointed but not defeated, I remove the Wonderbra and reach for stockings and garters, only to be disappointed again—this time because of a weird rubber-band-around-a-sausage effect I won't even bother to explain.

My little lingerie adventure continues for about thirty minutes, when I realize that lack of oxygen and circulation isn't going to rekindle anything. I slowly close the lingerie drawer and resolve to find another way to zap some wild passion into our marriage.

Over the next few days, I watch my husband closely, trying to determine the best way to top off our anniversary celebration. I see him with our children, reading stories to our two-year-old, helping with homework, coaching a basketball team of six- and seven-year-olds, and the million other daily parental duties that don't exactly scream romance. But then I look closer, and I see us sharing good morning hugs, holding hands at a ball game and always sharing goodbye kisses before work, and I realize that although it's not wild with reckless abandon, we still can't keep our hands off each other. In our own quiet, comfortable way, we are passionate, but now we know passion is more a state of mind than a state of undress.

So this year on our anniversary, as I sit across the candlelit dinner from my husband, I'll know it's okay to feel a little loss for the people we once were, as long as we remember to celebrate the people we've become.

~Renee Mayhew
Chicken Soup for Every Mom's Soul

I'm Gonna Write It on the Agenda!

If you think you're too small to have an impact,
try going to bed with a mosquito.
~Anita Roddick

"Theresa, would you rather talk about this now or at the family meeting?" I asked.

"At the family meeting? Dad, give me a break!" she cried. And she stomped into the breakfast room to write "quit piano" on our family meeting agenda. This was all preceded by a mini-explosion as Theresa, then seven, was practicing the piano after school one day. She slammed her hands on the keys and shouted, "I quit!"

I stormed into the room, saying, "You can't quit. It's the beginning of the month, and we've already paid for all four lessons. Besides, my mother let me quit the piano, and I regret it. And furthermore, quitting is irresponsible behavior, and irresponsibility is not tolerated in the McGinnis household!" Suddenly, I heard myself ranting and stopped. That's when I caught my breath and put the question above to Theresa: "Would you rather talk about this now or at the family meeting?"

Thank goodness, at the time of the outburst, our family had been using this alternative forum for conflict resolution and decision making for about three years. We had found a workable alternative to my authoritarian outbursts, to my need to control family decisions, to the kids' sense of powerlessness. Since friends had introduced us to this decision-making mechanism, it had served us well. Not that we were doing our family meetings "perfectly," whatever that means. And not that we still didn't have outbursts like the one above. But Kathy and I had gotten in touch with our "nonnegotiables" and "bottom lines," and had articulated those to our three children. And now, we as a family had a way of correcting ourselves and mutually working through problems and disagreements.

Our children (now adults) convinced us of the truth of all this on a number of occasions. Perhaps the most memorable example, and testimony to the value of family meetings, happened when Tom, our oldest, was thirteen. One Sunday afternoon, he informed me that he was putting "cable TV" on the next night's family meeting agenda. When I told him he was wasting his time, because we had decided only six months earlier that we couldn't afford cable TV, he said calmly, "Dad, let me worry about that."

The next night at dinner, which is when we had our weekly family meetings, Tom's "cable TV" was first on the agenda. When eleven-year-old David, as leader that night, asked him what he wanted to say about cable TV, Tom pushed his plate aside, stood, gathered some paper from the counter behind him, turned back to us and said, "Twenty-six reasons why our family should get cable TV."

What a shock! No one had ever written out a statement in five years of meetings; no one had ever stood, either. To give a sampling of his twenty-six reasons, he began with, "Mom and Dad, you value family togetherness. If we got cable with one of the movie channels, we could watch more movies together as a family." Next he stated, "You're concerned about the quality of the TV we watch. Well, I've researched the three movie channels and find that most of those X- and R-rated movies you don't like are on the other two channels. I think we should just get HBO. And you're concerned about how we spend our family recreation money. HBO and the works cost $13.90 a month. David, Theresa and I are willing to kick in $6 a month from our allowances. That leaves $7.90. I'm sure you realize that you go to at least one movie a month and pay $4 each. If you would stay home that evening with your children and watch a cable movie instead, your $8 and our $6 each would mean we could get cable without spending any more family recreation money than we do now." He went on through his list of twenty-six reasons, then sat down — and stared at Kathy and me.

Kathy looked at me, sitting there somewhat shell-shocked, and asked what I thought. I stammered at first, saying something like I couldn't think of any reason why not. Then David asked if we had a decision. Each one of us said we would be willing to try cable for a few months to see if it would work. Tom, with tears in his eyes, proclaimed, "This is the most emotional day of my life. This morning after the dentist pulled out five teeth, I thought I was going to die at school. But tonight, I've persuaded the family to buy cable TV. This is the most emotional day of my life!"

Kathy and I love to share this story, not because we are convinced of the value of cable TV, but because it convinced us of the power of the process of the family meeting. If a "recovering authoritarian" like me can do it, almost anyone can!

Not only did family meetings offer a corrective for an authoritarian father, it provided an outlet for an impulsive child. Contrary to the impression that family meetings may only work for highly verbal, well-behaved children, both Theresa and David were diagnosed with ADD (Attention Deficit Disorder), David's manifesting itself in volatile impulsivity. As a four-year-old, in the heat of rage, he punched out our dining room window. At twelve, he destroyed his bike because it wasn't working as he wanted. So when I heard his full-volume outburst coming from the bedroom that he and Tom shared, I raced upstairs hoping to save the second story of our home.

David was storming around their room, cussing out Tom because he had apparently taken one of David's things. "I can't stand living with that *#@%&! I'm so ^%$#@! angry, I'm gonna, gonna, gonna WRITE IT ON THE AGENDA!!!!!!" With that declaration, he stomped downstairs and into the breakfast room where he grabbed a pen and wrote "TOMMY! NOW!" on the family meeting agenda.

David had found a way of dealing with his issues besides

punching out a window — or his brother. He was putting the issue on our family meeting agenda and calling for an emergency meeting that night. In our family, writing "NOW" after an item signaled that the person couldn't wait until the next regular family meeting and needed a resolution right away. We were so proud of David for being able to take this approach. Eighteen years later, as a thirty-year-old, David looked back on that episode as a real step forward for his ongoing efforts to channel his anger and impulsivity in constructive ways. I can't help but think how different the news headlines would look today if only all the angry people in our world would... could... WRITE IT ON THE AGENDA!

~James McGinnis, Ph.D.
Chicken Soup for the Soul Stories for a Better World

Bonding with Notebooks

*D*ear *Chicken Soup for the Teenage Soul,*

I have always been a real fan of your books and the important lessons of love and understanding that are shared in each of the stories. They have helped me to see things that were not so clear to me. I have received a great deal of comfort from reading many of the stories.

I had been going through some difficult times not so long ago, dealing with the pressures of growing up and trying to communicate with my parents, particularly my mother. Our relationship had suffered because of this. When I would get frustrated or angry it seemed like we would end up in some sort of confrontation with each other and not talk about what we were really feeling. I feel like I have overcome those obstacles now, but not without a certain turn of events.

A while back, I ran away from home so that I could be far enough away to vent my anger and release some of the pain bottled up inside of me. I stayed away for many hours, well into the night, before I finally decided to return home. When I walked through the front door of my house, I immediately saw all the pain, anger and disappointment on my parents' faces, especially my mother's. For days after the incident, my mom and I were on unfirm ground, to say the least. Everything we did or said was filled with tension until we both eventually snapped. We knew we desperately had to have a talk. We agreed to have breakfast together the next morning. That morning will remain etched in my memory forever. It was a turning point in both of our lives and our relationship.

We decided to go to a local café. On our way to the table I noticed that my mother had two notebooks and some pens. I asked her what they were for. She explained to me that sometimes it is easier to write down our feelings rather than try to talk about them. She then handed me a notebook of my own and kept one for herself. The "rules" for that talk were that she would pick a topic, and we would write down our feelings about the topic in the form of a letter. It could be as long or as short as we wanted.

Our first topic was: "Why I am so angry." I had written a half page worth of stuff, and my mom filled up nearly three pages. I watched tears stream down her face as she wrote. I never realized anyone could hide so much anger and frustration. It could have been that I never paid much attention, either. Sometimes we think we are the only ones with problems, but I was reminded that morning that other people can be hurting just as much.

After she finished writing, we exchanged our notebooks and read what the other had written. As soon as I started reading my mother's words, I began to cry and so did she. When we were finished reading we discussed our feelings. Amazingly enough, it felt like all the anger I had welled up inside of me drained from my body. Our talk helped me realize so many things I had never thought of before, not only about my mother but about other people as well.

My mother and I continue to use our notebooks as a means of communicating our anger and frustrations, and our happiness also. We know that no matter how we feel about each other, our notebooks are a safe place to express it. We have made a pact that at the end of each letter we write, "I love you." Here are two of our more recent entries:

Dear Mom,

I just wanted you to know that some things I do are not meant to hurt or spite you. When I yell at you it's not because I hate you. And when I tell you I hate you, you should know that I really don't, although at times I feel like you hate me. Sometimes you just make me really mad and frustrated, and I don't know what to do with it. Like when you tell me you don't believe me even though I'm not lying, or when you do things that invade my privacy without my permission that you know I won't like. For instance, the other day you searched my room without me knowing or being there. I just wanted to hate you so much then. Then today you yelled at me, and it made me so mad. I really don't think there is much more to say right now. I love you.

Katie

And my mother's response to my letter:

Dear Katie,

I realize that you get mad and frustrated, but I do, too. I don't want you to think that since I am an adult I don't have feelings. As much as you think that I might like it, I don't like yelling at you. I just wish you would help out a little more with the family and around the house. It would make things easier on me. Some things I do, like searching your room or not believing you, are not done to be mean. I only do those things if I have good cause. Sometimes you worry me, but it's just because I care. Although you might not think so, you yell at me as much as I yell at you. It hurts my feelings as well.

Sometimes I just want to cry. I'm glad you told me how you felt about all those things. I'll try to work on my temper with you, and I'll try to be more patient if you will return the same courtesy to me and help me out a little around the house. If this is not okay, tell me and we can try to work something out. I love you.

Mom

We gained a special gift that day at the restaurant and we continue to be blessed with each other's everlasting love and patience. I am now a firm believer that we all need to express our feelings in order to live healthy lives. Thank you so much for letting me share this with you.

Sincerely,

~Katie Benson
Chicken Soup for the Teenage Soul Letters

A Reason to Celebrate

If you don't like something change it;
if you can't change it, change the way you think about it.
~Mary Engelbreit

Numbly, I left my husband, Marty, at the hospital where I had been visiting two of my children and headed for the grocery store. Since it was 11 P.M., I drove to the only store that I knew was open twenty-four hours a day. I turned my car motor off and rested my head against the seat.

What a day, I thought to myself. With two of my young children in the hospital, and a third waiting at Grandma's, I was truly spread thin. Today I had actually passed the infant CPR exam required before I could take eight-week-old Joel home from the hospital. Would I remember how to perform CPR in a moment of crisis? A cold chill ran down my spine as I debated my answer.

Exhausted, I reached for my grocery list that resembled more of a scientific equation than the food for the week. For the past several days, I'd been learning the facts about juvenile diabetes and trying to accept Jenna's, my six-year-old daughter's, diagnosis. In addition to the CPR exam, I'd spent the day reviewing how to test Jenna's blood and give her insulin shots. Now I was buying the needed food to balance the insulin that would sustain Jenna's life.

"Let's go, Janet," I mumbled to myself while sliding out of the car. "Tomorrow is the big day! Both kids are coming home from the hospital." It didn't take long before my mumbling turned into a prayer.

God, I am soooo scared! What if I make a mistake and give Jenna too much insulin, or what if I measure her food wrong, or what if she does the unmentionable — and sneaks a treat? And God, what about Joel's apnea monitor? What if it goes off? What if he turns blue and I panic? What if? Oh, the consequences are certain to be great!

With a shiver, my own thoughts startled me. Quickly, I tried to redirect my mind away from the what ifs. I gave myself an emergency pep talk and recited what I knew to be true, "I can do all things through Christ who strengthens me. I can do all things...."

Like a child doing an errand she wasn't up for, I grabbed my purse, locked the car and found my way inside the store. The layout of the store was different from what I was used to. Uncertain where to find what I needed, I decided to walk up and down each aisle.

Soon I was holding a box of cereal, reading the label, trying to figure out the carbohydrate count and sugar content. Would three-fourths a cup of cereal fill Jenna up? Not finding any "sugar free" cereal, I grabbed a box of Kellogg's Corn Flakes and continued shopping. Pausing, I turned back. Do I still buy Froot Loops for Jason? I hadn't even thought how Jenna's diagnosis might affect Jason, my typical four-year-old. Is it okay if he has a box of Froot Loops while Jenna eats Kellogg's Corn Flakes?

Eventually I walked down the canned fruit and juice aisle. Yes, I need apple juice, but how much? Just how often will Jenna's sugar "go low" so she will need this lifesaving can of juice? Will a six-year-old actually know when her blood sugar is dropping? What if...? I began to ask myself again.

I held the can of apple juice and began to read the label. Jenna will need fifteen carbohydrates of juice when her sugar drops. But this can has thirty-two. Immediately I could see my hand begin to tremble. I tried to steady the can and reread the label when I felt tears leave my eyes and make their way down the sides of my face. Not knowing what to do, I grabbed a couple of six-packs of apple juice and placed them in my cart. Frustrated by feelings of total inadequacy, I crumpled up my grocery list, covered my face in my hands and cried.

"Honey, are you all right?" I heard a gentle voice ask. I had been so engrossed in my own thoughts that I hadn't even noticed the woman who was shopping alongside of me. Suddenly I felt her hand as she reached toward me and rested it upon my shoulder. "Are you all right? Honey, are you a little short of cash? Why don't you just let me...?"

I slowly dropped my hands from my face and looked into the eyes of the silver-haired woman who waited for my answer. "Oh, no, thank you, ma'am," I said while wiping my tears, trying to gather my composure. "I have enough money."

"Well, honey, what is it then?" she persisted.

"It's just that I'm kind of overwhelmed. I'm here shopping for groceries so that I can bring my children home from the hospital tomorrow."

"Home from the hospital! What a celebration that shall be. Why, you should have a party!"

Within minutes this stranger had befriended me. She took my crumpled-up grocery list, smoothed it out and became my personal shopper. She stayed by my side until each item on my list was checked off. She even walked me to my car, helping me as I placed the groceries in my trunk. Then with a hug and a smile, she sent me on my way.

It was shortly after midnight, while lugging the groceries into my house, that I realized the lesson this woman had taught me. "My kids are coming home from the hospital!" I shouted with joy. "Joel is off life support and functioning on a monitor. Jenna and I can learn how to manage her diabetes and give her shots properly. And just as God met my needs in a grocery store, He will meet each and every need we have. What a reason to celebrate." I giggled to myself.

"I have a reason to celebrate!" I shouted to my empty house.

"Why, you should have a party!" the woman had exclaimed.

And a party there would be!

~Janet Lynn Mitchell
Chicken Soup for the Christian Soul 2

68

The Wonder Years

A women who creates and sustains a home,
and under whose hands children grow up to be
strong and pure men and women,
is a creator second only to God.
~Helen Hunt Jackson

One bleak day eighteen years ago, I was awash with self-pity. I was stuck in the "terrible twos"—a parenting stage that started early and lingered long at our house—and there was no hope in sight.

The morning began with the usual activities, but I tried to rush my small sons through them. Company was coming that evening, and I wanted a clean house. I'd finished cleaning the living room and begun the family room when I heard whispered giggles coming from my boys. With a sense of foreboding, I tiptoed to the doorway and gasped in dismay at the sight before me.

"Doesn't the living room look pretty, Mommy?" Tyler, my then-four-year-old, held a giant-sized empty jar of silver glitter, while two-year-old Landon danced around in happy circles. The entire room—carpet, couch, coffee table, everything—glittered like a giant Fourth of July sparkler!

Banishing the boys to their room to play with Legos, I dragged the vacuum back into the living room. By the time it was restored to its original condition, my schedule was in shambles and I was exhausted.

Stepping up my pace, I returned to the family room. "Look, Mommy! We're helping!" my boys shrieked in delight. This time the empty container was an economy-size can of Comet cleanser I thought I had placed in a locked cabinet. I was too shocked even to gasp as I surveyed the scene before me. The floor and every book, plant, knickknack and piece of furniture were covered with a fine layer of bluish-white grit.

The worst was yet to come. The last room to be cleaned was the master bedroom that we'd recently recarpeted. As I walked into the room, my attention was immediately drawn to a large, black spot smack in the middle of the floor. Beside it sat an empty bottle of permanent black ink I'd inadvertently left out. I crumpled to my knees in tears.

That's how most of our days went during those preschool years. We bounced from disaster to disaster: perfume poured on my new satin bedspread; the phone cord cut with scissors while I was talking on the phone. If it could be poured, dumped, sprinkled or sprayed, Tyler and Landon found a way to do it. There was no shelf the two of them could not reach, no lid they could not pry off.

After I discovered the ink spot that morning, I called my mom, but she didn't provide the sympathy I expected. "Honey, I know it feels as though this time will never end but believe me, a blink of your eye and it'll be gone. You have to find a way to cherish this season of your life."

This is not what I want to hear, I thought. But I knew she was right. I just didn't know how to switch from surviving to cherishing. So from that morning on, I asked God for help. And in the process, I became aware of some patterns that had squashed my capacity for joy. Life in the Mathers home lightened up as I worked to change some of my habits.

First, I realized I overused the word "no." Some days it seemed I'd forgotten how to say "yes." One afternoon I jotted down everything to which I regularly responded "no." Looking over the completed list, I discovered I denied far too many of my sons' requests because they would make a mess or take too much time.

For example, the boys loved to pull their chairs to the kitchen sink and play in the water while I did dishes, but this slowed me down and made a sudsy mess. I decided to remove this activity from my "no" list.

The next morning, to the boys' delight, I filled the sink with warm water and told them to bring their chairs and have fun. This simple activity kept them so entertained, I finished my morning chores in record time.

Removing just this one "no" made a tremendous difference. The boys thought I was wonderful, and I was pretty impressed with them. As a bonus, my kitchen was cleaner than ever, thanks to all the splashed water.

But avoiding the word "no" hasn't always been easy. As Tyler and Landon grew older, I discovered that overusing it made them feel untrustworthy. The first time Landon asked to go camping overnight with friends, I refused to consider it. He angrily accused me of not trusting him. Although Landon was wrong, I couldn't really explain the fear that made me deny his request.

When my husband suggested my refusal was based on a reluctance to let Landon grow up, I knew he was right. We sat down together and laid out clear plans for the campout. Landon had a great time and I survived, thanks to several calls he made from a pay phone to reassure me he was okay. Several weeks later, when he asked to go to an unsupervised party, I again declined. This time Landon was disappointed, but not angry. He knew I trusted him—just not the circumstances.

I also realized I didn't laugh enough. Proverbs 15:15 promises that "a cheerful heart has a continual feast." During the preschool years, however, I was becoming emotionally anorexic. I'd forgotten there's something humorous to be found in almost every situation.

After one particularly trying day with my preschoolers, I escaped to a long, steamy shower, leaving my husband to oversee the boys. I'd just dressed when our neighbor dropped by for coffee. As she followed me to the kitchen, she stopped abruptly.

"Interesting," she murmured, studying the dining room floor.

"We've always kept our catsup in the refrigerator." I followed her gaze to a giant red puddle circled neatly on the carpet. Husband and sons were nowhere to be seen. Instant embarrassment and anger inflated my chest. Then I caught the twinkle in my neighbor's eyes, and we both burst into laughter. Laughing can help shrink things down to manageable proportions.

I've definitely needed that healthy dose of humor in each stage of parenting. Learning to find the humor in difficult or embarrassing situations has often defused tension.

I compared my kids and my parenting to others. I routinely measured my success as a parent by this faulty yardstick—and came up short. As I scrutinized my friends' choices, I constantly second-guessed mine.

My insecurities increased as the boys grew older. One afternoon I was waiting in line to pick them up from school when I noticed a bumper sticker on the car in front of mine: "My child is an honor student at Pilot Butte School." Glancing around, I saw another vehicle with a similar sticker, then another. Suddenly, it seemed my car was the only one lacking a badge of success!

My temptation to compare raged strongest when it was time for my sons to pursue plans beyond high school. As I listened to other parents talk about the colleges to which their kids were applying or the scholarships they were receiving, my insecurities blossomed. I found myself being apologetic about Tyler's plans to work before going to school. Not until I caught the same tone in Tyler's voice did I realize I was passing my insecurities to him. That was the last thing I wanted to bequeath my son. Asking God's forgiveness, I determined to focus squarely on God—not on other people. That decision is one that I still renew every morning when I ask God for help.

Now as the parent of grown children, I see my mother was right. The preschool years passed in the blink of an eye. But it wasn't just those years that vanished in a moment—it was all of childhood! One moment we were reading Mother Goose together, the next, it was college catalogs.

As my sons have matured, I've found that everyday traumas that accompany each parenting stage come with valuable lessons. That became clear to me the day I found the ink on my new carpet. I called every cleaner in town for advice on removing the stain. The only solution was to cover it with a rug.

I just couldn't accept that. I had to try something. Getting a basin of water and a washcloth, I began soaking up the ink and rinsing out the cloth. Soaking... rinsing... soaking... rinsing. As I worked, tears spilling down my cheeks, chubby little hands patted me on the back.

"We're sorry, Mommy," they said. While Tyler ran to get more water, Landon brought a bar of soap. Together we worked and gradually, before our disbelieving eyes, the spot that should have been permanent disappeared.

That day I discovered God looks on mothers with a special kind of love. He knows our insecurities, our frustrations, our desire to be good parents. And sometimes, when we need it most, He goes out of his way to prove his love. Tucked away with my cleaning supplies is a reminder of that. It's the cloth I used to clean the carpet. To this day it remains stained with permanent black ink!

~Mayo Mathers
Chicken Soup for the Christian Family Soul

On, Being a Parent

Learning from the Kids

While we try to teach our children all about life,
Our children teach us what life is all about.
~Angela Schwindt

69

"Is It Fun Being a Mommy?"

The phrase "working mother" is redundant.
~Jane Sellman

I didn't know Rachel was paying close attention to me one ordinary evening. I did know that nothing slipped past my bright, inquisitive second-grade daughter. Like all mothers, I bragged about my child's brilliance, but once again I was caught off-guard by her insight into adult behavior.

From the time Rachel arrived home from school that particular Tuesday afternoon until after our family dinner, she observed me prepare a snack for her and her little brother, help her with her homework, cook dinner, wash dishes, and sweep and mop the floor. Then I prepared to begin the daily laundry routine. When her dad walked in the door from his day's work, she observed him leisurely reading the evening newspaper, working on a crossword puzzle, stretching out in the recliner, watching television, eating dinner and retreating to the backyard to play catch with her brother.

"Ummm," Rachel wondered what was wrong with this picture. In her mind, the score wasn't quite even. She decided this issue demanded immediate resolution.

As I checked a load of clothes in the dryer, Rachel approached me with a puzzled look.

"Mom, is it hard being a mommy?"

"No, dear," I moaned as I trotted to the bedroom with a load of hot sheets and towels to fold. "I love being a mommy."

"You do?" she asked in amazement.

"Yes, I do, sweetheart," I moaned again, as I gathered up a pile of grimy play clothes to start yet another washer load.

"Why do you ask?"

"Well, to me, it looks like mommies get all the hard work and daddies get all the fun."

"This is what stay-at-home moms do. It's part of my work. You didn't see Dad working hard all day at his office. Now it's time for him to relax and have fun with his family."

"Oh, okay," Rachel conceded. "So, when is it your turn to have fun?"

Good question. I wondered if I had a good answer. Before I replied, my son called for Rachel to come outside and play ball. As I folded and stacked towels, it occurred to me that as Rachel observed me that evening, she didn't see a contented homemaker, happy to stay home and care for her family by maintaining an orderly home. What my daughter watched was a madwoman frantically rushing about the kitchen throwing hamburger meat into the microwave. She witnessed an impatient woman who thought the story in the second-grade reader would never end. She saw a weary woman who seemed to prefer scrubbing sticky pots and pans to playing baseball in the backyard.

This wasn't the picture of motherhood my daughter needed to model. She deserved better. (I deserved better, too!) She needed not a picture of perfection, but one of joy and contentment in a mother doing the same old household chores again, and again and again.

In her daddy, Rachel noticed a man who took time out for himself and his family. It was my turn to try that approach to life as well. I decided immediately that the laundry could wait to be folded. I joined my half-pint ball team by the swing set. My relaxed, new and improved outlook on life paid immediate results. My family watched in amazement as my home-run baseball cleared the backyard fence.

~DeAnna Sanders
Chicken Soup for the Mother & Daughter Soul

Learning to Listen

Each day of our lives we make deposits in the memory banks of our children.
~Charles R. Swindoll

One year, I went out of town to attend a writer's conference. As I stepped off the jet back home in Atlanta, my family waited for me. After we had embraced, I started telling them about my trip. At least I tried to. Everyone wanted to tell me something—especially eight-year-old Jeremy. He jumped up and down in order to be heard, and his voice carried above the other children's, even above my husband Jerry's.

Everyone needs something from me, I thought. They don't want to hear about my trip. What is it Jeremy keeps saying?

"Poster paper, Mama! I have to have poster paper. We're having a contest at school."

I put him off, promising we'd talk about it later. Back at home I readjusted to the telephone, doorbell, sorting laundry, driving carpools, answering questions and wiping up spills. I fought off the creeping knowledge that, no matter how hard I tried, I couldn't keep up with the needs of my family. As I moved about hurriedly, trying to decide what to do next, Jeremy kept reminding me, "I need the poster paper, Mama."

Gradually though, he began to speak more softly, almost as though he were talking to himself. So I put Jeremy's request at the bottom of my long list of things to do. Maybe he'll just hush about the poster paper, I thought hopefully.

My third day home I managed to salvage about fifteen minutes to try to type an article. Sitting at the typewriter, I heard the dryer stop. Another load of clothes should be put in. Two important phone calls needed to be returned. One of my daughters had pleaded with me several times to listen to her recite part of *The Canterbury Tales*. For over an hour, one of the cats had meowed right in my face trying to get me to feed her. Someone had spilled orange Kool-Aid on the kitchen floor and smeared it around with a dry towel. It was past time to start supper, and I hadn't even eaten lunch. Nevertheless, I typed joyfully for a few delicious minutes.

A small shadow fell across my paper. I knew who it would be before I looked up. I glanced up anyway. Jeremy stood quietly watching me. Oh, Lord, please don't let him say it again. I know he needs poster paper. I need to type. I smiled weakly at Jeremy and kept typing. He watched for a few more minutes, then turned and walked away. I almost didn't hear his comment. "Contest is over tomorrow, anyway."

I wanted to write so much that, with a little effort, I could have tuned out his remark. But I couldn't ignore the silent voice that spoke urgently to my heart. Get him that paper—now! I shut off my electric typewriter. "Let's go get the paper, Jeremy." He stopped, turned around and looked at me without even smiling or speaking—almost as though he hadn't heard.

"Come on," I urged, grabbing my purse and the car keys.

He still didn't move. "Do you have something else you have to get, Mama?"

"No, just your poster paper." I headed for the door.

He lagged behind and asked, "You're going to the store just for me?"

I stopped and looked down at him. Really looked at him. Spots of whatever he'd eaten for lunch at school stained his shirt. Untied, flopping shoes and traces of orange Kool-Aid that turned up at the corners of his small, grim mouth gave Jeremy a clown-like appearance.

Suddenly, a look of utter delight shot across his face, erasing the disbelief. I don't think I'll ever forget that moment. He moved with amazing speed and running to the bottom of the stairs he threw his head back and shouted, "Hey, Julie, Jen, Jon, Mama's taking me to the store! Anybody need anything?"

No one answered him, but he didn't seem to notice. He sprinted out to the car still wearing the Christmas morning expression. At the store, instead of running in ahead of me, he grabbed my hand and started rapidly telling me about the poster contest.

"It's about fire prevention. The teacher announced it a long time ago, and when I first told you, you said we'd see later. Then you went out of town. The contest ends tomorrow. I'll have to work hard. What if I win?" He went on with endless enthusiasm as though he'd only asked me one time for the paper.

Jeremy didn't want an apology from me. It would have spoiled the joy. So I just listened. I listened to him as intently as I ever have anyone in my life. After he bought the poster paper, I asked, "Do you need anything else?"

"Do you have enough money?" he whispered.

I smiled at him, suddenly feeling very rich, "Yes, today I just happen to have lots of money. What do you need?"

"Can I have my own glue and some construction paper?"

We got the other items and at the cashier's, Jeremy, who usually doesn't confide in strangers, said, "I'm making a poster. My Mama brought me to the store to buy the stuff." He tried to sound matter-of-fact, but his face gave him away.

He worked silently and with great determination on the poster all afternoon.

The winner of the contest was announced over the school intercom two days later. Jeremy won. His poster was then entered in the county competition. He won that, too. The principal wrote him a letter and enclosed a check for five dollars. Jeremy wrote a story about the contest. He left it lying on his dresser and I read it. One sentence jumped out at me. "And then my Mama stopped typing and listened to me and took just me to the store."

And a few weeks later, a large yellow envelope came in the mail addressed to Jeremy. He tore into it and read aloud slowly and almost in disbelief the Certificate of Award. "This certifies that Jeremy West has the distinction of reaching the state finals in the Georgia Fire Prevention Theme and Poster Contest." It was signed by the comptroller general of Georgia.

Jeremy fell on the floor and did somersaults, laughing aloud. We framed his certificate and often when I see it I remember that almost—almost—I'd turned away from his request to get him some poster paper.

~Marion Bond West
Chicken Soup for the Mother's Soul 2

Happy Birthday, Jane!

The capacity to care is the thing
that gives life its deepest meaning and significance.
~Pablo Casals

Inwardly, I groaned. Couldn't our too-efficient receptionist have forgotten to consult her calendar just this once?

"Thanks, Carol." I tried to inject enthusiasm into my tone as I zoomed into my office. The less said about this momentous occasion the better.

However, by leaning forward at her desk, Carol could look through the open doorway right at my desk. This she did, beaming a huge smile at me. "Lordy, lordy, look who's forty! Planning a big celebration tonight?"

"Nah. Just family."

My mother would probably bring over a cake, and my sole hope for the day was that it would be her Heavenly Chocolate, full of fruit and nuts and spices. Kathy had the night off from the movie theater where she worked part-time—"shoveling popcorn," as she put it—and Stewart would have finished his paper route long before I got home. We would sit down together to something quick and simple, maybe the tacos the kids liked. No romantic candlelit dinners for this birthday girl.

Carol's smile widened, if that was possible. "It's nice with just family."

Faker that I was, I agreed, then grabbed my coffee mug and

scurried off. Unfortunately, to get to the kitchen, I had to pass through the art department. One of the designers looked up and chortled, "Over the hill now, huh, Jane?"

"Rub it in, Bill," I grumbled. Still on the sunny side of thirty, Bill just grinned.

Another designer, Dottie, was a little more perceptive, and with good reason. At about forty-five, she was even more shopworn than I was.

"You know what the French say, don't you?" She peered up at me slyly through her auburn bangs. "They don't think a woman is even worth noticing till she's forty."

I grimaced. "I don't know any Frenchmen."

She just gave me a throaty chuckle and went back to the ad she was comping. I filled my mug and skulked back to my office. My desk was turned so that my back was to the raw January day outside, but I seemed more than capable of making my own gloom.

Bill was right; I was over the hill. And I hadn't exactly reached much of a pinnacle on the way, either. As I slurped coffee, I summarized in my head: I had achieved no real career, just a low-paying job as a small-time copywriter. I had salted away no bank account. I had provided my children with none of the things they assured me all their friends had—VCR, microwave, answering machine, vacations. Worst of all for one who had spent her childhood playing Cinderella, I had failed—both in my marriage and during the three years since—to find true love.

Even so, the minutes were ticking away, as fast as they had for four decades, and the billing sheet in front of me was waiting for entries. So I applied myself to the task of writing a brochure for seed corn.

Seated as I was just five or six feet from the receptionist's desk, I had learned to tune out the opening of the front door, especially when I was under such enchantment as yield-per-acre. Therefore, I was a little startled when I heard an unfamiliar voice speak my name in a questioning tone.

I looked up. "Yes?" A man was standing in my doorway holding some sort of huge, shapeless mass covered in tissue paper.

"Flowers for you."

He stepped forward, deposited what he claimed to be flowers on the corner of my desk, and disappeared.

Carol took his place in the doorway and demanded, "Did somebody send you flowers?"

"I guess so," I replied, dazed.

"Some secret admirer you forgot to tell me about?"

I tried a shaky laugh. "I doubt that."

"Well, aren't you going to look at them?"

"Well... yeah." As I ripped away the tissue, I wondered if Carol could possibly be right. Had I somehow impressed one of the few men who had taken me out? My rational side butted in to say that wasn't likely. Maybe the people in the office had taken pity on me, or some kind client.

The bouquet that emerged from the tissue paper was an enormous sheaf of springtime color—irises, daisies, carnations—quite a contrast with the scene outside my window. I was stunned.

"Well, see who they're from," practical Carol ordered.

I fumbled for the card. The tiny envelope bore my name in the unfamiliar handwriting of someone at the florist shop. Then I pulled out the card itself.

"Dear Mom." I smiled as I recognized the self-conscious, curlicue letters I had watched develop for a dozen years. "Today, life begins, right? Love, Me."

My eyes stung. Of course. Who else could it have been but Kathy? Kathy, who had lent me her favorite top because she thought I had nothing suitable to wear to a party. Who had once found me sitting alone in the dark and whispered, "Mom, what's wrong?" Who had offered to split weekend nights out with me so someone would always be home with Stewart.

I reached out and started touching petals. Each festive pastel made a memory spring forth, and I thought with tender dismay that my hard-working daughter could ill afford such an extravagant gesture.

Dottie appeared next to Carol. "Oooh, flowers! Who from?"

I blinked against my tears and said proudly, "My daughter."

"Aaaw," Carol cooed. "That's so sweet."

I could tell it was more of an effort for Dottie. "That's very nice."

My only answer was the radiant smile a woman is supposed to wear on her birthday. I just couldn't hide the fact that I had found true love.

~Jane Robertson
Chicken Soup for the Soul Celebrates Mothers

Making Room for Shooting Stars

Alone we can do so little;
together we can do so much.
~Helen Keller

This was the big game. The bleachers were packed with parents and kids. Lights blazed down on the baseball field, giving it a real "big league" feel. The boys in the dugouts were nervous and excited. It was the bottom of the fifth inning, and our team was actually leading by one run. Andy, our son, was in right field, and behind him, at the edge of the lights, it was dark, with the black shape of the distant mountains rising up to the stars. It was a clear and chilly night, and Andy's Little League team, which had struggled all year and didn't even reach .500 in the final standings, had shocked two of the better teams by making it to this championship game. The mood was electric.

Only one out to go to end the inning. The other team's left-handed slugger, a big kid who always hit long balls and had that home-run swagger when he walked, was up. He was poised at the plate like a rattlesnake, dangerous and ready to strike.

Nervously, I looked out Andy's way. He had never really done well in the outfield. I was shocked to see Andy looking straight up at the night sky! It was obvious he wasn't paying attention to the game. I was horrified this slugger was going to launch the ball Andy's way and he wouldn't even know it was coming. They'd score a bunch of runs and break the game wide open.

"What's he doing out there?" I hissed to my wife, Mary.

"What do you mean?" she replied.

"Well, look at him — he's not paying attention; he's goofing off! This guy's gonna hit it right to him!" I muttered.

"Relax," said my wife. "He'll be fine. It's just a game."

"Come on, Andy. Wake up out there," I said more to myself than Mary.

I could barely watch. My body was tense. The pitch was on the way, a slow, enticing floater right in the middle of the strike zone. I squinted out at Andy, who was still gazing heavenward. Maybe he's praying, I thought. I heard the crack of the bat. "Oh, no," I said.

I was mostly worried that Andy would be really embarrassed, because he did take his performance seriously, and cared what his teammates thought of him. But I also realized I was worried that I'd be embarrassed, too. I prided myself on being a supportive and not-too-pushy dad. We'd go out and play one-on-one games and practice catching those high flies. I always tried to make it fun, yet pushed hard enough that Andy would improve. And I'd always say, "Just give it your best shot." So if Andy made a good try going after the ball and missed it — you know, stretched out with the glove and eating sod, or backwards over the fence — that was okay. But to miss it because he was off in a different dimension somewhere — that was embarrassing. Downright goofy. Not playing tough. Letting the guys down. I felt all that macho sports stuff churning around inside me like indigestion.

"Yes!" I shouted, as the play ended. Sluggo had grounded out to first. We (Andy and I) had been spared, and we still led by one run. It was imperative that I get Andy straightened out for the last inning.

We were sitting behind the fence near home plate, and as the kids came in from the outfield, Andy ran up to us, breathless. I was about to start my "What-do-you-think-you're-doing-out-there speech" when Andy exclaimed, "Did you see that shooting star? It was beautiful! It was so great. It had a long tail, and I thought it might crash into the mountain. But then it just disappeared, like someone turned the lights off inside. I wonder where it came from. It was so awesome. I wish you'd seen it!"

Andy's eyes were glowing with excitement (after all, we had spent as much time looking for meteors as we had practicing baseball). I paused. "Me, too," I said. "Well, one inning to go. You guys hold 'em now. Hit a home run!"

"Okay!" said Andy, and he ran back to his teammates in the dugout.

Mary smiled at me. We were thinking the same thing—that it was nice our son would take time out to appreciate the wonder and beauty in life, and that it was important to him. There was plenty of time for Andy to experience the suffocating crush of team sports, the peer pressure, the "at all costs" mentality. He was still a kid, thank goodness. And I was a little chagrined that I had been temporarily caught up in the same vortex.

As we grow up, it seems we have less and less time to seek beauty and wonder. As adults, it's way down the list somewhere. For many of us, just keeping up with everything we have going consumes most of our time and energy, and sadly there's not much room for shooting stars. So every once in a while I take time out to look around, even if I'm in the middle of something I think is too important to interrupt. You might be surprised by the beauty you can find when you least expect it—on the street, in the sky, even in the corporate boardroom—and how it can make your day better. Andy hit a triple in that last inning. But I still wish I had seen that shooting star, too.

~Mark Crawford
A 6th Bowl of Chicken Soup for the Soul

Let's Go Bug Hunting More Often

One fall afternoon I rushed home from the university where I taught. I prepared a hasty dinner, threatened my nine-year-old daughter, Christi, to hurry and finish her homework "or else," and properly reprimanded Del, my husband, for leaving his dusty shoes on the good carpet. I then frantically vacuumed the entryway because a group of prestigious ladies were coming by to pick up some good used clothing for a worthwhile cause; and then later a graduate student would be at our house to work on a very important thesis—one that I was certain would make a sound contribution to research.

As I paused to catch my breath, I heard Christi talking with a friend on the telephone. Her comments went something like this: "Mom is cleaning house—some ladies we don't even know are coming by to pick up some old worn-out clothes... and a college student is coming out to work on a thesis... no, I don't know what a thesis is... I just know Mom isn't doing anything important... and she won't go bug hunting with me."

Before Christi had hung up the phone, I had put on my jeans and old tennis shoes, persuaded Del to do likewise, pinned a note to the door telling the graduate student I'd be back soon, and set the box of used clothing on the front porch with a note on it that Del, Christi and I had gone bug hunting.

~Barbara Chesser
A 5th Portion of Chicken Soup for the Soul

Choosing Life

For nearly twenty years, my life revolved around two things: smoking cigarettes—and trying to quit smoking cigarettes. It was a vicious circle, one I couldn't break.

When I married Cassie ten years ago, I crumpled up my pack of cigarettes and swore I was quitting.

When we bought our first house eight years ago, I marked that rite of passage by pulverizing my pack of cigarettes with my shoe heel.

When my son, Cole, was born five years ago, I slam-dunked my cigs into a garbage can.

And when my daughter, Olivia, was born three years later, yet another pack of butts bit the dust.

I even began working out fanatically—lifting weights and running five days a week, rain or shine. I lost forty pounds and developed a rock-hard physique, but I never was able to outrun those cigarettes.

Smoking is an insidious habit; it scrambles your brain. Rationally, you know cigarettes are lethal—but every cell in your body screams out for that nicotine, skewing judgment and priorities. So I kept puffing away, the life slowly and invisibly being sucked right out of me.

One day the willpower I had lacked arrived with brusque force, from a most unexpected place: an unclouded corner of my son's mind.

As Cassie was driving Cole home from kindergarten, they passed a cemetery, which prompted the boy to ask: "Mom, what's under tombstones?"

She pondered the question for a few moments, trying to think of a delicate answer. Realizing there was no delicate answer, she bluntly said, "Dead people."

"Is that where Dad's going to be because he smokes?" Cole asked.

"I hope not," Cassie replied.

"Dad shouldn't smoke," Cole said, his voice rising in anger. He kicked the back of the front seat. "Dad's stupid for smoking. When I'm twenty, he'll be dead."

Cassie was speechless, stunned by Cole's intuitiveness. Then, just as quickly as he had exploded, he composed himself. "I hope he comes back as a ghost and talks to me," he said placidly. "Like Obi-Wan Kenobi did to Luke Skywalker in *Star Wars*."

When I arrived home from work that evening, Cassie recounted the story to me. Never one to mince words, she stared right into my eyes and said, "He's already written you off, Will. He's figured things out in his mind, come to terms with the fact that you won't be around. And if he can only have you as a ghost, that's what he'll take."

Call it an epiphany. Although Cole hadn't said anything I didn't already know, his words — delivered so honestly and innocently, as only a child can do — distilled everything into a simple, unavoidable truth. Smoking could only lead to one conclusion, and when they placed me under that tombstone, life would have to go on without me. If I couldn't even fool my own five-year-old kid, why was I continuing to try to fool myself?

Cole was, however, off the mark on one important count: As far as I knew, that ghost deal was a long shot at best. I wasn't coming back as some suburban Jedi Knight, a flickering ray of light in a golf shirt and khakis, dispensing pearls of wisdom to Cole and Olivia on how to combat the perils of their young adult lives. They'd be on their own.

Later that evening, I found Cole lying on the couch in the family room watching *Monsters, Inc.*

"Cole," I said. "I've been thinking about what you said to Mom today, and I'm going to quit smoking. But I need your help. It's too hard to do alone."

The seconds ticked by as he hatched his plan. His lips were pursed, a sure sign that he was deep in thought. Finally, he spoke. "Okay. Here's what we'll do: every morning and every night, I'll tell you not to smoke."

"You'll do that?" I said.

"Yes."

"Promise?"

"Yes."

"Sounds like a plan."

And, by God, it was. Every time I had an urge to smoke, I fought it off with thoughts of tombstones and Obi-Wan Kenobi and a little boy trying desperately to help his old man out of a jam. Those visions were like a psychic, industrial-strength nicotine patch.

So here I am, checking off the days that I've been cigarette-free. I miss those darn things, but I'm choosing life over the alternative. After all, my kids need me—although not nearly as much as I need them.

~William Wagner
Chicken Soup to Inspire the Body & Soul

75

A True Champion

This is the miracle that happens every time to those who really love;
the more they give, the more they possess.
~Rainer Maria Rilke

When our second child was born, Jim and I thought she was perfect, but the doctor pointed out that her feet were turned inward. "Left uncorrected, it would be a problem," he told us.

We vowed to do anything we could to help our baby. When only two weeks old, I brought her back to the doctor, just as he had directed, and the doctor put her tiny feet into casts, her precious baby toes just barely visible. Because she was growing, I had to take her back to the doctor every two weeks to have each foot recast.

Eventually the casting was finished and it was time for corrective shoes and bars. Jim and I watched with hope and concern as she struggled to walk. Those first, awkward steps made us so proud. By the time she entered preschool, her steps appeared quite normal. Encouraged by her progress, we looked for something else to help strengthen her lower body.

As it turned out, she loved the ice!

When she turned six, we enrolled her in skating lessons and soon she was gliding like a swan. We watched in wonderment as she skimmed the ice. She wasn't the fastest nor the most coordinated skater. She had to work hard at every new movement, but she loved the ice and her dedication paid off. At fifteen, she competed in both pairs-skating and the ladies' singles at the 1988 World Junior Championships in Australia, winning both events! At the senior World Championships in 1991, she won the ladies' singles. Then we found ourselves filled with love and admiration in France, at the 1992 Winter Olympics, as our daughter, Kristi Yamaguchi, won the gold medal.

I thought back to the early years of challenge for Kristi—the years of fear for us as her parents, and the same years of frustration for her as a child who simply wanted to walk; the endless doctor visits; the arduous first baby steps with bars and corrective shoes. During those years, we didn't expect gold medals and a stunning professional career ahead of her. We stood in awe of Kristi herself, respecting her strength and dedication, and how far she had come on two tiny feet that had once been bound in heavy casts. In our eyes, Kristi had always walked with the grace of a true champion.

~Carole Yamaguchi as told to Anita Gogno
Chicken Soup for the Sports Fan's Soul

76

Maple Leaf Wars

I watched him scamper outside, a bed of gold and red leaves beckoning him. Come play with us, little man!

He raced as fast as his little legs could carry him, and with a "wheeeee," threw himself into the arms of his autumn friends. They played with him, covered him, snuck down his jacket, tripped him and tickled him. My carefully piled leaves soon became a playhouse, a castle, a battleground, a spaceship.

"Come play, Momma!"

I smiled at him from the kitchen window and shook my head. It was an encouraging smile, but there was no way Momma was going to get out of her fuzzy slippers and oversized tee to go out there. C-c-c-cold...

Lost sight of him now... buried under there. Oh dear is he warm enough? I ran through a mental checklist and nodded yep.

"Woooooosssssshhhhhhhhh!!" My trouper surfaced.

"Captain to starship, we got the leaf leader, need backup!"

"He's gonna havta tell us where the others are hiding! Send Poliwhirl and Pikachu with double stun phasers!"

He spun around hit by a falling leaf, staggered, clutched his Star Wars tuque and keeled over.

"Aaargh... he got me, stoopid poxamity radar dint work."

"I'm wounded, gotta... get... to... ship."

He crawled forward to the tree trunk, his little mitted hands reached for the root of the tree that was his teleporter.

"Drop it, Human!"

He gasped and looked up.

There was Queen Momma Leaf, in full battle regalia with King Daddy's coat, scarf thrown decadently around my neck, ten starleaves stuck in my tuque signifying my position as Her Royal Autumness.

"We have you surrounded, Human, prepare to be tickled!"

I dove at him, wrestling him, aided by my trusty leaf regiment.

Hmm... not that cold out here after all.

High-pitched squeals filled the air as the leaf queen did battle with the miniature human. Momma-toned shouts echoed as we rolled and pummeled each other into submission. A chance glance at the home ship window revealed King Daddy looking through, concerned but half amused, considering his options of committing the queen on account of insanity. Other spaceship windows showed neighbors shaking their heads or nodding with smiles, depending on the amount of bran in their diets. This momentary distraction cost me dearly as, with a victory yell, the Captain grabbed my queenly tuque and raced off with it.

"I got the old bag's hat!" he yelled into his transponder.

Note to self: Be careful when discussing Aunt Gladys in front of the captain.

The now tuqueless queen recovers quickly since no hat meant disheveled hair festooned with leaves would ruin my reputation in the galaxy for coiffure perfection.

I race after the short but cute Captain.

"Give it back you tinytwoleggedtestosteronetesttube! Queen Leaf demands it in the name of all things falling south!"

He stared at me.

"Huh?"

"Never mind son."

I made a flying tackle, taking advantage of his temporary bemusement at his archenemy's obvious Alzheimer's.

"Arggggghh!!"

Falling prey to the universal mistake all Queen Autumnesses make after they've passed thirty by several light years, and still think they can accomplish flying tackles without squishing their boobs and causing trauma to bones carefully wrapped in cellulite space-suits, I managed to squish my boobs and hurt my cellulite-wrapped spacesuit.

"Mom? Are you okay?" asked the now-concerned Captain.

"Uhmm... yes, I'm fine."

Pride has a way of relieving most moments of destruction, especially since Spaceship 212 across the street had that nosy three-headed alien with her nose stuck to her window watching me.

I chased the Captain around the trees and into the leaf settlements until he tired.

"Momma? Can you and me do this every day?"

"No, baby, but I'm sure Daddy and you can."

I smiled at the Captain as I collected him in my arms and strolled back to home base.

Nope... not cold out here at all.

~Nathalie K. Taghaboni
Chicken Soup for the Soul Celebrates Mothers

On, Being a Parent

Thank You

As we express our gratitude, we must never forget that the highest appreciation is not to utter words, but to live by them.
~John Fitzgerald Kennedy

77

Spelling L-O-V-E

He didn't tell me how to live;
he lived, and let me watch him do it.
~Clarence Budington Kelland

"Betty! Bonnie! Bob! Paula!"

I blinked awake. The house that a moment before slumbered in early Saturday morning darkness was now alive with lights and groggy children. I pulled the covers back over my head. But it was no use. Daddy had brought us his usual Saturday morning offering of love.

"Good morning, girls!" he boomed. Already dressed for his half-day at work, his cardboard-stiff white shirt, rosy cheeks, prematurely silver hair and beaming smile glowed.

"Here, Bonnie, this is your list of words for this morning. Betty, here's yours. If you learn them right away, you can have some more before I go!"

For in our home, the delightful, carefree wonder of Saturday began, not with a chance to sleep in for a spell, but with spelling itself. As in s-p-e-l-l-i-n-g.

Protests got us nowhere. "Don't worry, children," Daddy would assure us cheerfully. "You'll thank me when you're older. I wish I could have done this when I was your age." And, believe it or not, he meant it!

Harold Compton's love affair with learning began as a precocious four-year-old. Every morning his father, Charlie, left their hardscrabble farm in the hills of Eastern Kentucky for his teaching post at a nearby hamlet. In bad weather, when getting back home over the rutted, muddy roads was impossible, he would board with a student's parents.

The schoolmaster's lot back then was a lonely, hard and poorly paid one. But to his young son, getting to spend the day in a world of books instead of chores seemed the ultimate luxury. And soon Harold's persistent begging broke down his weary father's resolve. After that, Charlie's faithful mule carried both father and son off in the predawn darkness. And soon Harold was blissfully immersed in the three Rs: reading, 'riting and 'rithmetic.

Devouring every book available, young Harold dreamed of high school, Latin, Greek and Shakespeare, and college—and all the wonders such an education would bring. Meanwhile, he wrote poetry in the delicate Spencerian script his father taught him, an art form in itself. He taught himself algebra and geometry from ancient, taped-together books, saved for penny by penny.

Then tragedy struck—his beloved father died. And, in quick succession, so did two brothers and a sister.

As the new head of his family, Harold had four funeral debts to pay and a large family of brothers and sisters to feed. This meant leaving school after the eighth grade for twelve hours a day, six days a week of backbreaking, unskilled labor in fields and forests for fifty cents a day.

But he never gave up his dream. And years later, bypassing high school altogether, he went on to a teachers' training college and became a teacher himself.

Eventually, he left the hills and hollows of Eastern Kentucky for the bustling cities of Chicago and Cincinnati as a highly skilled building estimator for Sears Roebuck's booming ship-to-site housing industry.

World War II brought an end to the housing industry. Immediately Harold became part of the even more booming defense industry.

Then peace. And suddenly he was out of work, his lungs filled with metal shavings. Thus, twenty years after Harold left that

Kentucky hollow, he found himself back in it, in poor health, and with a new family of children to care for. His own.

Even there though, in our tumbledown log cabin near where he himself had grown up, he kept his dream alive. For crowded around its 150-year-old fireplace were our treasures: a piano, crammed-full bookcases, a well-thumbed Bible and a weighty *Merriam-Webster's Unabridged Dictionary*.

Besides running the farm, both he and my mother taught in schools much like the ones they themselves attended as children and taught in as young adults.

Even there, busy as we were, our Saturday-morning spelling tests continued. And so did Harold's self-education. He pored over that dictionary at night by kerosene light, after the last chores were done, memorizing word by word.

And that was not all. When he plowed or harrowed his rock-strewn fields, he grandly orated full Latin conjugations to his startled mules. He had finally taught himself Latin, too, from the hand-me-down textbooks we children used in high school.

We were still dirt poor when my older sister Betty graduated from high school.

Determined that she continue her education, Daddy drove her to Georgetown College himself in our wired-together '37 Chevy. Admitting that he didn't have a penny to put on her account, he promised the school that if she were accepted, he and Mother would pay all her bills somehow.

Many a night we would wake up to hear Daddy and Mother praying over how to make ends meet. But eventually all six of us went to college. And all of the bills were paid.

Of course, even with all of us working during college as well as taking full class loads, there was nothing left over for extras. One time I managed to stretch six dollars for laundry, clothes and all other incidentals for a whole semester. But we never dared give up, even at our most discouraging point. Daddy was counting on us to make it.

By the way, those Saturday mornings "took." From them we

learned a world of words that helped one sister become a journalist, another a teacher, another a writer and our brother a lawyer.

But the word we learned best was: L-O-V-E.

~Bonnie Compton Hanson
Chicken Soup for the Father & Daughter Soul

78

Reconnecting

The most important things are the hardest to say,
because words diminish them.
~Stephen King

My son Kent and I always had a great bond. Our communications were cemented by his sharing grade-school notes on the refrigerator, long journal entries crammed on the back of postcards during climbs and treks, late-night e-mails that ended with, "Mom, I think I need a woman," and phone calls about interesting females, all of whom were apparently forgotten as soon as he met Janet. The minute he told me, "Mom, she's a park ranger, she paints her toenails and wears a toe ring," I knew that this attractive young woman was a good match for him.

They planned a June wedding in California, unaware that his parents' marriage had unraveled back home in Kansas. I was the one to tell both of the children, living far away, in a letter. My daughter came and worked through communication with both her father and me. Kent did not respond. I finally reached him by phone and was met by a vehement, "I don't want to hear about it, Mom!"

I managed to stay outwardly calm while we finished the conversation as quickly as possible. Asking about their wedding plans was painful and confusing for me, so I ventured, "How's work?" A one-word answer, "Fine," exhausted that subject. Weather was about the only topic that didn't evoke some reference to family or the chasm that loomed between us.

From that day, we exchanged civil calls and e-mails about mundane happenings and family news, but I had no clue what he was really thinking.

Each time I would start to write feelings once easily expressed and received, his denied anger echoed in my head. In fear that I would say something to turn him against his father—or further against me—I would hit delete, not send.

The grief was almost as heavy as with the divorce itself. I had also lost my son.

Months later, I awakened with the conviction that I must speak from the heart. I wrote an e-mail and hit send:

Dear Kent,

It came to me this morning that you're possibly having as much of a struggle coming to some kind of clarity over this divorce as I am....

I told him how wounded I felt at first, how I came to realize that the marriage couldn't be "fixed," that I would miss my in-laws until they got comfortable enough with my being outside the clan to reestablish friendship ties, and assured him that neither his dad nor I wished the other ill after thirty-six years.

I don't see a single thing you or your sister did or didn't do as affecting our decision to divorce. Dad assured me that he loves you both just as much as ever. I do, too, and always will.

Ramblings from an aging mom or, maybe, insights from within a cracked cocoon when I'd like to see from the perspective of a butterfly.

A three-page answer came immediately. Kent's old voice was there, honestly telling me what he thought and felt. He recounted his fiancée's quizzical look when he spoke of his parents' "perfectly balanced marriage," of Mr. Sequential vs. Mrs. Random, taciturn vs.

gregarious personalities, nightly TV vs. frequent travel, retiree vs. second-career seeker, stock market vs. spiritual reader. Our breakup had rocked Kent to the core. He was about to commit to a marriage when most of his friends scorned the convention, and his role models had just chopped it all off at their clay ankles. He was anxious about how we'd handle the upcoming wedding.

He wrote that our superficial communication had taken its toll on him, too, but it had given him time to decide what he did and did not want from married life. He would work to keep common interests alive in his marriage and thought he might actually be a better husband from what he had learned from us. Above all, he loved us both.

The sweet relief I felt is difficult to describe. I read his letter over and over, grateful for the healing passage of time that brought insight and courage (or desperation?), that helped me stick my neck out vulnerably, and risk that helped us both to grow. Mostly, I felt thankful for the mother-son bond, mended.

~Virginia Fortner
Chicken Soup for the Mother and Son Soul

79

One Wish

H appy birthday, dear Rhea, happy birthday to you...." Silence penetrated the room.

"Make a wish," my mom said in a sweet, half-whisper. Her eyes glittered above the white cake. Was she crying? It tore at my heart that she still looked so sad, now that everything was over. I looked around the room filled with my friends, cousins, uncles and aunties, and then finally my mom and dad standing right next to me. I couldn't help but smile.

I wish...

The December morning breeze brushed my long, black hair as I stepped towards the large russet doors of Hagenberg High. It was my first day of school. There were students all over, trotting around with heavy backpacks, slamming lockers and running to catch up with old friends. I wondered who my friends would be. I was a bit anxious because I was starting school two-and-a-half months late.

In first period English, Mrs. Farley immediately put me on the spot.

"We have a new student." Heart pounding wildly in my chest, I managed a weak smile.

"So, what school are you from?" Mrs. Farley asked, tilting her head.

"A... school in the Philippines," I replied softly, my voice rising slightly as if I were asking if that was the right answer. Only two weeks ago, my parents and I migrated to America, hoping for a bright new life. At that awkward moment in class though, I silently prayed that I would snap out of the bad dream I was in and wake up to the sounds of the sea back home.

"How long ago did you move here?"

"Uh... two... two weeks ago." I had never stuttered before, but there I was, sounding as if I learned English only last week.

"Welcome to America... Ree-ya?"

"Rhea."

"Ra-ya." Mrs. Farley made herself a little note on the roll sheet. Why hadn't my parents just named me Ashley? Or Mary? All I wanted was to be normal. I wanted to be somebody.

At home, my parents spoke to me in Tagalog, and I didn't have any friends yet who spoke to me in English. But what was I worrying for anyway? In the Philippines, I had many friends, all the teachers knew me, and I had been getting excellent grades.

Walking through the locker-lined hallways, my dreams shattered like broken glass around me. I was alone, roaming the halls like a lost little kid. I unknowingly avoided interacting with anyone because I was afraid they'd laugh in my face. When my English was better, I decided, I would finally come up to people and maybe manage to say, "Whussup?"

Finally in gym class, a friendly brown face. She almost looked like me, only happier. Her name was Caroline. At lunchtime we found ourselves enjoying the bland cafeteria food. She wanted me to meet her friends. "Don't worry Ate Rhea," she assured me, calling me "sister" in Tagalog. "You'll fit right in."

And I did. It was as if some foreign soul entered my body and made me do things against my will. I found myself drinking beer, smoking cigarettes and skipping school. I didn't even like the taste of beer. The moment it touched my tongue I felt like I had to spit it back out. But I didn't. I couldn't afford to look bad and lose my new "friends." I began to miss at least one day of school a week to hang out with them. Then I missed two, three, even four days in a row.

But while I was out having fun with my "friends," inside I was full of conflict, unhappiness and regret. I stopped practicing my English sentences in front of the mirror and instead practiced, "I don't know why the school called, mom. It was probably a glitch in the system because I did not miss school today."

One day the school counselor called my mom at the house while I was already at school, and the truth came out. I pushed open the heavy doors of the counselor's stuffy office, dreading the situation I had to face. When my mom lifted her tearful eyes and saw me, I knew I failed her.

"Why, anak ko?" she cried. Why, my child? I stood there, swallowing the lump in my throat, but I had nothing to say. I wished she would yell at me, embarrass me or tell me what a bad kid I was. But she didn't. She cried like her only daughter was lost and had run away. My dad flashed me an accusing glare. I looked down—I couldn't bear the hurt in their eyes.

I was so depressed that night—I was sure I had lost my parents' trust and love. But when I was at my lowest point, my parents came through for me, and I realized just how much they loved me, no matter what. My mom was just worried... so worried in fact that she looked older, as if the years of raising me had drawn lines on her lovely face.

"I'm sorry, I'm sorry..." I cried. I wanted to say I was sorry for the failing grades, for all the arguments... for all the lies. But a feeble "I'm sorry" was all I could muster.

"It's okay, honey. Everything will be okay," my mom whispered. My dad ran his fingers tenderly through my hair. Nothing else mattered at that moment. Not the laughing jokes at school, not my friends... not even the familiar teenage longing to be somebody. I was somebody in my parents' eyes.

My parents didn't change how they viewed me, despite everything I had done. They still loved me as their daughter, and I welcomed the forgiveness, understanding and unconditional love in their warm embrace. And now, staring at the yellow candles on my birthday cake, I only have one wish: That someday, somehow, I can repay my parents for raising me the way they did and for loving me no matter what.

My mom's voice roused me from my thoughts. "Have you made your birthday wish yet, sweetie?"

I looked at her, and then at my dad, tears of love and gratitude brimming in my eyes. "Yes, mom."

Then I hugged them both very, very tightly.

~Rhea Liezl C. Florendo
Chicken Soup for the Teenage Soul: The Real Deal School

80

A Mother's Love

A t one time children made May Day baskets to celebrate spring and the rewards of anonymous giving. When I was in perhaps the third grade, our class embarked on such an adventure. For several days, we worked on creating paper baskets. We cut colorful strips of construction paper and wove them together, following a magic formula shared by our teacher, Miss Anderson. We cut and wove and glued. Then we decorated them with our crayons and more cutting and gluing. Finally, we stapled handles onto the tops so that we could hang our creations on the doors of unsuspecting recipients: surely our mothers.

We were finished right on time. Miss Anderson brought armloads of flowers for us to use in stuffing our prizes. Lilacs and tulips and all the colorful flowers of spring. We had to wait until the day was nearly over before we were allowed to choose the flowers that were just right for our baskets. I chose the biggest, most beautiful blossoms, allowing myself to be selfish for the sake of my mother. Then we fidgeted away what remained of our day, waiting for the clock to tick down the minutes to our release.

Finally, mercifully, the bell rang! We threw on our coats, gathered our homework and our lunch pails, tied on our scarves and then, carefully, we cradled our offerings of love and off we ran to our individual homes!

I was so excited! I ran as fast as I could down the hill, across the street, up the block, heading home. I paused at the corner of my house, behind the hydrangea, to catch my breath and savor the moment. Then I glanced down to admire my offering one last time before I hung it lovingly over the doorknob. Horrors!! Shock, dread and dismay! My flowers were gone! Apparently, bouncing out on my mad dash home, all that was left was a sad, smudged-up, wrinkled little paper-simulation of a basket. An empty vessel! I stood on the porch and burst into mournful sobbing tears.

By and by, my mom came to the door to discover the source of the anguish. As she let me in and helped me off with my coat and relieved me of my school things, I tried to relate my horrible dilemma. Through spasmodic agonies of hot teary mutterings, I tried to communicate the depth of my sorrow. As she listened, she wiped my brow with a cool damp cloth and stroked my hair with the other. Finally spent, I collapsed into her arms. Next, she did what I will never forget. She retrieved a paring knife from the kitchen and my poor little empty basket from the coffee table, and we went outside. Along the west side of the house there was a flowerbed. Many of our flowers had already bloomed. And, for more varieties, it was too soon for their showy displays. But we had blue bells! A whole big row of blue bells! She cut one and placed it in my basket. Then, she looked at me and handed me the knife (yes, she entrusted me with a SHARP KNIFE!) Then she retreated to the house to start dinner.

Slowly, as I cut the flowers and arranged them in my little paper basket, my enthusiasm began to return. I became intrigued with the little blue bells. Instead of a kaleidoscope of competing colors, my basket was in harmony with itself and nature. All a serene shade of blue. And, simultaneously, I was becoming serene. Cut and arrange, cut and arrange. Soon, once again, my gift was ready to be offered.

Now, a new emotion came over me. It dawned on me that the element of surprise, so essential to my deed, was now totally gone. Awkwardly, I placed the paper handle over the knob, knocked hesitantly, and made an embarrassed retreat. Mother slowly came and answered the door. Oh! She was SO surprised! Could it be that she had forgotten? Yes! She had totally forgotten! The May Day surprise worked! She had no idea, no idea whatsoever, who had left the lovely gift! I stepped out of my hiding place. "Well, Mary Kay!" she exclaimed! "Look what someone left on our porch! Aren't they lovely!" With her excitement all my trepidations vanished. I fairly danced across the yard and into her arms. We went into the house and found our loveliest vase, a fruit jar, and placed the surprise gift of love into fresh water to display on the kitchen table. My pride of giving barely allowed me to maintain my anonymity. Mother was so thrilled to have been remembered on May Day that she didn't even ponder the identity of her benefactor.

That was around forty-five years ago. The blue bells and little woven basket are long gone. But the love endures.

~Mary K. Schram
Chicken Soup for the Soul Celebrates Mothers

81

Donuts

My mother passed away when I was six, and my dad became the only parent for my siblings and me.

Every morning before Dad went to work, he frequented his favorite neighborhood donut shop. He always left with a bear claw pastry and a cup of coffee. Occasionally, Dad would take me fishing on weekends or to his work during the summer, and we always stopped at Dad's morning hangout, where he would share conversation and jokes with the employees and customers alike.

When we left, accompanying the bear claw in a small box was a chocolate-covered donut for me. Dad would help me up and into his truck. My ankles just cleared the seat as my shoes stayed clear of dirtying the upholstery. I sat close to Dad, just under his wing, feeling honored, safe and comfortable. My job during the journey was to hold Dad's coffee between my knees to keep it from spilling. Even though the cup had a lid, I took my job seriously and the coffee never did spill.

After catching my first rainbow trout, Dad was so proud, we stopped by the donut shop on our way home to show off the trophy. The applause they gave me felt good, but to see how proud Dad looked was the real gift.

As time passed and I grew older and bigger, the donut shop became a special place for us to celebrate my wins from swimming and downhill skiing competitions. Even if I didn't win or place, Dad would still take me to that familiar place of sharing. We always left with the little box holding one bear claw and one chocolate-covered donut.

Eventually, I grew up and left Dad's home. On my wedding day, before he walked me down the aisle, Dad handed me a small gift box. When I opened it, I found a small chocolate-covered donut. My heart melted quicker than the chocolate frosting would have in an oven. We held each other and cried. He told me how proud he was of me and that I would always be his little girl.

Dad continued going to his favorite donut shop long after I left. I only returned there once, with my first baby daughter. Dad glowed with pride, holding what seemed to be the best trophy yet to share with his friends.

In October 1989, Dad found out he had inoperable cancer. We lived an ocean apart, and our visits were few.

A year later, I was attacked and beaten, landing me in the hospital, undergoing three back surgeries for crushed vertebrae. Dad's cancer had progressed so much that his body was barely able to hold him up. Against doctor's orders, he flew to the hospital to comfort me. When he arrived, I was in traction and barely able to move. Dad's frail body lay over my chest, and with his skeletal arms he hugged me, saying if he could give me any gift in the world, he would trade places with me at that very moment.

As they prepared me for surgery, I watched Dad's eyes pour tears that would fill a dam. He asked the anesthesiologist to take care of his little girl. They wheeled me out of the room and into surgery. When I woke up, I was back in my room. Nobody was around. As I reached for the telephone to call Dad, I saw a paper plate holding a donut covered with chocolate.

I never saw Dad again. He'd become so weak he had to return home. The cancer took him just days after he left my bedside.

Now when I drive past donut shops, I can't help but smile, recalling those memories, my greatest trophy.

~Gail Eynon
Chicken Soup for the Father & Daughter Soul

82

Island Girl

earest Mom and Dad,

Having just given birth to little baby Ella Bleu, and now that I'm the mother of two amazing children, I've been thinking back to my own childhood and all the wonderful experiences I had. Lots of the lessons I learned back then make me smile, but it's the conclusion that I wanted to share with you.

There are so many memories: piling into the back of Auntie Kathy and Uncle Joe's pickup and heading for Jackass Ginger—what a paradise for a little girl—just twenty minutes from our house! We'd arrive at the storybook setting of ponds and waterfalls, and best of all, a whole mountain filled with enormous mudslides! Then came the very important job of finding just the right ti leaves to fit underneath all our backsides. Once chosen, we'd head up through the tropical growth to the top of the well-worn paths, grasp the stalks of the ti leaves firmly in front, position our okole (backsides) carefully and whoosh!—the ancient Hawaiian luge! I'll never forget the sheer joy of riding those ti leaves down those well-worn grooves, hitting the twists and turns at what seemed like hundreds of miles an hour, arriving at the bottom grinning and covered head to foot with mud and finally, splashing under the waterfall to get the top layer off, then running back up to do it all over again.

I remember catching crawfish for hours in the ponds (though we always threw them back!), and how much Chris and I loved diving for puka shells at 'Ehukai Beach. Do you remember the year puka shell jewelry became all the rage, and we were the proudest girls around, because we had made our own?!

Mom, I'll never forget you baking the greatest lemon meringue pies and oxtail stew and shoyu chicken, and Dad helping us build a tree fort in the banyan tree in front of our house.

I would sometimes hear that other kids felt their lives were boring or a drag, but you taught us purpose, you taught us love and responsibility. You also taught us to choose to live with laughter and joy, that life could be fun. How I loved riding down Ma'laekahana Beach on horseback, or walking along the bay looking for glass balls at dawn. I loved driving out to the "country" and always stopping along the way at that little local roadside stand to order the same thing—rice and gravy with two scoops of mac salad. No one does comfort food like they do at home!

You also gave us a sense of heritage. The Hawaiian part of our heritage means so much to me, and I'm so glad I got to study hula. I loved dancing with my ha'lau, my hula group on May Days and reveling in our wonderful culture. I loved staying at Nani's little house on the beach where Mom grew up, and feeling roots going back for generations.

'Ohana means family, and we sure had one of the best. All those Sunday picnics in Kapi'olani Park with Jimmy, Steph, Chula, Bob and all the cousins. And who could forget holidays at Uncle Sen's and Auntie Maudie's castle on Maui—a real live castle with turrets and a spiral staircase and a library wall of books that would really turn around if you took out the right book! And a dungeon filled with toys and a pool table. The Easter egg hunts there were great. But nothing beat their house at Halloween, when all the grown-ups would wear dark capes and hide in the darkened castle, and Chris and I would have to make it, running, from one end to the other, screaming and successfully surviving who knew what scary snares along the way!

You also nurtured my dreams—letting me perform all those gymnastic routines for your friends after dinners at the Aukai house. And the magic acts—tricks learned from a box. If the routines were a bit lame, no one ever let on! You were always so tolerant.

You also instilled in me a sense of wonder. In Hawai'i, there is magic everywhere you look, and the trick is never to see it through jaded eyes. I remember traveling with Nani through the Ko'olau Mountains, and every single trip, the incredulous look on her face. "Kelly, Chris, look! The colors! The sky! Have you ever seen the shower trees so vibrant? Do you see?" Even as she aged, having lived in this paradise forever, she never took it for granted.

Now that I've grown, I'm so glad that my own family feels so at home in the islands. I knew they would from the moment I brought "my new fiancé" home. Our whole family came over to the house to meet Johnny for the first time—aunties, uncles, cousins and of course, Nani. When Nani told Johnny what a wonderful dancer he was, he swept her off her feet, held her in his arms and led her through a waltz. She was beaming—and so was he. Nani even uncharacteristically allowed me to take her picture. It's something I treasure to this day.

Johnny has certainly come to love it here. When we get off the plane, the air, the sweet fragrance just envelops us. It's so beautiful and relaxing. Johnny says he's destimulated—he can't touch work. (In our lives, this is a wonderful thing!) When we're here, our days are shaped by long walks and by the pull of the ocean. Both Ella Bleu and Jett are water babies. Jett is in the ocean 24-7. Johnny and I practically have to pull him out of the waves just to get him to eat! Ella Bleu loves splashing in the water, too, even though she's still a baby. (She should—she was in the ocean often enough when she was inside me!)

I'm so sorry Nani is gone now; but I can't tell you what it means to me that Johnny and I now have our own house on "her" beach, four doors down from the house that was Nani's—the house that Mom grew up in.

And the other day, showing some friends around O'ahu, I heard myself saying, "Oh! Look at those shower trees! They're so beautiful and in full bloom. The yellow! The pink! Do you see?" I could almost feel Nani smile.

I guess what I want to say is that our family, and these islands, mean so much to us that we want to come back as often as we can. The reason for all of this, I realized, is that you are the best parents ever. You raised Chris and me with unlimited love, guidance and fun. When Johnny or Jett tell me I'm a wonderful mom, I know it's because of the two of you. Mahalo nui—there aren't enough words to tell you thanks. I love you with all my heart.

~Kelly Preston
Chicken Soup from the Soul of Hawai'i

Somebody Else's Children

Biology is the least of what makes someone a mother.
~Oprah Winfrey

I am often told what beautiful children I have. Many people even comment that they look like me. Pamela, my daughter, I am told has my blue eyes; my son James has my red hair. The truth of the matter is Pamela has her father's eyes, and James, well, his hair color was inherited from his mother—his biological mother. James and Pamela are my husband's children, and I am their stepmother.

Shortly after I met my husband, Carl, his children came for a visit. The visit was to last for two weeks, and then the children would return to their mother. When the two weeks came to an end, their mother called to say she had a job working in a resort community. She would be living in a room provided by the hotel where she worked. The children would have to stay with us until the end of the summer.

But by the end of summer the children's mother had joined the military, and again, they could not live with her. The military does not accept single parents who do not have somebody living with them to care for their children.

Although their mother's military career did not last through basic training, for a variety of reasons, she never returned for them. Carl and I realized the children were going to stay with us, permanently. I can't say I was thrilled by this realization. I had not wanted children of my own, and raising someone else's children did not appeal to me.

The kids weren't crazy about the idea either. Months earlier, when they had first arrived for their visit, I had been quickly made aware of their feelings toward me. "You're not my mommy! I want my mommy!" they had often shouted at me. After a couple of weeks or so of this, I grew to hate the word "mommy." Then, one day everything changed.

James, who was three years old at the time, had been in the middle of one of his "mommy tantrums" when he suddenly stopped screaming and looked up at me. His face was filled with terror and sadness. "I don't have a mommy no more," he calmly told me.

"James, you do have a mommy," I told him. He didn't believe me, looking at me as if I was crazy.

"No, I don't. Her went away." It was hard to defy his three-year-old logic.

"James, your mommy wants to be with you, but she can't right now. She has to work." When the children asked about their mommy, we had decided this was the best way to explain.

"I don't have no mommy." Fat tears began to roll down his cheeks, and I was beginning to panic. This child needed to know he had a mother, and I didn't know how to make him believe me. I knelt down to wipe the tears from his face.

"Are you my mommy?" he asked. At that moment, I wished that kids came with a manual. I needed answers—fast.

"I'm whatever you want me to be," I said and prayed I was saying the right thing. "No matter what that is. I'll be your friend, and I'll love you." At that moment, I realized that I meant every word I had just said. I did love this child.

James seemed to be satisfied with the explanation I had given him and as quickly as his questions began, they ended. James went outside to play, while I was left to figure out what had just happened.

With Pamela, it had been easier, once we'd come to an understanding. One day while watching television, Pamela looked up at the photographs hanging on the wall. She identified each person in the pictures and who they were to her. When she reached the one of her father, she told me "my daddy."

"Yes, that is Daddy," I told her. My response did not seem to satisfy her.

"My daddy!" Pamela said again, pointing to herself. I suddenly understood what she was trying to tell me.

"Pamela," I began, "I don't want to take your daddy away. I know you love him, but I love him, too. Maybe if you will let me, we can both love him. Can we share, if I promise never to take your daddy away from you?"

"Okay. We can share." Pamela was smiling at me. "We both love my daddy."

Carl and I married Christmas Day, the children standing next to us while we exchanged vows. They quickly began telling anyone who would listen, "We got married." I suppose "we" did. Then shortly after the wedding, James and I cleared the mommy issue up once and for all.

It was his fourth birthday, and I had taken the children to the grocery store to get a few things for the party. James, excited about his birthday, was talking a mile a minute. Exactly what he was talking about, I doubt I'll ever remember, because James had said one word that had immediately caught my attention, and I didn't hear anything else he had to say. When James realized what he had said he looked up at me. "I called you Mommy," he giggled.

"Yes, I know." I was trying to behave as if nothing out the ordinary had just happened.

"I'm sorry." James twisted his mouth a bit.

"You don't have to be sorry," I explained. "I don't mind if you call me Mommy."

"Are you my mommy, too?" Why couldn't he just once ask an easy question?

"I'm like a mommy, but you have your mother, and she is your mommy. As I told you before, I am whatever you want me to be."

"Okay, Mommy," James said, smiling at me. He was telling me what he wanted.

Recently, James came home from school with a drawing he'd done. "Look what I made for you, Mommy. It's our family. This one is you."

As I looked at the paper he handed me, I felt the tears begin to form in my eyes. He had drawn four red stick figures, holding hands and smiling. James was telling me in his own wonderful way that I am not raising someone else's children—I am raising my children.

~Trudy Bowler
Chicken Soup for the Mother's Soul 2

Voicing My Wish

So, like a forgotten fire,
a childhood memory can always flare up again within us.
~Gaston Bachelard

One evening, while writing the first draft of my book, I attended a writer's group for feedback. There were so many people there that discussion was limited to just a few stories. When I arrived home, my thirteen-year-old son shrugged off my disappointment and asked me to read the excerpt to him instead. So I settled into a chair and read a rough draft of my reflections on spending my allowance as a nine-year-old child.

The experience I wrote about was a metaphor for how choice and risk were handled by a child affected by alcoholism. Each week at Woolworth's lunch counter, I dreamed of someday ordering a banana split. Above the counter twirled an umbrella with colorful balloons hanging from each rib. The sign read: Pop a balloon and pay 1 to 63 cents!

Imagine paying one cent for a banana split! But I never had more than fifty cents, and I shuddered at the thought of Woolworth's calling my parents for more money if I got the sixty-three-cent balloon, so I kept my wish to myself. I never thought of asking anyone for more money. It seemed way too risky, and risks were dangerous in a world where alcohol made even benign requests subject to rage.

Frankie sat at my feet, listening intently, as I read the final sentences of the chapter.

Each week as I watched others select a balloon to pop, I fantasized about proudly taking my chance. But it never happened. Pink, blue, orange and yellow balloons called out to me, daring me, taunting me and, eventually, defeating me. Inevitably, when the waitress strolled up to my spot at the counter and smiled, indicating that she was ready to jot down my order, I mumbled, "I'll take a Coke, please," and then turned my back on the umbrella.

Frankie was silent. After thinking for a moment, he said, "So you never got the banana split?" A long discussion ensued, and eventually he seemed to understand that it was my own belief that limited me. I never took the chance of voicing my wish. It was a pattern that took years to break.

The next morning, Frankie casually announced that he was going out for a little while. When I asked where, he smiled and said, "I can't say."

My mother's instinct told me he wasn't up to anything dangerous, so I agreed. Frankie left, and I busied myself upstairs packing for an upcoming camping trip.

In a short time, I heard the back door open and then the sounds of chairs scraping, kitchen cabinets slamming and muffled conversation. Soon my nine-year-old daughter Sarah announced through giggles that I could come downstairs. "Eyes closed—except for stairs," she said.

Once downstairs, Sarah held my hand and helped me stumble my way through camping equipment and into the kitchen.

"Open your eyes!" Frankie and Sarah shouted in chorus.

I couldn't believe what I saw. The kitchen table was covered in a pile of balloons. Frankie walked up to me and handed me two quarters and a fork. His eyes were lit with anticipation. "Pop one!"

Tears welled up in my eyes. I stared at the balloons in disbelief and then jabbed one. When it popped, Frankie and Sarah laughed as I let out a loud whoop. A piece of paper fell out of the balloon. I opened it and recognized Frankie's awkward scrawl.

"What does it say?" he prompted.

"Fifty cents," I whispered, too choked up to speak loudly.

Frankie got business-like and asked, "Well, do you have fifty cents?"

I handed him the two quarters he'd given me moments earlier.

"Okay then!" Frankie walked over to the refrigerator, pulled out a homemade banana split on a Tupperware plate and handed it to me. Mounds of vanilla ice cream were covered in chocolate sauce, Cool Whip and peanuts. Underneath it all was a banana, split in two. I hugged Frankie hard and kissed the top of his head, still sweaty from all the effort. My eyes stung with tears as I held the banana split Frankie lovingly made to right an ancient wrong.

~Theresa Goggin-Roberts
Chicken Soup for the Mother and Son Soul

The Things You Never Did

Looking back across the years
To when I was a kid,
I find myself remembering
All the things you never did.

You never made me feel unloved
When I did something wrong,
You just helped me learn my lesson,
And you never stayed angry long.

You never went back on a promise,
You were never too tired to play,
No matter what else there was to be done
In the course of your busy day.

You never forgot to kiss me good night
As you tucked me snug in my bed,
You never rushed out in a hurry,
Without a story being read.

You never said no when I asked for a ride
To a practice, a friend's or the mall,
You never missed one softball game,
Even though I never once hit the ball!

You never acted like I was a failure
When I didn't do well on a test,
With your encouragement I came to learn
The importance of doing my best.

You never skimped on giving advice,
(Whether I listened or not!)
I swore I would never admit it,
But your words always helped a lot.

You never made fun of my trendy clothes
Or the makeup I put on all wrong,
You were there to wipe away countless tears
When I felt like I'd never belong.

You never turned one of my friends away,
Or for that matter, ten,
You never complained when the music got loud
Or they all spent the night in our den.

You never made fun of my boyfriends
Or made light of my tales of woe,
And if you felt relieved at each break-up,
You never once let it show.

Now that I'm a mother too,
I finally understand
How hard it can be to say the right thing
Or reach out with a tender hand.

I haven't said this near enough,
But Mom, I hope you know—
That all those things you never did
Are why I love you so.

~Lisa Inquagiato Benwitz
Chicken Soup for the Soul Celebrates Mothers

On, Being a Parent

It Takes a Village to Raise a Child

In spite of the six thousand manuals on child raising in the bookstores,
child raising is still a dark continent and no one really knows anything.
You just need a lot of support, love and luck — and, of course, courage.
~Bill Cosby

Swans Mate for Life

What I need to live has been given to me by the earth.
Why I need to live has been given to me by you.
~Author Unknown

The end of my sophomore year was approaching. Mom called me at the dorm one muggy evening during the last week of May. My summer break would be spent with Grandma and Grandpa, helping out around their farm. The arrangement made good sense to all the family. I wasn't fully convinced of that myself but figured it was just one summer. Next year would be my little brother's turn.

I packed my car after my last exam and said my goodbyes until the fall. My friends would keep until then. Most of them were going home for the summer anyway.

The farm was about a three-hour drive from school. My grandparents were both in their seventies, and I knew they really needed the help around the farm. Getting in the hay would be something Grandpa couldn't do by himself. He also needed help with repairs to the barns and a host of other chores.

I arrived late that afternoon. Grandma had fixed more food than the three of us could possibly eat. She doted over me entirely too much. I figured all the attention would taper off once she got used to having me around, but it didn't. Grandpa wanted to bring me up to date on literally everything. By the time I settled in for bed that night, I'd decided things would be okay. After all, it was just for one summer.

The next morning, Grandpa fixed breakfast for the two of us. He told me Grandma had tired herself out yesterday and was going to rest in bed a little longer. I made a mental note to myself to not ask her to do things for me while I was there. I was there to help, not be a burden.

Grandpa surprised me that morning. Once we were out of the house, he seemed more in his own element. The farm was his domain. Despite his age, there was confidence in the way he moved about the place. He didn't seem like the same person who had fallen asleep last night on the couch before the six o'clock news was finished. As we walked the pastures getting a close-up look at the livestock, Grandpa seemed to know each cow. And there were nearly two hundred of them!

We didn't do much real work that first day, but I gained a sense of appreciation for what Grandpa had done all those years before I was even born. He wasn't an educated man, but he had raised and provided for four children on this farm. I was impressed by that.

Weeks passed. By June we had already baled one cutting of hay and gotten it safely into the barn. I gradually settled into a routine of daily work with Grandpa. He had a mental schedule of things that needed doing, and we worked on part of it each day. In the evenings I usually read or talked with Grandma. She never grew tired of hearing about college or anything I was involved in. She told me stories about her childhood, family and the early years after she and Grandpa had married.

The last Saturday in June, Grandpa suggested we go fishing, since we were caught up on everything. The pond was in a low pasture near the woods. Years before, Grandpa had stocked it with fish. We drove the pickup to the pond that day, looking over the livestock as we went. We hadn't expected what we saw when we got to the pond that morning: One of the swans was dead. Grandpa had given the pair of swans to Grandma on their fiftieth anniversary.

"Why don't we see about buying another one," I suggested,

hoping the situation could somehow be righted. Grandpa thought for a few moments before answering. He finally said, "No... it's not that easy, Bruce. You see, swans mate for life." He raised his finger to point, holding the fishing pole in his other hand. "There's nothing we can do for the one that's left. He has to work it out for himself."

We caught enough fish that morning for lunch. On the way back to the house, Grandpa asked me not to tell Grandma about the swan. She didn't get down to the pond much anymore, and there was no sense in her knowing about it right away.

A few days later, we drove by the pond while doing our morning check on the cows. We found the other swan lying near the same spot we had found the first one. It, too, was dead.

The month of July started with me and Grandpa putting up a new stretch of fence. Then July 12th came. That was the day Grandma passed away. I'd overslept that morning. Grandpa had not knocked on my door, either. It was nearly eight o'clock by the time I could hurriedly dress myself and get down to the kitchen. I saw Dr. Morgan sitting at the kitchen table. He was a neighbor my grandparents' age, long since retired. He'd come to the house several times before on social calls. I immediately knew something was wrong. This morning, his tattered old black bag was by his feet, and my grandfather was obviously shaken.

Grandma had died suddenly that morning of a stroke. By the afternoon, my parents were there. The old house was soon crowded with relatives and Grandpa's friends.

The funeral was held the next day. Grandpa had insisted on having it as soon as possible. On the second day after the funeral, Grandpa announced at the breakfast table, "This is a working farm. We have a lot of things to do. The rest of you should get back to your own lives." Most of the family had already left, but this was Grandpa's way of telling the rest it was time for them to go home. My parents were the last to leave after lunch.

Grandpa was not a man who could outwardly express his grief around others, and we all worried about him. There had been talk of his giving up the farm. My parents thought he was too old to live out there alone. He wouldn't hear of it, though. I was proud of the way the old man had stood his ground.

The rest of the summer flowed by. We stayed busy working. I thought there was something different about Grandpa but couldn't quite put my finger on it. I started to wonder if he would be better off living with someone after all, but I knew he could not leave the farm.

September was nearing, and part of me did not want to leave. I thought of skipping the fall semester and staying around a few more months. When I mentioned it, Grandpa quickly told me that my place was back at college.

The day finally came for me to pack my car and leave. I shook his hand and chanced a hug. As I drove down the driveway, I saw him in the rearview mirror. He waved to me and then walked to the pasture gate to start the morning livestock check. That's how I like to remember him.

Mom called me at school on a blustery October day to tell me Grandpa had died. A neighbor had stopped by that morning for coffee and found him in the kitchen. He died of a stroke, same as Grandma. At that moment, I understood what he'd clumsily tried to explain to me about the swan on that morning we fished together by the pond.

~Hal Torrance
Chicken Soup for the College Soul

Love at First Sight

Just because somebody doesn't love you the way you want them to,
doesn't mean they don't love you with all they have.
~Author Unknown

Renee was four years old when we adopted her. Cute, tiny, talkative and strong-willed are all words I used to describe our new daughter. "Prodigal" was not in my vocabulary.

But as the years passed, it became apparent that Renee had an insurmountable problem bonding. Her first four years of neglect had changed her irreversibly. I often wished I could have held her as a baby, rocking and singing her lullabies. Certainly she would know how to return love if she had been given love as a baby.

I often wondered what she had looked like as an infant. I knew she was an extremely tiny preemie, but did she have her same dark hair and olive complexion? I had no way to know; there were no pictures.

Most of all, I wondered how to cope with her refusal of our love, year after year after year. As a teenager Renee rebelled against all authority and eventually left home, calling only when she got into desperate trouble. Finally, I could no longer handle the pain of her coming and going, and our communication ceased.

So it was a surprise when Renee contacted me one December. She was married. She had a baby girl. She wanted to come home. How could I say no? Yet, knowing my daughter and our painful, tumultuous history, how could I say yes? I couldn't bear having a grandchild ripped from my heart, too, when Renee, tired of her present situation, would move on—her pattern of many years.

I tried to resist the urge to see her and the baby, feeling it was best for all of us, but something stirred in my heart. Maybe it was the Christmas spirit. Maybe it was my desire to hold the new baby. Maybe I just wanted to see my daughter again. All I know is I found myself telling Renee that she and the baby could come for a visit.

On the day they were to arrive, I grew apprehensive. What if she doesn't come? That wouldn't be a shock by any stretch of the imagination. In fact, it was the norm for Renee. Then I wondered, What if she does come? What will I do? Will we have anything to talk about? Anything in common? The hours stretched by, and I kept myself busy with the multitudes of things I needed to do before Christmas.

Then the doorbell rang.

I opened the door. Renee stepped inside, clutching a wrapped bundle in her arms. She pulled the soft blanket away from the baby's face and placed Dyann into my arms. It was love at first sight. This tiny baby—my granddaughter—grabbed my heart, never to let it go. She had dark eyes and a head full of straight, black hair that begged for a lacy headband. In her features, I saw her mother's lips, her cheeks and her slight build, and instantly knew I was looking at an incredible likeness of the baby I was never able to hold—my daughter.

Dyann wiggled and made sweet gurgling sounds as I cuddled her to my heart, knowing she would be there forever, no matter what happened in the future.

In those first years of my granddaughter's life, I bonded with her in a special way, offering the security and unconditional love that she so desperately needed in her unstable environment. I bought frilly dresses and lacey tights, and I took hundreds of pictures and hours of video of this effervescent child.

Dyann is now thirteen years old, and I cherish her with all my heart. And though her mother eventually deserted her, Dyann still keeps a sweet spirit and visits us often. On those summer and holiday visits I often mistakenly call her by my daughter's name. Dyann giggles and asks, "Grandmother, why do you keep calling me Renee?" I tell her the words she longs to hear as she snuggles into my embrace. "Because you look just like your mother, and I'll love you forever."

~Laura Lawson
Chicken Soup for the Grandma's Soul

Alone Together: A Grandmother's Tale

I am a reflection of my past generations
and the essence of those following after me.
~Martha Kinney

We are alone. Blissfully alone. She is lying in my arms sleeping so soundly that I need constant reassurance that she is breathing.

Her mother has been sent out of the apartment, her father is at his office, and there is not a single distraction.

No TV blares.

No phones ring.

And for a blink of very precious, very remarkable time, it's just Hannah and her grandmother. What takes some getting used to is that I am that grandmother!

My oldest daughter, Jill, and her husband bestowed that title on me and, in the process, transformed me into a humbled, overwhelmed, slightly mad woman.

In the blur of those first days, Hannah and I were often in the same place at the same time, but never alone together. And I had such a longing for that experience that, I admit, I engineered my own opportunity by offering Jill an afternoon out at the precise moment when cabin fever was threatening to overcome her.

Jill succumbed. But not to the entire notion.

She would leave for an hour. Just an hour.

So, it came to pass that on a recent afternoon, I rushed my own daughter out the door to have the pleasure of her daughter's company.

Hannah is a perfect companion. She fits perfectly into the hollow where my shoulder meets my neck and nestles there, soft, pink and warm, without stirring. It has been too long since I've felt this blissful weight—and the perfect peace and contentment it brings.

For a full hour, Hannah asks nothing of me.

No searching questions about life or philosophy or morality or fairness.

No pouts about why I was too critical, not interested enough, too prying, too controlling.

Just an occasional, tiny little lurch or turn and, once, a small wail, just to remind me that, yes, she's really there.

The afternoon sunlight dances on the rug as Hannah and I dream our separate dreams. I marvel at her miniature perfection, kiss her tiny fingers, stroke her silky, sparse hair. I stare at a face that I am still trying to memorize, looking for clues to who this lovely little infant will turn out to be.

Will she have her mother's iron will? Her father's gentleness?

Will she be a sober, serious child or a laughing one, an eruption of joy?

Will she do to her mother what her mother did to me during that enchanting period twixt twelve and twenty, that era of slow torture called "coming of age"?

Hannah—tiny Hannah—already has a disposition, a natural bent, a network of traits that will someday define her. The notion that in my arms is a creature with all of us in her bone marrow still leaves me breathless, grateful, awed.

Suddenly, I feel tears streaming down my cheeks. Silly, sentimental, new-grandmother tears.

I realize, sitting with Hannah on a sunny afternoon in the middle of my life and the beginning of hers that she represents the last phase of this complicated, endless, precious process called parenting.

She is renewal and hope, and the person who makes waves of love swirl through rooms as she holds us, already, in her tiny grip.

And for all those reasons, my tears keep coming. I've barely composed myself when Jill rushes breathlessly into the apartment to ask, "So, how did it go?"

And I can't begin to tell her.

~Sally Friedman
Chicken Soup to Inspire a Woman's Soul

89

Same Agenda

Our grandchildren accept us for ourselves,
without rebuke or effort to change us,
as no one in our entire lives has ever done.
~Ruth Goode

We were sitting in the crowded auditorium waiting for the program to view the performance of our seven-year-old grandson, Tanner, in his school's annual Christmas pageant.

It was difficult to say who was more excited—the children or the audience. I looked around and spotted my son and his wife, with their four-month-old baby boy, and Tanner's maternal grandparents seated several rows behind us. We acknowledged each other with a smile and a wave.

Then I saw them—Tanner's "biological" paternal grandparents. My son and Tanner's mother had dated briefly as sixteen-year-olds, split up, then became reacquainted shortly after their high school graduation when Tanner was just six months old. Even though my daughter-in-law never married Tanner's father, his parents had fought for grandparents' rights and won. Tanner may call my son "Daddy," but Tanner is bound by court order to go every other weekend for visitation with the parents of his "biological" father.

We had taken Tanner into our hearts as our own, and we weren't very willing to share him.

This had always been a particular sore spot for me. We did not know them well, and I feared the worst when he went with them on their weekend. In retrospect, we should have viewed it as commendable that they were interested enough in Tanner to pay a lawyer and go through the complicated legal system.

So there we were, separated by a few rows of folding chairs. There were only a few instances where we had been thrown together, and each of these meetings had been uncomfortable. I saw the woman look at us, nudge her husband and whisper in his ear. He immediately looked back at us as well.

My ears were burning as if on fire. I attempted to remember why we were here — our common bond, a child who meant so much to us.

Shortly thereafter the program started, and for the next hour we were enthralled. Before we knew it, the lights were on, and we were gathering our things to leave. We followed the crowd into the hall and searched for our grandson.

We soon found him, and suddenly three sets of grandparents were thrown together, each waiting to take our turn in congratulating Tanner on a fine performance. We eyed each other and spoke a brief "hello."

Finally, it was our turn to hug Tanner and discuss his job well done. His eyes were shining brightly, and he was obviously proud to be the object of so much adoration.

I leaned down to hear what he was saying. "Grandma, I'm so lucky!" Tanner exclaimed, clapping his hands together.

"Because you did such a fine job?" I innocently asked.

"No, because all my favorite people are here! My Mom, Dad, little brother, and all my grandmas and grandpas are here together, just to see me!"

I looked up, stunned at his remark.

My eyes met those of the "other" grandma, and I could see she was feeling the same shame as I was. I was horrified at my thoughts and feelings over all these years.

What had given only me the right to love this little boy? They obviously loved him as much as we did, and he obviously loved each of us. They also no doubt had their own fears about us. How could we have been so blind?

As I looked around, I could see we were all ashamed of our previous feelings on this subject. We visited briefly, said our goodbyes and went our separate ways.

I've thought a lot about our encounter since that night, and I admit I feel that a weight has been lifted off my shoulders. I don't fear Tanner's weekend visits like I used to.

I discovered that we all have the same agenda—to love a little boy who truly belongs to all of us.

~Patricia Pinney
Chicken Soup for the Grandparent's Soul

90

Of Needs and Wants

Everyone needs to have access both to grandparents and grandchildren in order to be a full human being.
~Margaret Mead

I was thirteen. It was 1967, the year I started hanging around with a handful of kids a grade older than I was. The year I learned to smoke and swear. The year my baseball coach told us to take a lap around Cloverland Park and, halfway around, a bunch of us just quit and walked. The previous year, I had made the twelve- to thirteen-year-old all-star team as a rookie. This year, as a "veteran," I not only wouldn't make that team, I wouldn't care about not making it.

Around me, the revolutionary sixties swirled, ushering in an invitation to freedom, to experimentation, to breaking away from the shackles of authority and boldly going one's own way. I was poised for a summer of nothingness, the idea of irresponsibility happily wallowing in my teenage brain.

At which point I learned that my mother, in all her wisdom and foresight, had arranged for me to spend the next ten weeks mowing a fraternity lawn with her father—my grandfather—an ex-Army officer.

"Now, Bob," he said, looking at me and my tattered tennis shoes on the first day of work, "what you really need is a good pair of work boots."

What I really needed, I felt, was to be back in bed, not mowing a lawn the size of the Arlington National Cemetery in ninety-degree heat while being watched by Sgt. Perfectionist. This lawn job, you see, was not some here-and-gone task that could be completed whenever I had a spare couple of hours. This was a full-time job. I was expected to show up virtually every day at 8:00 A.M.—not to be confused with 8:05 A.M.—and complete a list of jobs that my grandfather had written on three-by-five index cards the previous night: mowing, edging, watering, weeding, fertilizing, sweeping, pruning, planting, trimming, painting, sanding, scraping, taping, chipping and clipping.

For this, I was to be paid $1.50 an hour.

Boots? Get real, I wanted to tell the old man. It was bad enough that I'd be spending my summer trying to scrape unwanted grass from sidewalk cracks, but did I have to wear a ball and chain in the process? Boots restricted. Boots were clumsy and time-consuming. But more importantly, in the mind of a thirteen-year-old boy who was knocking on the door of sixties coolness, boots simply looked—well, stupid.

From the beginning, it was clear my grandfather and I were separated by more than two generations; more like two universes. We saw the world differently. We saw this job differently. We saw proper work attire differently. He showed up each morning in a uniform that was part U.S. Army, part Home & Garden: well-pressed beige pants with cuffs, a long-sleeve shirt that often buttoned at the top, an Oregon State University (OSU) baseball hat and, of course, boots. Well-oiled boots.

At sixty-eight and retired, Benjamin Franklin Schumacher presided over the grounds of the hallowed Sigma Alpha Epsilon (SAE) fraternity at OSU, where he was treasurer and self-appointed "guardian of the grounds." To him, this was not a fraternity. It was a block-wide, split-level shrine. Nearly half a century before, he had been a member. After college, he had continued to be involved in the fraternity, becoming affectionately known around town as "Schu of '22." In the years after World War II, my father and uncle had been SAEs here, too.

"Now, Bob," he once said, "tell that daughter of mine [my mother] that she should invest in some good boots for you. Get the ones with the steel-shanked toes. They'll protect you." Then he laughed his hey-hey-hey laugh, a kind of laugh that sounded like a lawn mower that sputtered but wouldn't turn off, even when you hit the stop button.

Yeah, yeah, yeah.

Needless to say, he wasn't all that pleased when I over-fertilized the Harrison Street quadrant and the grass turned the color of beef Stroganoff—nor when, upon returning from a weekend camping trip, I realized I'd accidentally left the sprinklers on for three solid days and created Fraternity Lake. But as the days turned into weeks, I noticed something about the man: He never got mad at me.

"I'll tell ya, Bob, nobody's perfect," he said after the sprinkler incident. Instead of berating me for doing something wrong, he would simply take whatever tool I had used inappropriately and show me how to use it right.

"When you do a task," he'd say, "do it as well as you can, even if nobody is watching. When you try to fix something and find yourself stuck, improvise; use your imagination. When you take out a weed get the whole root or 'the guy' will be back in a few weeks."

He always talked about weeds as if they were human and part of some top-secret military operation, as if dandelions had generals who devised intricate plans to invade and capture, say, eastern arborvitae (a type of evergreen tree).

He led, I followed. While I did my work, he did his. Only when he did his work, it was with a certain enthusiasm that I couldn't muster, as if he found a deeper purpose to the job.

One day, when I was changing the southeast sprinklers, a guy in a car turned onto Harrison Street, rolled down his window, and said, "Hey, looks great."

After he drove on, I looked at the landscaping and realized the man was right. It did look great. I realized people actually noticed the job we were doing here. I realized, as deeply as a thirteen-year-old can realize, that I was somehow part of something. Something good.

Gradually, I began caring about how the SAE place looked almost as much as Schu did.

For three summers, I helped my grandfather take care of the SAE grounds, and I came to realize ours was the best-kept fraternity or sorority in Corvallis, probably in the entire world. But I learned more than how to keep grass green, sidewalks swept and trees trimmed. I learned that work was good and honorable. I learned that what something looked like on the outside said a lot about what it was like on the inside. I learned there is a right way and a wrong way to do something.

More than anything, I learned how to grow up. To care more and swear less. Just like the Gravenstein apple trees along 30th Street needed pruning so the fruit would be better, so did I need some pruning, Schu figured. And he was right.

In February of my sophomore year in high school, I was sitting in Mrs. Shaw's English class when an office worker brought me a pink-slip message. All eyes turned to me. My heart pounded. It read: "Your grandfather is waiting for you in the office."

The possibilities swirled in my mind as I hurried down the hall to the office. My father was dead. My mother was dead. But there stood my grandfather, and nobody was dead. "Bob," he said, "I've arranged to take you out of school for a short time."

"Why?" I asked.

"Let's just say it's a little birthday surprise," he said, laughing his hey-hey-hey laugh. We got into his gold Oldsmobile, which was roughly the size of the USS Teddy Roosevelt, and drove a mile down Buchanan Street to a one-stop shopping store. I slumped low so nobody would see me.

I couldn't figure out what was going on, but he led, so I followed him into the store. We stopped in the sporting goods section.

Some kids get cars on their sixteenth birthday. Some get stereos, ten-speed bikes, skis or skateboards. But my grandfather cared too much to give me something I wanted. Instead, he gave me something I needed.

"Now, Bob," he said, "take your pick." And he gestured toward a huge display of work boots. The kind with the steel-shanked toes.

~Bob Welch
Chicken Soup to Inspire the Body & Soul

91

Grandmother's Language of Love

I didn't speak Polish and she didn't speak English, but we both spoke love. That's how I remember my grandmother, especially during one holiday a long time ago. On a very cold Christmas Eve in a Polish neighborhood in Detroit, I opened the door to my grandmother's house and ran right into her arms.

"Busha," I called, smiling with my whole body, delighted to see her.

She hugged me, then placed her soft hands on both sides of my face. Cupping my cheeks gently, she spoke lovingly to me with her eyes. Grandmother's face was inches from mine, and I loved looking into her beautiful eighty-year-old eyes—those eyes that said so much.

Bending over, she kissed my forehead. I stretched my six-year-old arms around her aproned front and inhaled her Christmas-cookie-dough smell. She motioned for me to hurry to the dining room. I fumbled around, trying to unbutton my scratchy wool coat with the silky lining. Grandmother came and helped me, then watched me stuff my earmuffs into a pocket and my hand muff inside the sleeve in the "don't want to lose it" spot. I remember feeling so happy to have earmuffs and not to have to wear a babushka, that old-fashioned scarf. My grandmother pointed me to the bedroom, where I put my coat on the bed, already piled high with the coats of my cousins, aunts and uncles. She caressed my new dress, took my hand and smiled. She twirled me around to get a good look, then we snugly walked to the dining room to join my cousins. I hoped they too would notice my new dress and shoes. They, being mostly boys, didn't notice. They were all sitting on the floor, impatiently waiting for my grandmother's clocks to chime. I gave up my ladylike pose, shrugged, sat down and wiggled in next to the only cousin who had red hair just like mine. Grandmother left me and went to the kitchen to be with my aunts.

I tucked my black, shiny, patent-leather shoes with the pokey buckle underneath me and joined the wait. Grandmother collected all kinds of clocks. I never knew all the types, but there were a lot of them and I believed they were magical. The chiming would start with the deep sound of the tall grandfather clock with the gold pendulum, then the small sound of the table clock on the buffet, then the bong-bong-bong sound of the skinny grandfather clock. Sound from the other clocks moved all around the room. The chimes didn't sound the same, but they all spoke "clock." Each of them was very special and had come from Poland, just like my grandmother.

The last clocks finished chiming, signaling us to follow my parents, aunts, uncles and cousins to the kitchen, where they sat chattering and laughing in Polish. I looked around at some of the special things my grandmother did to create Christmas magic. She knew the language of love. There was the embroidered tablecloth draped across the table, the green smells-like-the-forest branches carefully placed all around the rooms, and the sound of the china clinking and the silverware clanging. My mom said, "All Grandmother's china and silverware came from Poland, too."

When the adults were ready, we began the oplatek ceremony. Grandmother motioned for me to stand up from the little bench I was sitting on and she gave me an oplatek, a wafer like the ones used in Communion in the Catholic Church. They had pictures of Baby Jesus, Blessed Mary and angels on them. My dad said that oplateks are known as the bread of love.

Grandmother started. Being the oldest, she held her oplatek out to me and I, the youngest, held mine out to her. She wished wonderful things for me. I know because my mother translated what she said. As Grandmother wished, she broke off my wafer—a small amount broken off for each wish. Then I wished my grandmother wonderful things. Again my mother translated, but this time in Polish. We put the broken wafers in our mouths and kissed. The ceremony continued throughout the family until my wafer was reduced to a crumb.

I loved all the kind things people wished. Sometimes it was all in Polish, sometimes in English and other times it was some kind of mixture of Polish and English. My aunt would wish, "Get good grades in school, stay healthy, and maybe you'll get that bike."

My mother would say, "Be good and we can talk about that puppy."

So many wonderful wishes—except for my brother's goofy wish, like, "I wish Trudy would get lots of toys for Christmas so she'll leave mine alone."

After the ceremony, my grandmother stacked my plate with dumplings filled with sauerkraut, cheese and potatoes called pierògies, cheese-filled crepes called nalesnikies, chruscikies—pastries sprinkled with powdered sugar—and apple strudel.

There were many other foods. Borscht, horseradish and sauerkraut were tasty, but I didn't eat everything—the pickled herring and mushrooms were yucky.

My grandmother sat at the head of the table on the other side of the room. She smiled at me with her eyes, and I smiled back with mine. She knew how to hug across a room. I felt loved all over, in Polish and in English.

Later, I fell asleep on a little bench off in the corner of the warm kitchen. Grandmother reached down and gently touched my face. As I woke and stood up she looked at me lovingly, reached over and hugged me. As we were getting ready to leave for church, she helped me with my coat and earmuffs. I left my hand muff on the bed. I didn't need it. She would keep me warm. I held her hand. She held my heart.

~Trudy Reeder
Chicken Soup for the Grandma's Soul

92

The Family in My Heart

The bond that links your true family is not one of blood,
but of respect and joy in each other's life.
Rarely do members of one family grow up under the same roof.
~Richard Bach

One Labor Day weekend I was enjoying a peaceful bike ride with my family on spectacular Mackinac Island in northern Michigan. My two-year-old son, Justin, was napping behind me when I heard, "Aunt Shelly, I have a question for you!" Without a second thought I replied, "I have an answer!" I was expecting six-year-old Tyler, who was trailing behind me on his two-wheeler, to ask if I was up for an ice cream cone and a break from the long ride. Boy, was I wrong.

"Why is it that Justin's my brother and you are his mom, but my mom is my mom and you and Justin live in a different house than me?"

Somehow, I managed to appease Tyler with a simple response and successfully change the subject. The complicated answer is that he and Justin share a father, something Tyler knew, but obviously didn't understand. I spent the rest of the ride reflecting on the amazing twist of events that had occurred in my life over the previous three years.

In April 2000, as a single mother, I gave birth to my beautiful son. Before my baby was born I had learned that Justin's father also had another son with a young woman named Heidi.

When Justin was eight months old and a full two months had passed without a word from his father, I decided to contact Heidi. We had known each other from a distance, and although we had had some minor confrontations in the past, it didn't feel awkward to connect with her, as I knew she was the one person who could understand what I was feeling. I was new at being a single mother and valued her experience. We began talking and e-mailing every day, nonstop. The funny thing is, we found out we were alike in so many ways!

Shortly after our initial conversation we decided to bite the bullet and meet with the boys. I'll never forget that night. Tyler, who was four at the time, presented me with a rose, and Heidi had a cake decorated that said, "I love you, Justin." Everything was perfect. By the end of the evening, Justin had taken his first steps toward Heidi. With those first steps, we both knew it was the beginning of something very special for all of us.

From that evening on, Heidi and I have become practically inseparable. Even today, it truly feels like a miracle. We are now in our fourth year of sharing the ups and downs of parenting. Where others might let jealousy, anger and resentment get in the way, we have chosen a decidedly different path. We are single mothers joined together by fate, and we have chosen to see this as a great blessing.

Tyler, now eight, loves the fact that he has another aunt, and in turn, I have fallen head over heels for him. Heidi is known as Aunt "Didi" to my rambunctious, now four-year-old Justin, and the two brothers horse around and get into all kinds of mischief, as brothers typically do. When I look at the two of them, Tyler and Justin side by side, both with caramel-colored skin, curly hair and soulful brown eyes—and both with dimples so deep you could sink quarters into them—I know that we were meant to become a family. Heidi and I have vowed to raise our two children together as much as possible. It really is a testament to the love we both share for our children and for each other.

As for me, I've learned two very important lessons: first, your "family" is who you choose to hold in your heart, not necessarily those who share your bloodlines. Not only did I gain a nephew in Tyler and a sister in Heidi, but also Heidi's mother, Nancy, has "adopted" me as her own and Justin as her grandson. Heidi's two sisters, Monika and Lisa, have embraced us as well. I am very blessed to have become a part of such a wonderful family.

The second very important lesson I've learned is to never tell Tyler that I have the answer before I know the question. I'll let Heidi answer the tough ones.

~Michelle Lawson
Chicken Soup for the Single Parent's Soul

93

Three Times the Lover

Anyone can catch your eye,
but it takes someone special to catch your heart.
~Author Unknown

On Valentine's Day, Tom asked me to have dinner with him. He insisted that my two daughters, ages nine and eleven, be at home when he picked me up.

When he arrived, he asked us to sit on the couch. From his pocket, he took three small boxes. One contained a diamond engagement ring. Each of the other two contained a heart-shaped ring with a tiny diamond in the center.

He proposed to all three of us and, needless to say, I didn't have a chance.

The four of us have been married now for almost thirty years.

~Sherry Huxtable
Chicken Soup for the Romantic Soul

On, Being a Parent

No Place I'd Rather Be

Hem your blessings with thankfulness so they don't unravel.
~Author Unknown

94

Alaska Time

*My prayer is that Alaska will not lose the heart-nourishing
friendliness of her youth — that her people will always care for one another...
and that her great wild places will remain great and wild and free.*
~Margaret Murie

My husband Greg worked the Bristol Bay salmon season
every summer. For years Greg had urged me to join him
with the kids, and when our youngest turned three, I
said, "Yes."

I imagined six weeks in a cozy cabin with a lush landscape outside our door, the perfect escape from the tedious deadlines, duties
and responsibilities that had become our life. The kids and I watched
the movie The Wilderness Family and saw a happy clan sawing logs
and saving a baby cougar. Adventure beckoned! With anticipation
we flew to King Salmon, Alaska.

Greg arrived at the airport in a battered truck. Wedged together
in the cab, we bounced down a highway of potholes. The tundra
stretched before us, flat and peculiar, the sky a vault of scattered
clouds. There were no discernible features to orient ourselves. No
rise of peaks or spine of hills to navigate with. My eyes slid uninterrupted to the wide horizon. I drew a breath and looked away.

We pulled into a rutted drive and lurched to a stop before a
structure that vaguely resembled a trailer.

"Here it is!" Greg said. "Home! I have to get back to the boat. I'll
see you in the morning."

He gave big hugs of encouragement and left us standing in the dust with our bags as we watched him drive off.

Home was a truck container. Someone had cut windows from the sides, called it a trailer and set it upon a scraped-off patch of tundra. We stepped gingerly on the plastic fish box that comprised the threshold to the door.

"This can't be it!" our nine-year-old daughter cried. "I could never, ever live here!"

It smelled like a swamp on a warm day. Greasy towels hung on a rack. The faded sofa was missing a leg. The water ran tea-colored from the faucet, and to our horror we discovered a strange trumpet-shaped lichen growing from the carpet of the bedroom. Home sweet home!

I rolled up my sleeves and went to work while the kids fled outdoors to dig rivers and channels in the dirt that was our yard.

The days unfolded endlessly; there was no darkness at this latitude. The light did strange things to our appetites, to our sleeping habits. Bedtime became a battle when the sun called my children out to play at midnight. Squalls blew in and, to the kids' delight, filled their river world with currents of water joining mud, skin, clothing and children in a happy marriage of mess. The mosquitoes drove us like cattle from tundra to trailer to car. In the evenings bears nosed around the margins of the trailer searching for garbage. We had twenty hours of available light to see what had become of my Wilderness Family.

One sun-filled night I hung clothes on a line strung between scrub alders, then sat down to watch the kids play baseball with neighboring children. They moved the bases around in the dirt at will. The three-year-old was allowed ten strikes. One girl declared that older boys could hit only within the base lines or they were out. She glanced over at me.

"You wanna play?" she asked.

I shrugged, thinking there was something else I should do.

"She's a good player!" my son cried.

I smiled. I hadn't played since high school, but I rose to the plate.

"Batter up!" the girls shouted.

I hefted the bat... pitch... and swung. A home run deep into the tundra.

I was in league with the big boys now. We played for hours under that midnight sun, laughing and shrieking, changing rules, shaking the dust from our bodies. Suddenly, I was a girl again, unfettered and breathless with the crazy fun of it all.

The next morning, I changed the rules. Our days would be governed by the urges and appetites of our bodies, not the clock. We began to rise at whatever time we woke, eat when we were hungry and sleep when we were tired, even if that meant dinner at ten and bedtime at two. Problems that seemed overwhelming a few days earlier suddenly fell away, and the weeks stretched long, empty of duties. We called it Alaska Time.

With Alaska Time I became a willing ear for listening to worries and dreams. My arms were idle for holding, for pouring plaster in bear tracks, for throwing a baseball. Once again, my newly opened eyes could see the treasures available to children: Mud. Boundless light. Midnight drives to watch caribou graze and eagles wheel in the sky.

Alaska Time is watching a radiant sunset at home and naming the stars that bloom in the heavens. Alaska Time is when the rules change, the dishes wait, the phone goes unanswered.

Alaska Time is in the words, "Yes, I want to play!"

~Nancy Blakey
Chicken Soup for the Nature Lover's Soul

Ricochet

Love is nothing in tennis, but in life it's everything.
~Author Unknown

"Don't worry, Mom. If you're at net and someone hits the ball at you, just hold up your racquet."

"Are you sure about this?"

David had started playing tennis when we moved to a new state and Neil, the only other eleven-year-old boy on our block, played tennis. When you're entering a new middle school in the fall, don't know a soul, love sports and want a friend, learning to play the same game seems incredibly important.

"I need," David had said, "to at least know how to hold the racquet and serve."

My tennis career began and ended in my sophomore year in college. The only instruction I recalled was something about shaking hands with your racquet and love — as a score, or lack thereof.

The town tennis courts and Little League field were only five minutes away. Since neither of us owned tennis racquets and I didn't want to invest a lot of money, I responded quickly to a two-for-one sale ad. It became apparent, after a morning at the court, that David's great athletic skills allowed him to volley the ball over the net several times before missing a shot. My own shots lacked finesse, positioning or anything approaching power.

David and Neil became fast friends, and within a week I took David to Marshalls department store, bought him two white polo shirts, a pair of tennis sneakers and several cans of vacuum-packed yellow tennis balls.

One day, David announced that Neil's mother had signed him up for tennis lessons. So David signed up, too. Every morning for two weeks, David and Neil used a bungee cord to secure a racquet, a can of balls and a Thermos to their bike holders, and they rode off for lessons.

About that time, I noticed a local newspaper ad: *Wanted: someone who is a beginner to play tennis—Barbara and a phone number.* Because I also didn't know anyone in my new town and my appetite for tennis blossomed after playing with David, I called Barbara, and we met to play.

Over the next five years, David's love of tennis increased, and he took more lessons, played on the high school team, entered the town tennis tournament, won in his division and grew to over six feet tall. My own tennis improved with lessons, but not being athletically inclined, I never really acquired a decent backhand shot. My lob-like serves landed within the appropriate box, at best.

David's friend Matt played on the high school team, and his mother belonged to a tennis club, hit a wicked serve, played four or five times a week, and towered over me. One day David came home and announced that Mrs. Armsley's tennis club was sponsoring a mother-son doubles tournament.

"Mom," said David, who excelled in tennis and the art of debating, "how can we go wrong? The money goes to a charity that helps kids." Since I taught in a school for children with disabilities, David knew what tack to take.

"Suppose I make a donation?" I offered.

"But," countered David, "how often do we get an opportunity like this? You were the one who first showed me how to shake hands with a racquet and keep score. Besides," he added, "it's just for fun, not really competitive."

He convinced me I could handle the net and fast approaching balls. We went to the town court and practiced against Barbara and another friend. David gave me some pointers and a lot of one-liners. "Don't worry. Hold up your racquet like this, and the ball will simply ricochet back across the net. Remember, it's for charity. No one is going to play for blood when you're at the net."

The day of the tournament, we both wore whites. By that time, David owned a metal racquet with taut strings, and I owned one with a large head. The tournament director divided the boys into age-appropriate groups.

"There are eight teams in my age bracket. If we survive three matches, we'll be in the finals."

"You don't really expect to win, do you?"

David had been right: No one went after the mothers when they played net. The boys quickly assessed if the mother played well. If so, they went all out. If not, they saved the spin and velocity for her son.

We survived three matches. David knew how to move the ball from side-to-side, and I enjoyed the fun of playing with him. The championship game in our age group came down to a match between us and Mrs. Armsley and Matt.

"David, do you realize that the top of my head is even with the second button on her polo shirt?"

All the rules evaporated when we played them. When I stood at the net, it felt like target practice.

"Mom," said David, "I can take the net the entire time. You just pull back, and I'll go to the net."

We did just that. Moving back and forth like a well-oiled machine. The score was tied.

Then a yellow ball, like an errant rocket, came whizzing at me. There wasn't time for David to get to the net, and I remembered, "Hold up your racquet like this, and the ball will simply ricochet back across the net." More for protection than game, I held up my racquet; the ball hit the strings with a resounding ping and rebounded across the net like an unexpected intruder.

I walked away with the prize wristbands, balls and a small trophy—and my son's amazed admiration.

~Linda Watskin
Chicken Soup for the Mother and Son Soul

Falling in Love with Molly

Sometimes being a brother is even better than being a superhero.
~Marc Brown

My son Joe knew about Molly even before I did.

He was fourteen years old and had just walked through the open door of the bathroom, where I was standing at the sink. "Just need to grab my hair gel," he said, reaching up to the shelf above my head. I was startled and turned slightly away from him. But it was too late. He had already noticed that I was holding something in my hand.

"What's that?" he asked.

For a moment, I didn't answer him. Just mumble something, I said to myself. He doesn't listen to most of what you say anyway. But there was something about the depth of his voice behind me, something about the fact that it was coming from a good five inches above me, that made me turn and tell him the truth.

"It's a pregnancy test," I said, looking down at the little white wand. "I... I don't really think I'm... you know... it's just a possibility... a remote possibility... your Dad said I should try one of these kits...."

I looked up at Joe as my voice trailed off. His face had gone white. He didn't look so grown up after all.

"How do you know if it's... positive?" he asked.

"Well," I said, reaching for the instruction leaflet, "it says here that a little red line would appear."

Just then, the phone rang. I had been waiting to hear from my husband all day—I didn't want to miss his call. "Hold this for a minute," I said, handing the wand to Joe. "Don't tip it. I'll be right back."

It wasn't my husband. "Okay," I said, heading back into the bathroom. "Sorry about all this, Joe, the time's up anyway. I'll just throw that thing in the—" I stopped. The wand was lying in the sink. Joe was staring down at it. Slowly, he raised his head, turned, and looked straight at me.

"There's a line," he said. "A little red line." His eyes narrowed. "A gross, disgusting, little... red... line."

And then he walked past me, out of the bathroom, down the stairs, out the side door, and as much as was possible for the next nine months, out of our lives.

By the time our daughter Molly was due to be born, I had grown accustomed to my elder son's embarrassment and animosity. I had grown accustomed to a lot of things, not the least of which was having an unexpected child at the age of thirty-nine, long after we thought our family of two boys was complete. My husband, to his eternal credit, was delighted. Our younger son, eleven-year-old Shea, pored over the baby books with me, keenly following the week-by-week progress of his little sister's in utero development. Throughout it all, Joe rarely spoke to me, except to say, "You don't have to come to my school," and—after a marathon baby-naming conference—"Molly is Ron's dog's name."

When Molly finally arrived—tiny, quiet and perfect—six family arms were there to draw her close. But Joe's remained tightly crossed over his chest, on the far side of the hospital room. It was an effort to step outside my bliss, to call to him, to beckon him into our circle of adoration. Shaking his head just slightly, he backed up farther into the corridor. I could see him standing there, arms still folded, staring straight ahead.

Joe arranged to be at a friend's cottage when Molly and I came home from the hospital. He was still gone ten days later when I took our daughter for her first check-up. He arrived home just as I was coming back, tears streaming down my face. "The doctor thinks she might have a hearing problem," I sobbed. "She's too quiet, she's not responding like she should. We have to have her tested."

As my husband soothed me, downplaying my worry, I noticed that Joe had stopped beside the baby, sound asleep in her car seat. He reached out to her, shifting her slightly away from a bump in the carpet. "She's okay," he said, looking down at her. "There's nothing wrong with her. She's just little."

He looked up at us. I stopped crying. I held my breath. "I'm going in-line skating," he said. "I'll put my stuff away when I get back."

Three months later, as I walked the floor at 4:00 A.M. with a fretful, inconsolable (and otherwise perfectly healthy) baby in my arms, I stumbled into Joe's room and nudged him awake. "Joe, could you take her? Just for a few minutes? I can't settle her down, Dad's at work, I just really need a break."

Saying nothing, but throwing off his covers, Joe took his little sister from me. He laid her briefly on his bed, tightly rewrapping her blanket. Putting her over his shoulder, he patted her back, spoke to her softly, slowly walked her up and down the hall outside his room. It wasn't his first night with Molly, and it wouldn't be his last.

In the months before Molly was born, a lot of people told us about the pleasures of a baby who comes late. "A do-it-yourself grandchild," said one old gentleman. "We had one of those, the best thing that ever happened to us." "A change-of-life child," said another. "What a blessing." "A caboose baby," said an aunt. "They're always the sweetest." They assured us that we would cherish this unexpected detour in our lives.

They were right. But they didn't mention the bonus. They didn't tell us about the sight of a baby stroller parked perilously close to a backyard basketball net, a mop-haired one-year-old shrieking in delight as lanky teenagers tore back and forth in front of her. They didn't talk about a chubby toddler, dressed in a size-large hockey jersey, scooping up the puck that always slid directly into her over-sized glove. They didn't describe a two-year-old, sitting high atop a stack of cushions at the kitchen table, "helping" earnestly with grade-eleven math. Or the four-year-old wrapped tightly around the legs of the smiling graduate, in each and every photo.

No one ever predicted the first family visit to a college dorm, where sixteen drawings of the same two stick figures competed on the wall with air-brushed, leggy calendar girls. They didn't portray newly muscled arms holding up a struggling swimmer, a shaky skater, a first-time skier. They failed to account for an impish little face hanging out the window of a rusty, rumbling car, or prepare me to be bypassed on the platform for tiny outstretched arms. Certainly, no one ever warned me that I would have to will my heart to stay intact one Christmas Eve, when a seven-year-old with a brother on the other side of the world asked if she could trade all the presents under the tree for "our Joey at the door."

No one ever told me about the joy of seeing your own little girl perched on the shoulders of your own grown-up son, her arms reaching down toward him, his grinning, handsome face turned up toward her laughter. They couldn't tell me. Because they couldn't describe it.

~Liz Mayer
Chicken Soup for the Sister's Soul

97

Sonar

High up in an oak tree, the five hairless, newborn squirrels nursed, curled tightly against their mother for warmth. Using her bushy tail like a blanket, she draped it over her latest family. When the time came for her to feed, she covered the babies with the leaves and bits of bark that made up her nest. Eyes still tightly closed, barely two ounces at birth, the little ones were completely helpless.

By the time the squirrels were three weeks old, soft, distinctive gray fur covered their bodies. Somewhere between five and six weeks of age, their eyes opened, giving them their first glimpse of their new world. Already agile and swift, with sharp curved nails, they played tag up and down the oak tree's trunk, experimenting with jumps from branch to swaying branch. All but one.

At eight weeks, four of the young were foraging for acorns, hickory nuts, pinecones and other seeds. The littlest one was still eating from the stored supplies.

By the time they were four months old, the babies moved out of the nest, and mother squirrel was having her second litter of the year.

The smallest female from the first litter half crawled and fell out of the oak tree onto the forest floor. Her siblings had already scattered. She could hear her mother chattering nearby. Carefully, nose sniffing, whiskers twitching, she groped her way toward the fading voice. Her hunched, shuffling gait prevented quick movement. Turning her head side to side, she listened intently. By now, her family had departed, leaving her behind. It was survival of the fittest in the woods.

Soft paws scraped over rocks and roots as the squirrel hauled herself over the obstacles. Her tail twitched with anxiety as she shrilly shrieked her distress. Nothing answered her calls for help. Heart pounding rapidly in her narrow chest, the squirrel continued her journey.

Within a short time, the little female panted her panic. Her body trembled with exhaustion. Curling into a tight ball, tail wrapped around and over herself, she waited.

Suddenly, a strange vibration rumbled the forest floor. Twigs crackled. Closer. Closer. The cadence pulsated throughout her body. Unfamiliar sounds made the squirrel tremble.

"Mom!" Johnny's keen eyesight had spotted the frightened baby. As the son of a licensed wildlife rehabilitator, he had helped raise many wild babies and knew that one lying so still on the ground was unusual. With gentle hands, he scooped the gray ball of fur off the forest floor.

"What is it?" I walked up alongside my son to find him petting the squirrel baby. The little one snuggled into the warmth of his cupped hands, relaxing as a finger delicately stroked her. His soothing voice calmed her as it murmured assurances of safety and comfort.

"Look, Mom," Johnny held her out for my inspection. Dark slits with tiny eyelashes showed where her eyes should have been. "She has no eyes. She's blind. I guess this one's a keeper, huh?"

Carefully cradling his precious find, Johnny and I took the little girl home. It was love, with or without first sight.

We set up a cage, and Johnny christened the newest arrival to our household "Sonar."

"Sonar. Sonar Squirrel, because of how well she hears," he explained.

Soon water, peanut butter, sunflower seeds and corn on the cob satisfied her thirst and hunger. Tentatively, she explored the safe confinement, a miniature forest complete with branches, stones and leaves. She discovered a bed of something soft and warm. Satiated and content, she cuddled into her new nest.

The blind squirrel had a name, a home and Johnny.

Sonar adored Johnny above the rest of the family. She eagerly responded to his voice, dashing into his arms as soon as he opened her cage door. "You're my squirrel-girl," he'd whisper as she would nibble his ears and run her soft paws through his hair.

Each morning, Sonar would search Johnny's shirt pocket, squeaking in delight when she discovered the treat he'd carefully hidden there. After school, she'd curl around his neck as he did his homework. He'd tenderly brush her tail out of his eyes so he could see his books. Occasionally, Sonar ventured down his arm to help him, nibbling at his pencil or papers.

Evenings would find her sleeping contentedly on his chest while Johnny watched TV in the living room, stroking her soft fur. Before heading off to his own bed, he'd carefully tuck Sonar into her nest, wishing her sweet dreams.

Two years and one day after Johnny found her, Sonar passed away nestled in my son's arms. Wrapping his little friend in his shirt, Johnny gently held Sonar one last time before burying her among our other departed critters.

At sixteen, my son was not too old to cry.

~Linda Mihatov
Chicken Soup for the Nature Lover's Soul

98

Sugarplums

'Twas the night before Christmas and all
    through the street
Not a creature was sleeping, my body was beat;
The stockings were taped to the chimney
    quite snug,
In hopes that my kids wouldn't give them a tug;

My daughter was jumping on top of my bed,
While visions of broken things
    danced in my head;
And Mamma getting ready, and I with a comb,
Were almost prepared to drive
    to my folks' home,

When somewhere downstairs there arose
    such a clatter,
I sprang from my room to see
    what was the matter.
Away to the stairs I flew like an ace,
Tripped over the Legos and fell on my face.

The bruise on my head and my
    pain-swelling side,
Gave a luster of midnight to objects inside,
When, what to my crestfallen eyes
    should appear,
But my rambunctious son,
    with a face full of tears,

With a little hors d'oeuvre plate,
    so empty and bare,
I knew in a moment he dropped it downstairs.
More rapid than squirrels my anger it came,
and I whistled, and shouted and
    called them by name;
"You dropped fruit! Rocky road! The truffles!
    And sweets!
The tea cakes! The crackers!
    What will Uncle Dutch eat?!
To the top of the stairs!
    To the rooms down the hall!
Now sweep it up! Sweep it up! Sweep it up, all!"

As mad dogs that before the wild tornado fly,
When they meet with their parent-folk,
    fit to be tied,
So out to the auto my family we flew,
With an armful of gifts
    and the damaged treats, too.

And then, in a flurry, we arrived at my folks'
Their puppy was barking,
    my kids gave it pokes

As I fell in a chair and was spinning around,
Down the hallway my mom and dad came
    with a bound.

Mom was dressed all in red,
    from her feet to her yoke,
And her clothes were all blemished with Jell-O
    and smoke;
A trayful of food she had spilled on her lace,
And she looked like a toddler
    just feeding her face.

My dad—how he hugged us! His laughing
    how jolly!
My kids jumped on his back, and called him
    a trolley!
My tight little mouth was drawn up like a bow,
And I shot words off my lips like darts at a foe;

"Children be careful, Papa's back is quite bad!
If he throws a spinal disk,
    you'll make Grandma mad!"
The plates were set and the dinner was ready
My son gave the prayer that included his teddy,

The room was jammed with people, tables
    and chairs,
My nephew threw stuffing into his dad's hairs;
A flash of Gram's eyes and a shake of her head,
Soon gave him to know he had something to
    dread;

We spoke many words and went straight to
        our meals,
And ate all the fixings despite how we'd feel,
Then sometime around twelve
        we expressed our last joys,
And returned back home to assemble the toys.

We placed the last gifts, and I gave a tired yawn,
I made a silent prayer, to sleep hopefully
        past dawn.
But my son did exclaim,
        as I walked past his door,
"Happy Christmas, dear Dad, I'll wake you
        'round four."

~Ken Swarner
Chicken Soup for the Soul Christmas Treasury

A Mother's Day Review

Ah, Mother's Day. Used to be it was a day to sit back and relax. Who could ask for more than a wake-up call of toast heaped with chunky peanut butter and dripping with jam, coffee lukewarm, half sugar, half cream? I loved being able to take it easy for at least that one holiday.

But a recent conversation with a neighbor gave me a case of the guilts. "How can you let such a great opportunity for self-improvement pass you by?" she chided. "Now's the time to examine how you're doing in your role as a mother. Think about all you've learned that you never read in books! Think about all you've learned about yourself. Think about what it means to be a real mother!"

As much as I try to avoid getting too philosophical while piecing together Mr. Potato Head or trying to pull gum out of someone's socks, I decided to give the self-evaluation stuff a try. I started with thinking about the early days.

Amazingly enough, I realized I did know something I'd never read in a book—all babies are born with an innate sense that urges them to cry and demand immediate attention if their mother should attempt any of the following: a warm meal, a long-distance phone call, a good book, a hot bath or sex. My kids are older now, and about the only changes I've noticed are that food can be good cold, magazines are quicker to read than books and cold showers diminish the desire for sex.

Then I thought of something else I learned. It's perfectly normal for kids to get sick when the doctor's office is closed. This habit used to send me into a panic, trying to determine what rare disease my child had and if I should call the doctor's service or just head straight for the hospital. I'm smarter now. My first call is to a friend who has five kids, for her opinion.

I've learned some unpublished facts about nutrition, too. I know a two-year-old can survive on yogurt, Cheerios and raisins for extended periods of time; that at first, raisins come out looking pretty much like they did going in, and that anything covered in ketchup is gourmet to kids. I also know that peanut butter, besides being almost impossible to clean off a high chair, is a great hair conditioner.

Further thought made me realize that I have learned some things about myself. I've learned that if I could find someone who would pay me a nickel for every time I thought, "My kids will never..." and they did, I'd be a millionaire. And even though my wonderful offspring sometimes do not react at all when I'm speaking, I do still speak English and can be heard and understood by other people in the room. In addition, I've discovered that if I don't have some time to myself, I tend to get ugly. I've learned that for me to be a good (most of the time) and sane (some of the time) mother, I need a good friend who shares the same ideas and ideals of motherhood. I've also learned that if every once in a while I think how peaceful it would be without my kids, it doesn't mean I don't love them—it simply means I need a break.

And I do know what it means to be a real mother! It means that on our very bad days, my method of survival relies on reciting, "This, too, shall pass" and that on most days, I know that this, too, shall pass—too quickly.

Bring on the toast!

~Paula (Bachleda) Koskey
A 5th Portion of Chicken Soup for the Soul

Goose Island

My children call it Goose Island, although "island" is an obvious exaggeration. A little rock pile with a half-dozen scraggly shrubs, it doesn't even appear on most charts. At high water it measures less than six feet by twenty.

The goose part is accurate, though. Every spring, for the past fifteen years, a pair of Canada geese has chosen the rock pile for its nesting site. But not just any spot on Goose Island will do. Each year they form their nest in exactly the same location, a little indentation between a couple of flat rocks on the highest point above the water line.

Mother Goose gathers small twigs and vegetation to frame the nest, then plucks down from her breast to create a soft lining. Two flowering dogwoods provide a little camouflage, and by maintaining her perfectly immobile stance, she is able to escape detection. Fishermen regularly pass within yards of her hiding place, unaware that she is there.

One spring, I decided to visit Mother Goose regularly, while she incubated her eggs. My early-morning, five-minute paddle to the island was a great way to start the day. I always brought a few crusts of bread on these visits, which the nest-bound mama would hungrily devour. While she was busy filling up on the bread, she would allow me to examine her nest and its contents—six large white eggs.

By the second Saturday in May, she had been sitting on the eggs for twenty-four days. She greeted me with less civility than usual and was especially protective of her nest area. As she reached for a piece of bread, I discovered the source of her newfound surliness—a number of grayish-yellow fluffballs peeked out from beneath their mother's breast.

Five adorable baby geese filled the nest, but it was the egg that caught my attention.

Normally, all the eggs in a clutch hatch within hours of each other. While Mama gave me suspicious glances, I slowly lifted the remaining egg from the nest and held it to my ear. No sounds came from within, so I gave the egg a gentle shake, expecting it to be empty. To my surprise, I could feel something inside. I realized that the gosling had not been strong enough to break from its shell and had probably exhausted itself in the effort.

Carefully, I cracked the egg on a rock, not knowing what to expect. Inside was a wet mess of down, with a bill at one end and two gangly grey feet at the other. There was no sign of life.

Using my shirt, I lightly patted the pathetic creature dry. The head hung limply. There was no response to my coaxings, so I placed the unfortunate bird in amongst its brothers and sisters and resigned to let nature take its course.

The next morning, I awoke early. It was Mother's Day.

As my daughters and I prepared a special breakfast for my wife, I couldn't help but think about the gosling that hadn't been strong enough to escape its shell. I decided to paddle over to the islet after breakfast and bring a Mother's Day breakfast for Mother Goose to help her celebrate the birth of her quints.

As I headed toward the canoe, bread in hand, I was greeted by a marvelous sight—Mama Goose and all six of her goslings lined up behind her.

She had come to show off her brood and, just maybe, to let me know my efforts had not been in vain

~Tom Lusk
Chicken Soup for the Nature Lover's Soul

My Children

Sometimes I sit and wonder
where I would be today,
had I made different choices,
changed my path along the way.

Could I have mastered greatness,
had a lifetime full of bliss?
Which roads could I have taken,
and which ones did I miss?

But when I see your faces,
a reflection of my life,
all worldly goods diminish
under years of toil and strife.

For you my darling children,
are the masterpiece I'll leave.
The greatness that I longed for,
at last, I did, achieve.

~Donna J. Calabro
Chicken Soup for the Soul Celebrates Mothers

Share with Us

We would like to know how these stories affected you and which ones were your favorites. Please e-mail us and let us know.

We also would like to share your stories with future readers. You may be able to help another reader, and become a published author at the same time. Please send us your own stories and poems for our future books. Some of our past contributors have launched writing and speaking careers from the publication of their stories in our books!

Your stories have the best chance of being used if you submit them through our web site, at:

www.chickensoup.com

If you do not have access to the Internet, you may submit your stories by mail or by facsimile. Please do not send us any book manuscripts, unless through a literary agent, as these will be automatically discarded.

Chicken Soup for the Soul
P.O. Box 700
Cos Cob, CT 06807-0700
Fax 203-861-7194

Great books on Parenting
from the Chicken Soup Library...
for the Soul.

The Wisdom of Dads

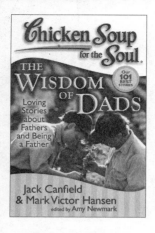

Children view their fathers with awe from the day they are born. Fathers are big and strong and seem to know everything, except for a few teenage years when fathers are perceived to know nothing! This book represents a new theme for Chicken Soup—101 stories selected from 35 past books, all stories focusing on the wisdom of dads. Stories are written by sons and daughters about their fathers, and by fathers relating stories about their children.

Dads & Daughters

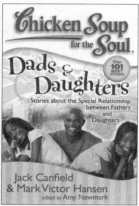

Whether she is ten years old or fifty – she will always be his little girl. And daughters take care of their dads too, whether it is a tea party for two at age five or loving care fifty years later. This wide-ranging exploration of the relationship between fathers and daughters provides an entirely new reading experience for Chicken Soup fans, with selections from forty past Chicken Soup books. Stories were written by fathers about their daughters and by daughters about their fathers, celebrating the special bond between fathers and daughters.

Grand and Great

A parent becomes a new person the day the first grand-child is born. Formerly serious adults become grandparents who dote on their grandchildren. This new book includes the best stories on being a grandparent from past Chicken soup books, representing a new reading experience for even the most devoted Chicken Soup fan. Everyone can understand the special ties between grandparents and grandchildren — the unlimited love, the mutual admiration and acceptance.

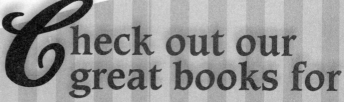

Check out our great books for

Moms Know Best

"Mom will know where it is…what to say…how to fix it." This Chicken Soup book focuses on the pervasive wisdom of mothers everywhere, and includes the best 101 stories from Chicken Soup's library on our perceptive, understanding, and insightful mothers. These stories celebrate the special bond between mothers and children, our mothers' unerring wisdom about everything from the mundane to the life-changing, and the hard work that goes into being a mother every day.

Like Mother, Like Daughter

Fathers, brothers, and friends sometimes shake their head in wonder as girls "turn into their mothers." This new collection from Chicken Soup represents the best 101 stories from Chicken Soup's library on the special bond between mothers and daughters, and the magical, mysterious similarities between them. Mothers and daughters of all ages will laugh, cry, and find inspiration in these stories that remind them how much they appreciate each other.

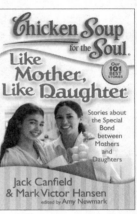

Moms & Sons

There is a special bond between mothers and their sons and it never goes away. This new book contains the 101 best stories and poems from Chicken Soup's library honoring that lifelong relationship between mothers and their male offspring. These heartfelt and loving stories written by mothers, grandmothers, and sons, about each other, span generations and show how the mother-son bond transcends time.

Families

Everyone loves Christmas and the holiday season. We reunite scattered family members, watch the wonder in a child's eyes, and feel the joy of giving gifts. The rituals of the holiday season give a rhythm to the years and create a foundation for our lives, as we gather with family, with our communities at church, at school, and even at the mall, to share the special spirit of the season, brightening those long winter days.

978-1-935096-15-3

Check out our

Books for Pet Lovers

Loving Our Cats
Heartwarming and Humorous Stories about
Our Feline Family Members
978-1-935096-08-5
We are all crazy about our mysterious cats.
Sometimes they are our best friends; sometimes
they are aloof. They are fun to watch and often
surprise us. These true stories, the best from
Chicken Soup's library, will make readers appreciate their own cats and see them with a new eye. Readers will revel
in the heartwarming, amusing, inspirational, and occasionally tearful
stories about our best friends and faithful companions — our cats.

Loving Our Dogs
Heartwarming and Humorous Stories about
Our Companions and Best Friends
978-1-935096-05-4
We are all crazy about our dogs and can't read
enough about them, whether they're misbe-
having and giving us big, innocent looks, or
loyally standing by us in times of need. This
new book from Chicken Soup for the Soul
contains the 101 best dog stories from the company's extensive
library. Readers will revel in the heartwarming, amusing, inspirational, and occasionally tearful stories about our best friends and
faithful companions — our dogs.

Favorites!

Chicken Soup for the Soul

Who Is
Jack Canfield?

Jack Canfield is the co-creator and editor of the *Chicken Soup for the Soul* series, which *Time* magazine has called "the publishing phenomenon of the decade." Jack is also the co-author of eight other bestselling books including *The Success Principles™: How to Get from Where You Are to Where You Want to Be*, *Dare to Win*, *The Aladdin Factor*, *You've Got to Read This Book*, and *The Power of Focus: How to Hit Your Business and Personal and Financial Targets with Absolute Certainty*.

Jack has recently developed a telephone coaching program and an online coaching program based on his most recent book *The Success Principles*. He also offers a seven-day *Breakthrough to Success* seminar every summer, which attracts 400 people from fifteen countries around the world.

Jack is the CEO of the Canfield Training Group in Santa Barbara, California, and founder of the Foundation for Self-Esteem in Culver City, California. He has conducted intensive personal and professional development seminars on the principles of success for over a million people in twenty-three countries. Jack is a dynamic keynote speaker and he has spoken to hundreds of thousands of others at more than 1,000 corporations, universities, professional conferences and conventions, and has been seen by millions more on national television shows such as *The Today Show*, *Fox and Friends*, *Inside Edition*, *Hard Copy*, *CNN's Talk Back Live*, *20/20*, *Eye to Eye*, and the *NBC Nightly News* and the *CBS Evening News*.

Jack is the recipient of many awards and honors, including three honorary doctorates and a *Guinness World Records Certificate* for having seven books from the *Chicken Soup for the Soul* series appearing on the *New York Times* bestseller list on May 24, 1998.

To write to Jack or for inquiries about Jack as a speaker, his coaching programs, trainings or seminars, use the following contact information:

Jack Canfield
The Canfield Companies
P.O. Box 30880 • Santa Barbara, CA 93130
phone: 805-563-2935 • fax: 805-563-2945
E-mail: info@jackcanfield.com
www.jackcanfield.com

Who Is
Mark Victor Hansen?

Mark Victor Hansen is the co-founder of *Chicken Soup for the Soul*, along with Jack Canfield. He is also a sought-after keynote speaker, bestselling author, and marketing maven. For more than thirty years, Mark has focused solely on helping people from all walks of life reshape their personal vision of what's possible. His powerful messages of possibility, opportunity, and action have created powerful change in thousands of organizations and millions of individuals worldwide.

Mark's credentials include a lifetime of entrepreneurial success. He is a prolific writer with many bestselling books, such as *The One Minute Millionaire*, *Cracking the Millionaire Code*, *How to Make the Rest of Your Life the Best of Your Life*, *The Power of Focus*, *The Aladdin Factor*, and *Dare to Win*, in addition to the *Chicken Soup for the Soul* series. Mark has had a profound influence in the field of human potential through his library of audios, videos, and articles in the areas of big thinking, sales achievement, wealth building, publishing success, and personal and professional development.

Mark is the founder of the *MEGA Seminar Series*. *MEGA Book Marketing University* and *Building Your MEGA Speaking Empire* are annual conferences where Mark coaches and teaches new and aspiring authors, speakers, and experts on building lucrative publishing and speaking careers. Other MEGA events include *MEGA Info-Marketing* and *My MEGA Life*.

He has appeared on *Oprah*, *CNN*, and *The Today Show*. He has been quoted in *Time*, *U.S. News & World Report*, *USA Today*, *New York Times*, and *Entrepreneur* and has had countless radio interviews, assuring our planet's people that "You can easily create the life you deserve."

As a philanthropist and humanitarian, Mark works tirelessly for organizations such as Habitat for Humanity, American Red Cross, March of Dimes, Childhelp USA, and many others. He is the recipient of numerous awards that honor his entrepreneurial spirit, philanthropic heart, and business acumen. He is a lifetime member of the Horatio Alger Association of Distinguished Americans, an organization that honored Mark with the prestigious Horatio Alger Award for his extraordinary life achievements.

Mark Victor Hansen is an enthusiastic crusader of what's possible and is driven to make the world a better place.

Mark Victor Hansen & Associates, Inc.
P.O. Box 7665 • Newport Beach, CA 92658
phone: 949-764-2640 • fax: 949-722-6912
www.markvictorhansen.com

Who Is
Amy Newmark?

Amy Newmark was recently named publisher of Chicken Soup for the Soul, after a thirty-year career as a writer, speaker, financial analyst, and business executive in the worlds of finance and telecommunications.

Amy is a graduate of Harvard College, where she majored in Portuguese, minored in French, and traveled extensively. She is also the mother of two children in college and has two grown stepchildren.

After a long career writing books on telecommunications, voluminous financial reports, business plans, and corporate press releases, Chicken Soup for the Soul is a breath of fresh air for Amy. She has fallen in love with Chicken Soup for the Soul and its life-changing books, and found it a true pleasure to conceptualize, compile, and edit the "101 Best Stories" books for our readers.

The best way to contact Chicken Soup for the Soul is through our web site, at www.chickensoup.com. This will always get the fastest attention.

If you do not have access to the Internet, please contact us by mail or by facsimile.

Chicken Soup for the Soul
P.O. Box 700
Cos Cob, CT 06807-0700
Fax 203-861-7194

Chicken Soup for the Soul

Thank You!

Our first thanks go to our loyal readers who have inspired the entire Chicken Soup team for the past fifteen years. Your appreciative letters and emails have reminded us why we work so hard on these books.

We owe huge thanks to all of our contributors as well. We know that you pour your hearts and souls into the stories and poems that you share with us, and ultimately with each other. We appreciate your willingness to open up your lives to other Chicken Soup readers.

We can only publish a small percentage of the stories that are submitted, but we read every single one and even the ones that do not appear in a book have an influence on us and on the final manuscripts.

As always, we would like to thank the entire staff of Chicken Soup for the Soul for their help on this project and the 101 Best series in general.

Among our California staff, we would especially like to single out the following people:

- D'ette Corona, our Assistant Publisher, who is the heart and soul of the Chicken Soup publishing operation, and who put together the first draft of this manuscript

- Barbara LoMonaco, our Webmaster and Chicken Soup for the Soul Editor, for invaluable assistance in obtaining the fabulous quotations that add depth and meaning to this book

- Patty Hansen for her extra special help with the permissions for these fabulous stories and for her amazing knowledge of the Chicken Soup library

- and Patti Clement for her help with permissions and other organizational matters.

In our Connecticut office, we would like to thank Madeline Clapps for her wonderful editorial assistance.

We would also like to thank our master of design, Creative Director and book producer, Brian Taylor at Pneuma Books, for his brilliant vision for our covers and interiors.

Finally, none of this would be possible without the business and creative leadership of our CEO, Bill Rouhana, and our president, Bob Jacobs.

Chicken Soup for the Soul

www.chickensoup.com